Polygons: Cultural Diversities and Intersections
General Editor: **Lieve Spaas,** *Professor of French Cultural Studies,*
Kingston University, UK

LONDON EYES

Reflections in Text and Image

Edited by

Gail Cunningham and Stephen Barber

Berghahn Books
New York • Oxford

First published in 2007 by

Berghahn Books

www.berghahnbooks.com

© 2007 Gail Cunningham and Stephen Barber

Library of Congress Cataloging-in-Publication Data

London eyes : reflections in text and image / edited by Gail Cunningham
and Stephen Barbe.
    p. cm. -- (Polygons : cultural diversities and intersections)
Includes bibliographical references and index.
    ISBN 978-1-84545-407-4 (hardback : acid-free paper)
    1. London (England)--In literature. 2. English literature--19th century--
History and criticism. 3. English literature--20th century--History and
criticism. 4. London (England)--In motion pictures. 5. London (England)--
In art. 6. City and town life--England--London--History--19th century. 7.
City and town life--England--London--History--20th century. 8. London
(England)--History--19th century. 9. London (England)--History--20th
century. I. Cunningham, Gail. II. Barber, Stephen, 1961-

PR468.L65L66 2007
820.9'32421--dc22

                     2007040569

British Library Cataloguing in Publication Data

A catalogue record for this book is available from the British Library

Printed in the United States on acid-free paper

ISBN: 978-1-84545-407-4 (hardback)

CONTENTS

PART II: THE MODERN AGE: LONDON IN IMAGE

LIST OF ILLUSTRATIONS

ACKNOWLEDGEMENTS

The editors would like to thank Lieve Spaas, the Polygons series editor, for her friendly, imaginative and constant support.

Gail Cunningham would like to thank Chris French of Kingston University's Centre for Local History Studies, and Vesna Goldsworthy and colleagues in Kingston University's Centre for Suburban Studies, for their help with and enthusiasm for the study of suburbia.

Stephen Barber would like to thank Mark Shiel and Gareth Evans for their guidance.

Andrew Smith's essay has been previously published in a different form in his book *Victorian Demons: Medicine, Masculinity and the Gothic at the Fin de Siècle*, 2004. It is published here by kind permission of Manchester University Press. Ana Parejo Vadillo's essay contains material previously published in 'Immaterial Poetics: A. Mary F. Robinson and the Fin de Siècle Poem' in Joseph Bristow (ed.) *The Fin de Siècle Poem*. This material is reproduced here by kind permission of Ohio University Press.

INTRODUCTION

Gail Cunningham

London occupies a unique position in England's – and probably the
Anglophone world's – imagination. From at least the Middle Ages,
when Chaucer's pilgrims left for Canterbury from a south London inn,
the city has stood for the literary, social and political centre against
which the rest of the country is in various ways contrasted. From the
Industrial Revolution onwards, it has also been the primary site in
which notions of emerging urban modernity have evolved and been
tested in writing, in photography, and – with the invention of film –
through the moving image. Though all cities are the same in
contrasting experientially and symbolically with the countryside, and
thus in creating an essential experience of urbanism recognizably
transposable from one city to another, none are in reality sufficiently
alike to make this experience identical in detail or in nuance whatever
the city in which it occurs. London, formed through accretion over
more than 2,000 years, even in the modern period apparently unable,
unlike Paris or New York, to subject itself to any serious urban
planning, lacking an obvious centre but composed rather – in the
common phrase – of a 'series of villages', is perhaps uniquely reflective
or constructive of urban modernity. If the understanding of the
modern city is expressed primarily in a discourse of fracture,
alienation, anonymity, then London – sprawling, unfocused, so huge
as to be virtually unknowable – provides a peculiarly appropriate
locus in which to explore this experience.

This volume focuses on the London of emerging modernity through
to postmodernity, the later nineteenth century to the present day. It
covers the period, in other words, that formed our relations to and
understanding of the city from the period of late industrialization to the
digital age. Our aim is to explore ways of seeing and of apprehending
London as a city uniquely centred in the growth of modernity, and our

choice is to concentrate on the dominant artistic and imaginative media of the nineteenth century (literature) and the twentieth century (film). We explore both the diversity of the city and its interconnections, its shapelessness and its form. Though the literature of London is immense and ever-growing, we make no apology for adding to it through a collection of essays that each, we believe, contributes something new and significant to our understanding of the modern city. We could reach for an example from any number of historical or imaginative writings of the past 150 years to represent our vision. The following, from Margaret Drabble's *The Middle Ground*, aptly merges the literary and the filmic view and brings together, through its aerial perspective, the 'London eyes' that encompass, in one take, the iconic public monuments and the private backyards, the randomness and the pathways that comprise this unique city:

> London stretched away, St Paul's in the distance, and the towers of the City, and beneath them, nearby, the little network of streets, backyards, cul-de-sacs, canals, warehouses, curves and chimneys, railways, little factories tucked into odd corners; unplanned, higgledy-piggledy, hardly a corner wasted, intricate, enmeshed, patched and pieced together, the old and the new side by side, overlapping, jumbled, always decaying yet always renewed: London, how could one ever be tired of it?[1]

Notes

1. Margaret Drabble, *The Middle Ground*, London, 1980, 218.

PART I

VICTORIAN AND EDWARDIAN LONDON ON THE PAGE

INTRODUCTION

Gail Cunningham

The essays in this part of the book are all concerned, in their different ways, with issues of spatial relations in London and the way these are perceived and communicated. The culturally dominant figure of modern urbanism in the nineteenth century, at least in contemporary critical discourse, is the *flâneur*, the man who moves randomly through the streets, observing but apart from the crowd, alienated and disconnected, yet deriving stimulus and indeed identity from the city. These essays adopt a different approach, all in various ways interrogating the dominance of this perspective. The London that is seen through these eyes is more diverse, more multi-layered, certainly more inclusive in terms both of class and of gender, than the London gazed upon by the *flâneur*. It is still, though, very much the London of emerging modernity, where boundaries – between home and street, for example, between private and public or human and mechanical – are unstable or contested, where the gendering of space and the relation of the individual to the mass are increasingly significant issues, and where unexpected or unfamiliar connections are revealed between the fragmentary spaces and lives of the modern city. The London seen from a commuter train or through the lens of a street camera is often fleetingly intimate, unexpectedly connected, and with a dynamic, direct and authentic relationship between observer and observed. At the same time there is the London, fragmented, sometimes dangerous, of Conrad's 'topographic mysteries', most effectively rendered in painterly style – impressionist, for example, in the poetry of Mary Robinson, cubist or futurist in Conrad's *The Secret Agent*. There is the London of the suburbs, culturally and spatially neglected in most critical discourse, but for the rebellious young an imaginatively powerful site of parental dominance, social conformity and desexualization. And perhaps above all there are the London streets, spaces constantly shifting in character, sites of performance and narrative, anxiety-provoking but also secure in providing anonymity.

Writings and representations of Victorian and Edwardian London laid the ground for many ways of apprehending the city today. Both imaginatively and through direct social commentary, observers of the city grappled with the gap between the leisured and the destitute, the rich and the poor. Questions of gender – how men and women respond differently to the city, which spaces are dominated by which sex – are raised by the writers studied in a number of essays. The nature of the city's spaces pose urgent questions at this period as they do now: is London developing as a site of affluence, consumption and entertainment? Is it primarily a focus for wealth creation and work? Does its physical nature make it inherently dangerous, whether through crime or terrorism? These are some of the general questions that occupy commentators on urbanism and the city in the nineteenth century as in the twenty-first.

The essays in this section, however, all address these issues through a focus on aspects of London specificities, whether in locations, groups, behaviours or media. They explore particulars not abstractions, and in so doing, it is hoped, reveal aspects of London and the London experience that are usually unexamined. My own essay, on London commuters, investigates the early representations of what has become a near-universal experience for Londoners. I argue that the figure of the commuter, largely neglected in the writings of the city except as a representative of the dehumanized mass, in fact experiences the city in a highly particular and significant way, negotiating on a daily basis the contrasting spaces of home, work and journey. Lindsay Smith's exploration of the revolution in visual representation brought about by photography reveals how photographic images both support and – sometimes inadvertently – extend the textual writing in which they are embedded. The photograph, she argues, is uniquely mimetic in capturing images unseen by the photographer and thus in evading selection and subverting intent. Andrew Smith notes that, despite Sherlock Holmes's close identification with London in the cultural imagination, Doyle in fact sets most of his stories in the countryside or the suburbs, and he contrasts the forensic, masculine gaze of Holmes's intelligence with the feminization of his London space in Baker Street and its surroundings. As Smith argues, masculine rationality was, during the period of the Sherlock Holmes stories, being progressively squeezed out of the city by the encroachment of feminine activities, as city spaces became increasingly gendered. Ana Parejo Vadillo investigates a different, and unexpected, kind of gendered space, that of the literary salon of a woman poet towards the end of the nineteenth century. She shows how the literary salon occupied a hybrid space between the public and the domestic, and how different London locations became the focus for the literary and artistic networks at the forefront of modern movements. And spatial relations – the social, physical and psychological geography of life in London in the 1890s – also form the focus of Deborah Parsons's essay on agoraphobia, which explores the links between domesticity and independence, claustrophobia and agoraphobia, in Dorothy Richardson's *Pilgrimage*. Finally, Roger Webster's essay on Conrad's *The Secret Agent* takes an early modernist London text and investigates the ways in which London is 'seen' through modernist eyes. Arguing that Conrad's representations of London draw heavily on techniques of cubist and futurist painting, Webster examines three film versions of *The Secret Agent* to assess which of them most successfully reworks Conrad's vision in film. His conclusion, interestingly, is that the version least faithful to the period and plot of the novel is closest to producing a visual realization of Conrad's textual construction of a fragmented and dehumanized city. The essay deftly demonstrates the potential overlap of textual and filmic representations of London, setting the scene for the succeeding section on London in film and text.

CHAPTER 1

LONDON COMMUTING: SUBURB AND CITY, THE QUOTIDIAN FRONTIER

Gail Cunningham

It rushes home, our own express,
So cheerfully, no one would guess
      The weight it carries

Of tired husbands, back from town,
For each of whom, in festal gown,
      A fond wife tarries....

Sometimes as I at leisure roam,
Admiring my suburban home,
      I wonder sadly

If men will always come and go
In these vast numbers, to and fro,
      So fast and madly.[1]

Dollie Radford's poem 'From the Suburbs' captures some of the contemporary ambivalences and anxieties about what was in 1895 the comparatively new phenomenon of commuting. Her poem evokes technological speed, cheer, the promise of domestic comfort and affection; but equally it contains images of exhaustion, melancholy, depersonalization and stress. The new suburbs that surrounded London in the latter part of the nineteenth century, which were growing at an astonishing rate, offered clean air, quiet, family space, and gardens. But they also exacted a price in the breadwinner's daily journey to and from work, and in the consequent growth of gender separation. 'To commute' means to change or mitigate; the commuter had his (and at this period the masculine pronoun is appropriate) train fare mitigated or commuted by reduced-price season tickets or lower-priced fares on working-men's trains. The earlier sense of 'change', however, is significant in a number of ways. Not only did commuters, as a group, represent a social and cultural shift in relations between different categories of space, but the individual commuter himself experienced a daily spatial and temporal change, mediated by train, Underground, omnibus, tram or foot-slog, between widely distanced environments. For these individuals, the London commuting terminus became, in V.S. Pritchett's words, 'a quotidian frontier, splitting a life, a temple of the inexorable'.[2] Commuting was a new experience, made possible by large-scale suburban development and by the transport that linked the suburbs to the city. It was an experience, too, that created new – though in current critical discourse largely neglected – ways of relating to and apprehending the city. The predominant terms for understanding the modern city largely rest on notions of alienation, disconnection and anonymity, with the *flâneur*, from Baudelaire through Benjamin and onwards, as the privileged representative of urban modernity. The commuter, I would argue, provides not only an equally significant but also a more empirically grounded alternative figure through which to apprehend the relations between individual and city, the personal and the mass.

This significance may perhaps be gauged by contrasting commuting with some of the more familiar ways of experiencing London. Philip Davis, for example, tracing the early Victorian move from the rural to the urban, argues that 'the city, roofed-in and smoked-over, became almost literally a huge separate world of its own, sealed-off spatially and historically', and cites Engels's *The Condition of the Working Class in England* in support:

> A town, such as London, where a man may wander for hours together without reaching the beginning of the end, without meeting the slightest hint which could lead to the inference that there is open country within reach, is a strange thing.[3]

But suburban living, of course, was promoted on precisely the opposite premise. The city was not sealed off from any hint of open country; on the contrary, in suburbia some form of the rural or pastoral was within reach of even a humble clerk, and for the more affluent professionals the *rus in urbe* ideal was neither an illusion nor a travesty. The commuter did not 'wander' within central London, but travelled daily between the distinct spaces of suburb and city. By contrast with the city, the suburban habitat provided low density housing, comparatively clean air, single-unit family dwellings, private gardens and tree-lined streets. And because the suburb was by definition attached to the city, suburbia created for its occupants what Ana Parejo Vadillo calls a 'dual spatial identity': the city for work, consumption, entertainment, the public sphere; the suburb for recreation, family, domesticity, love.[4] The commuter, who moved twice a day, six days a week, between these contrasting spaces took on a triple spatial and indeed temporal identity. Not only did he occupy a work space in the city and a domestic space in the suburb, but the journey between the two, commonly occupying up to an hour twice daily, became itself a distinct space and time.[5] Arguing in 1901 for increased suburban development and improved transport links as a means of solving London's housing problem, Charles Booth found that 'a new measure has to be applied to space and time in city life.'[6] For the London commuter, this new measure was a daily experience that shaped his relations with the city and constructed his identity in both home and work.

Although the word 'commuter' itself did not become current in Britain until the twentieth century,[7] the phenomenon of daily mass travel in and out of the city engaged the imaginative attention of writers throughout the Victorian period. Walter Besant, for example, observing the mass movement of commuters at Cannon Street station, was struck by the sheer human volume involved:

> See them pass out – by the hundred – by the thousand – by the fifty thousand. The brain reels at the mere contemplation of this mighty multitude which comes in every morning and goes out every afternoon.[8]

Quite how mighty this multitude of commuters actually was is of course difficult to estimate accurately, though it is clear that the numbers increased dramatically throughout the period. The London and Greenwich, for example, which was credited with being the first suburban railway, carried 1,500 passengers a day in its opening year of 1836, increasing to 5,500 by the mid-1840s.[9] John Kellett estimates that in the 1850s 27,000 rail passengers entered London each day, though this figure was dwarfed by the 244,000 who travelled by bus or on foot.[10] The Cheap Trains Act of 1883, which laid obligations on railway companies to run early morning trains at special rates for working men, led to claims that by 1891 between eleven and twelve million passengers per annum were being carried from the suburbs to the city.[11] The District Line Underground, which Christian Wolmar argues did more for suburban spread than the earlier and more commuter-associated Metropolitan Line, was carrying fifty-one million passengers a year by 1904.[12] Such figures confirm Besant's perception of the mind-boggling volume of commuter traffic and could incline us towards the by now commonplace assumption that the commuter was one of an undifferentiated mass. This would be, though, to ignore the distinctions concealed within the numbers. Unlike Paris or New York, the development of London's transport systems was characterized by degrees of prejudice and poor planning that ensured a lively if maddening variety within the mass.

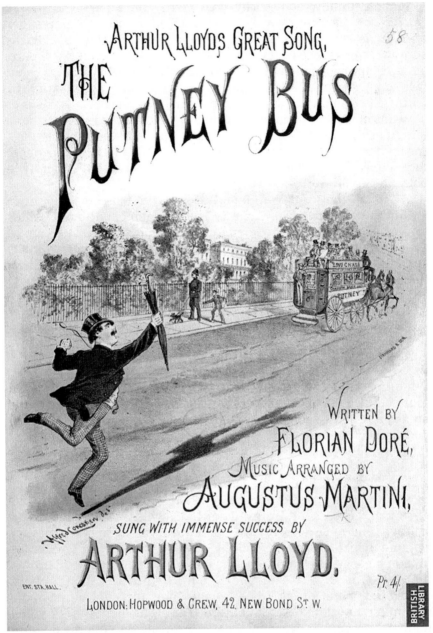

Figure 1.1: Cover to the sheet music of Arthur Lloyd's 1884 music hall song
The Putney Bus. Courtesy of the British Library.

Demarcations of social difference were embedded in the means of
transport and the timing and cost of journeys. Trams, for example,
which provided a comparatively efficient form of horse-drawn
transport, were associated with the working class. They ran earlier in

the mornings than omnibuses (which started at 8.00 a.m., making them useless for the working-class commuter) and were excluded from the West End and the City on the grounds that the lower orders should not be encouraged by cheap transport to travel to these areas. All London's major rail termini were situated on the periphery of the central areas because of the difficulties of purchasing city land from wealthy and usually aristocratic landowners. The Underground, which was planned to alleviate the traffic congestion in London largely caused by the absence of rail links in or across the centre, was allowed to develop piecemeal so that the different lines did not easily interconnect even when sharing a station. Working-men's trains deposited passengers at their city destinations well before 8.00 a.m., whereas the clerks and professionals often began their journey as late as 9.00 a.m. Frederick Willis wryly notes the status-based rhythms of the city commuters: at 4.00 p.m. 'the Very Great Men began to return to their solid, suburban comfort, and as the time advanced so the grades of returning business men descended until the flood-tide of clerks left the City to the police, the pigeons, and solitude'.[13] And Donald Olsen notes that by the end of the century Liverpool Street station received 19,000 early morning passengers each day on working men's fares, 35,000 slightly later on reduced fares, followed after 9.00 a.m. by 9,000 season ticket holders – 'a three fold segregation of commuters by fare and time of arrival'.[14]

These waves of suburban commuters may have been differentiated by class or occupation, but nevertheless rapidly became a daily signifier of the depersonalized mass that characterized the city space. They are 'sucked into the City at daybreak, and scattered again as darkness falls',[15] 'bobbing in and out of the City every day',[16] 'swallowed up' by 'the Underground and the bulgy buses'.[17] Such metaphorical depersonalization of the commuter, figuring him as passive flotsam on the twice-daily tide, or human fodder for the commercial machine, was perhaps fixed in the cultural imagination by Eliot's crowd of the undead that 'flowed over London Bridge' in *The Waste Land*.[18] For earlier observers, though, the commuting mass provoked more varied responses. George Sala sees that the omnibuses 'disgorge' commuters 'by hundreds' but the visual effect of this is, strikingly, that 'the pavement of the Strand and Fleet Street looks quite radiant with ... clerks', their silk hats shining in the sunlight.[19] For Frederick Willis the clerks at London Bridge station 'were rather amusing figures, very solemn, very respectable ... always flourishing a half-penny morning paper'.[20] Both Sala and Willis respond more positively to the commuting mass, but neither attribute it agency. Other writers, by contrast, interpret the commuter as engaged in near-heroic activity. Pett Ridge sees the male inhabitant leave his fictional suburb each morning 'in search of gold',[21] while in the evening, 'the detachment which went off in the morning to attack the City, and to loot it, returns'.[22] Charlotte Riddell, in a virtuoso passage that brilliantly evokes the sheer scale of the London commuting crowd, takes the individual commuter to be a 'soldier of the great army' that floods in daily from suburbs to city:

> Whichever quarter you take, North, East, South or West, it is the same – over London Bridge they come, seventeen conveyances a minute; down the City Road and Shoreditch, down Goswell and St. John Streets, pour the inhabitants of Holloway and Highbury, of Islington, of Pentonville, of Hackney, of Bethnal Green, of Kingsland, Dalston, Cambridge Heath, Hoxton and Hommerton, and Barnsbury and Ball's Pond; along the Commercial and Mile End Roads troop the dwellers in Stepney, Bow, Limehouse, Shadwell, Poplar, Whitechapel and Wapping. Down Holborn and through the Strand sweeps the West End tide, bearing with it the denizens of Kensington and Bayswater, of Notting Hill, of St. John's Wood, of Paddington, Tyburnia, Belgravia, Pimlico, Chelsea, Hammersmith, and Fulham. As for the South – across the bridges it sends its tributaries to the great human stream. By train, by omnibus, on foot, they come to swell the flood: from Greenwich and Blackheath, from New Cross, Peckham, Lewisham, Camberwell, Sydenham, Norwood, Walworth, Brixton, Bermondsey, Deptford, Kennington, Lambeth, Clapham, Battersea, Vauxhall … they come to work.[23]

Riddell's use of proper nouns – litanies of suburban place names that quarter the capital's outskirts – gives a sense of individual identity within a mass, of difference subsumed in the common purpose of work. The commuter may be one of a crowd but is not thereby rendered inhuman or passive. On the contrary, argues Sidney Low, 'the perpetual going and coming, the daily journeys by rail or tram or steamer … have sharpened his faculties' – to such an extent, indeed, that 'the young men of Wimbledon or Putney … could make up a regiment which would hold its own on a battle-field against a *corps d'élite* selected from any army in the world'.[24]

All these writers deal with the commuter as an observed phenomenon of the urban environment, a particular instance of the London crowd. Yet all, whether deliberately or unconsciously, foreground the aspect of commuters that distinguishes them from the crowd as normally figured in the discourse of urban modernism. This is a crowd that *moves*, and that moves, moreover, in a purposeful and patterned manner: it is not the randomized, disconnected mass that occupies the idle gaze of the *flâneur*. Indeed, a botanizer on the asphalt, to paraphrase Benjamin's description of the *flâneur*,[25] would be likely to find himself summarily trampled in the throng if he were to undertake his project in the streets surrounding a London station at rush-hour. Pett Ridge and Riddell liken the commuting mass to an armed force, and Low argues in all seriousness that the conditions of commuting produce the strength, vigour and quickness of faculty needed in an actual army. All acknowledge the sheer scale of purposeful movement and activity that is constituted in commuting. But within the crowd the individual commuter is engaged through this movement in a daily negotiation of difference and connection between distinct spatial and temporal identities. It is these distinctions, and the nature of negotiation between them, that, I suggest, give the commuter his particular form of relationship to urbanism.

John Stilgoe claims that the commuter provides the real link between city and fringe. Taking 'commute' to mean 'to mitigate or to lessen,' he argues that the suburbs 'began and developed as a spatial means of grappling with and lessening the difficulty of urbanization ... based on industrialization and corporate capitalism'.[26] The Victorian commuter engaged daily with an individual negotiation of differences between and connections with contrasting spheres – work and home, city and suburb, male and female – and in so doing grappled with and found means of mitigating difficulties inherent in urban existence. The rhythms of mass movement likened by many writers to flood tides or advancing and retreating armies were at the individual level marked by rituals that signified important elements of difference and connection. For the suburban commuter, 'the home' is not only a distinct physical location widely separated from work, but also a sphere that defines one part of his selfhood. Shan Bullock's London clerk, Robert Thorne, discovers this in his first suburban marital home: 'in this great London, we were centre of our own little world. Home. Ourselves'.[27] Commuting constitutes a process of leaving and returning to this centre of self that acquires significant and revealing routines. The parting kiss in the morning, for example, physically connects the individual man and woman while at the same time signalling the ritual disconnection of male from female, work from home. It can be used as a useful signifier of emotional vacancy: Edwin Pugh's Harry Cummers, who 'every morning, at nine o'clock ... kissed his mother and started for the City',[28] displays a dullness of routine that reflects the hopelessness of his aspirations to success as a writer. Charles Pooter, by contrast, notes in his diary only those occasions when some mild assertiveness from Carrie comically disrupts the normal harmony of their daily parting:

> I was so entirely taken aback by this onslaught ... I could say nothing, and as I heard the 'bus coming, I left with a hurried kiss – a little too hurried, perhaps, for my upper lip came in contact with Carrie's teeth and slightly cut it. It was quite painful for an hour afterwards.[29]

The return of the male from work is often represented as similarly freighted with significant ritual. W.H. Hartley (May Laffan) shows her tea-merchant commuter coming home 'as usual ... laden with little parcels' including 'a rush basket containing a ptarmigan' as a delicacy for the evening meal.[30] Frederick Willis notes such behaviour as characteristic of the conscientious male: 'It was considered "the thing" for paterfamilias to return with a rush basket, probably a link with primitive man returning to his cave with the thigh-bone of a diplodocus.'[31] And Charles Pooter, after yet another morning quarrel with his wife, uses a home-coming gift as conciliation: 'Fearing disagreeables at home after the "tiff" this morning, I ... bought a little silver bangle for Carrie.'[32] Such propitiatory gifts serve not merely to reconnect the male to the domestic sphere, but also to remind the female that his absence from home has granted him superior purchasing power. They symbolize the continuing linkage of the working male self with the home, even across distance, while at the same time displaying his independent economic status.

These small-scale daily rituals of connection and separation can be made to stand for the larger issues of split selfhood that the commuting male had to negotiate. Suburban living exacerbated the separation of home and work not merely through distance, but also, and more importantly, through difference. The suburbs constituted a type of spatial environment that was significantly different from the city; this, after all, was the point of them. And as Stilgoe suggests, the nature of this difference was ideally such as to mitigate the difficulties of urbanism. For most Victorians, the decision to live in suburbia was the result of an active choice: being newly built, the suburbs, unlike either the city or the country, had few native-born inhabitants. In selecting a physical environment, therefore, the suburb-dweller was in some direct sense creating a selfhood within a deliberately selected and distinct space that was in contradistinction to the self of the city. Conan Doyle is as explicit as any writer of the period in pointing out this difference when, in *Beyond the City*, he describes a stroll in the 'quiet tree-lined roads' of a south London suburb on a summer's day:

> The sky was of the deepest blue ... and the air was filled with the low drone of insects or with a sudden sharper note as bee or bluefly shot past with its quivering long-drawn hum, like an insect tuning-fork. As the friends topped each rise which leads up to the Crystal Palace, they could see the dun clouds of London stretching along the northern skyline, with spire or dome breaking through the low-lying haze.[33]

The trope of country purity opposed to urban corruption, familiar from classical times, is in the nineteenth-century literature of London commuting often transposed to suburb versus city. The suburb provides clear skies of 'deepest blue' contrasted with the 'dun clouds' covering London, and the life of the city is represented as 'brutalising',[34] or a 'taint',[35] threatening a corruption of self that can be mitigated only through physical separation in suburban domesticity. Dickens exploits this trope with characteristic verve in his depiction of Wemmick in *Great Expectations*. Wemmick's home in suburban Walworth is literally his castle (albeit 'the smallest house [Pip] ever saw'[36]) with miniature flagpole, drawbridge and cannon ('the Stinger') signalling

Figure 1.2: Poster advertising the new extension to Golders Green of the Charing Cross, Euston and Hampstead Railway, opened in 1907. Courtesy of the London Transport Museum.

it as a symbolical stronghold against the outside world. As Pip discovers, Wemmick maintains different selves in his two different spatial locations. At home he is a caring son, a proud householder and a devoted cultivator of cucumbers, rabbits and chickens; in the city he is a hard man of business who advises Pip to throw his money into the Thames rather than use it charitably to help a friend. As he says himself, accounting for his harshness: 'Walworth is one place, and the office is another. ... They must not be confounded together. My Walworth sentiments must be taken at Walworth; none but my official sentiments can be taken in this office.'[37]

Wemmick splits himself into two selves, consciously distinct in his demarcation of sentiments that 'must not be confounded together'. But the metamorphosis of the Walworth Wemmick into the office Wemmick is not mentally internalized but is, rather, inscribed on his body. Walking with him back to the office, Pip notes that:

> By degrees, Wemmick got dryer and harder ... and his mouth tightened into a post-office again. At last, when we got to his place of business and he pulled out his key from his coat-collar, he looked as unconscious of his Walworth property as if the Castle and the drawbridge and the arbour and the lake and the fountain and the Aged, had all been blown into space together by the last discharge of the Stinger.[38]

Conan Doyle's commuter Harold Denver, by contrast, consciously understands domesticity in suburbia as the only means by which he can attain morally acceptable selfhood. He proposes to Clara in a scene of idyll in suburbia ('the sloping gardens, the brick villas, the darkening sky with half a pale moon beginning to show over the chimney pots'[39]) explaining:

> You do not know how degrading this City life is, how debasing, and yet how absorbing. Money for ever clinks in your ear. You can think of nothing else. ... There was but one way in which I could defy the taint, and that was by having a home influence so pure and so high that it may brace me against all that draws me down.[40]

The novel concludes with a statement that could stand for the ideal of the city/suburb split, likening the process of commuting to a reconciliation of commercial duty with spiritual purity: 'As he goes back every evening from the crowds of Throgmorton Street to the tree-lined peaceful avenues of Norwood, so he has found it possible in spirit also to do one's duties amidst the babel of the City, and yet to live beyond it.'[41]

Conan Doyle's conclusion explicitly foregrounds the daily rhythm of the commuter's interconnections of dual identity ('as he goes back every evening ... so he finds it possible ... '). Yet as I have suggested above, commuting in some important senses creates not merely a dual but a triple identity. The journey between home and work, typically an hour twice daily, frees the commuter into a time which is dictated neither by home nor by work and into a space or series of spaces that is separate from both. While many writers stress the visual impact within urban space of commuters en masse, others note the significance of the commuter as observer rather than observed, of the particular gaze of the commuter. As John Kellett points out,[42] the economic and social conditions dictating the construction of suburban rail links to the major termini (smashing a route directly through slums, for example, while leaving untouched the houses of the poor on either side) meant that in a peculiarly literal sense the domestic conditions of the workers became visible to the middle-class commuter. Trains running high on embankments between houses brought the commuter's gaze directly on a level with upper windows, allowing an immediate visual contact from first-class carriage to working-class interior which can – perhaps should – provoke reflections in the gazer on social inequality. Dickens notes this phenomenon in *Dombey and Son* as Mr Dombey looks out of his train window:

> Everything around is blackened. … There are jagged walls and falling houses close at hand, and through the battered roofs and broken windows, wretched rooms are seen, where want and fever hide themselves in many wretched shapes. … As Mr Dombey looks out of his carriage window, it is never in his thoughts that the monster who has brought him there has let the light of day in on these things: not made or caused them.[43]

Some sixty years later, C.F.G. Masterman links the commuter still more directly with political identity. Constructing the typical suburban male as a timid, conformist, conservative type anxiously watching the rise of socialism, Masterman writes of the commuter's journey as a daily dash of the respectable middle-class individual through the danger zones of the mass:

> he has constructed in imagination the image of Democracy – a loud-voiced, independent, arrogant figure, with a thirst for drink and imperfect standards of decency, and a determination to be supported at some one else's expense. Every day, swung high upon embankments or buried deep in tubes underground, he hurries through the region where the creature lives.[44]

Gustave Doré's engraving *Over London by Rail* (plate 1) depicts a scene similar to the one described by Dickens, and shows the elevated perspective from which the middle-class commuter looked down on and into the lives of the poor. For Masterman, the commuter's carriage is a protected area allowing the middle classes to travel through such scenes in safety. His images imply deliberate separation from and blindness to the regions travelled – 'swung high … buried

Figure 1.3: Gustave Doré. 'Over London by Rail'. Courtesy of the British Library.

deep'. For a woman writer, though, the carriage window acts as a screen which the gaze and the empathetic imagination can permeate. Lucy Clifford's story, 'The End of Her Journey,' shows her protagonist turning to look 'aimlessly out of the window' of her train and becoming immediately engaged with the emblems of other lives that pass before her eyes:

> There were the squalid dreary backs of houses – she wondered if the people who lived within were ever happy? – the ugly unkept gardens, with the clothes hanging out to dry, or the crooked dirty lines, where they had been hung, left forgotten. The gardens were worse than the houses, and she looked up at the windows again. She could see into some of the rooms, corners of beds, backs of toilet glasses, now and then a cheap ornament, and she recoiled a little. It was all so tawdry.[45]

Here the train allows connection across classes in a degree of intimacy, making publicly visible details of daily life which are normally hidden from outside gaze such as beds and toilet glasses. Notably, though, in all these examples the connections are between the individual within the train, and objects, abstractions or collectives – rather than particular people – outside it. In transit, in the third space, the commuter is transformed from part of an objectified, gazed-upon mass to an individual subject whose gaze connects with but objectifies the world that passes beyond the screen of the carriage window.

The qualities of this third space, neither home nor work but the journey between, a space in which the individual is detached from, yet stimulated by, the objects of his gaze, may suggest that the commuter is a sort of high-speed *flâneur*. In the above examples, he may indeed seem to share some characteristics of the *flâneur* as outlined by Benjamin or Simmel: part of, yet separate from the crowd, his dulled senses awakened through the stimulation of the urban scene, enclosed in a private space from which he languidly casts scopic attention towards the spectacle beyond his subjectivity. Yet as I have suggested above, the commuter is in certain important respects the antithesis of the *flâneur*. The third space constituted by the journey is one of temporary leisure, but the commuter, unlike the *flâneur*, is by definition a working man moving through the urban scene towards a defined purpose. More importantly, whereas both Benjamin in *Charles Baudelaire* and Simmel in *Soziologie* argue that the urban stimulus is visual rather than aural, and, particularly, that on public transport the individual connects with his fellow travellers through silent gaze rather than conversation, the commuter's third space is commonly represented as one of community and social interaction. Numerous examples from both imaginative and life writing support this. In *City and Suburb*, for example, Charlotte Riddell recounts the 'schoolboy cheerfulness' of an omnibus full of ageing commuters:

> They were all old, they were all wrinkled, they had all known trial, and care, and trouble; they were all engaged in business, which ... carries anxiety with it to the end. ... Yet these staid, venerable merchants, travelling at once to and from the business of their lives, were happy as children, as pleased at small jokes, as keen in their pursuit of wealth, as eager for political news, as loath to stay at home for a day as had been the case twenty, thirty, forty, aye, fifty years previously.[46]

Riddell constructs the commuter's space between home and work as one that releases men into a secure masculine environment in which youthfulness can be recaptured away from domestic or business cares. Charles Pooter, too, finds reinforcement of self-esteem through social connection on the way to work: 'As I happened to be sitting next the driver going to town on the 'bus, I told him my joke about the frayed shirts. I thought he would have rolled off his seat.'[47] Thomas Burke stresses the importance of conversation amongst men. The free space of commuting travel allows their focus to shift from the serious and abstract to the possessive and personal: 'In suburban railway trains, dusty talk of hard times and political knavery is shelved, and bright hopes are expressed for "my early peas," "my Lady Gays," and "my crocuses."'[48] And for V.S. Pritchett, commuting as a teenager during the First World War, the interlude between home and work provides secure time and space in which he can test his identity and project his future:

I actually enjoyed standing in a compartment packed with fifteen people. ... I saw myself a junior clerk turning into a senior clerk, comfortable in my train, enjoying the characters of my fellow travellers, talking sententiously of the state of affairs in France, Hong Kong and Singapore and, with profound judiciousness, of government. Over the years one would know those season ticket holders ... as well as the characters in a novel. ... There was the curious satisfaction, in those months, of a settled fate and the feeling that here was good sense and, under the reserve, humour and decency.[49]

The communal spaces of omnibus or train are thus represented as social rather than anonymous, places of shared humour, conversation and continuity. In the brief interludes of travel, with no demands either from home or work, male commuters bond in groups small enough (no more than fifteen people in a 'packed' carriage) to constitute intimate if temporary communities within the colossal scale of total commuting numbers.

This community of commuters, though primarily masculine, was not of course exclusively so. Women may have been in a minority on the suburban commuting routes but they did constitute an important presence, and one that interestingly complicated the third space of the journey. In her recent biography, Kathryn Hughes quotes memories of Mrs Beeton, an early example, in the 1860s, of a woman commuter whose unfamiliar presence disrupted the masculine community into which she intruded.

Mrs Beeton used to go up to town every day by the business train with her husband, a quite unusual thing for any woman of those times to do, and really more or less resented by the other travellers, who were mostly young men who all knew each other but had to curb their exuberant spirits when a lady was present.[50]

Half a century later, in a novel of 1909, H.G. Wells turns the sudden sexualizing of a safe male space to comic effect when Mr Stanley, father to Ann Veronica, finds himself unexpectedly travelling to work at the same time as his daughter. Meeting a fellow commuter – Mr Ramage, who will later attempt a clumsy seduction of Ann Veronica – he is manoeuvred into exchanging his normal first-class carriage for second class so that the three can travel together. To his horror, Ramage and his daughter fall into a discussion of 'one of those modern advanced plays':

'His love-making,' she remarked, 'struck me as unconvincing. He seemed too noisy.'
    The full significance of her words did not instantly appear to him. Then it dawned. Good heavens! She was discussing love-making. ... Could she understand what she was talking about? Luckily, it was a second-class carriage, and the ordinary fellow travellers were not there.[51]

The commuting space, both passages imply, curiously mingles the public and private. Conversation amongst daily companions is constituted of routine familiarity within a privately shared and enclosed social framework. When the community is fractured, however, by the presence of a woman and amongst a different class of fellow travellers, conversation becomes exposed to public hearing and judgement.

Mr Stanley's middle-aged shock at encountering for the first time his daughter's adult sexuality is mitigated only by the relief that he is out of his usual community and that the conversation is thus heard by strangers. For younger men, on the other hand, the daily journey provides time and space for both anonymous and personal encounters with women. Thomas Burke recalls the sexualization of commuting as both general, providing space for encountering girls en masse, and particular, in enabling his first tentative encounters with a selected individual:

> There were many others – girls met on the way to work – girls in the train. ... There was the little girl in the Woolwich train. ... We met every day on the platform ... when the train came in, I would stand back until she had chosen a carriage, and then make for that one. ... And in the evenings I would often lose my train from Charing Cross, waiting about to travel home with her.[52]

Once casual admiration grows into courtship, the daily routine of commuting can be turned to erotic game-playing. Bullock exploits the eroticism of the male's fixed gaze on the particular female within the anonymous crowd as Robert Thorne follows the woman he is later to marry from her place of work:

> I let Nell walk on for some distance, my eyes full of her as she went in and out of the hurrying crowd; and it was not till she had crossed Cannon Street and turned down towards Southwark Bridge that I overtook her. I did not speak. She did not look round. She hurried, I kept pace with her. She crossed the road, I stayed by her side. And with that she turned, a flush ... on her face. ...
> 'I've been following you from Gresham Street. ... Only that I wanted to hear your voice and see your face, I think I could have followed you longer.'
> 'Could you indeed?' Nell looked round. ... Her face was still a-flush. ... 'Well, it's a pity you didn't wait longer, for then you might have admired the way I climb an omnibus.'[53]

Thorne follows Nell as a prospective client follows a prostitute, his mounting excitement mimicked in the panting, simple sentences. And Nell colludes willingly, conscious of her body as an erotic object of a spectator's gaze that is detached and anonymous but also personal and loving.

Figure 1.4: 'Home' by
F.C. Whitney, the
frontispiece for *The
Art and Craft of
Homemaking* by
E.W. Gregory (1913),
Courtesy of the
British Library.

The commuter's journey, therefore, is a release – away from home or work, and into experimentation, observation and eroticism; it is a world enclosed in time and space where connections are made both socially within and visually outside the carriage, bus or street. In this third sphere the commuter creates a selfhood that is independent of both domesticity and employment, a temporal interlude which creates a separate identity as well as a space for negotiation between the worlds of work and home, public and private, city and suburb. Though the *Building News* claimed that the suburban commuter must 'lose an hour each way,' the testimony of both imaginative and life writers is rather to the personal gain that these journeys bestowed.[54] The tensions and ambivalences entailed in commuting occur to the observer in viewing the undifferentiated mass of commuter crowds, and to the commuter or his wife at the points of dis- or reconnection between separate worlds, rather than in the journey itself.

The poem with which I began, Dollie Radford's 'From the Suburbs', is significantly titled: it depicts the commuter train from the perspective of the abandoned wife looking from the suburbs for the returning male, rather than from the point of view of the husband going away *from* the suburbs towards his place of work. The poem thus provides a rare female perspective on the phenomenon of commuting, and, as I suggested above, captures some of the anxieties created by it. The train 'rushes home ... cheerfully' yet it carries a 'weight'; the 'fond wife' spends her leisured day 'admiring [her] suburban home' yet reflects 'sadly' on the 'vast numbers' of men shuttling 'to and fro/So fast and madly'. Radford writes against the idyllic picture of suburban commuting promulgated by the rail companies, as depicted in the advertisement for Golders Green (plate 1.2). Here wife and child sit at leisure in the suburban garden; the returned male worker has removed his jacket to water the garden as later travellers stroll home from the station (visible but tactfully distanced) down a tree-lined avenue. The image is one of idealised harmony through integration of different worlds, as indicated in the poster's text, an extract from William Cooper's 'Sanctuary':

'Tis pleasant, through the loopholes of retreat,
To peep at such a world; to see the stir
Of the great Babel, and not feel the crowd.

By contrast, F.C. Whitney's 'Home' (plate 1.4) is sombrely ambiguous. The returning male's hand hovering apparently indecisively above the garden gate, the woman framed in the open door, hand on hip, and the twisted, dark trees framing the path, are as suggestive of looming conflict as they are of warmth and welcome. The picture is a wonderfully distilled evocation of the tensions evoked in the commuter's negotiation of difference, his daily interconnections of contrasting spheres.

I have argued, then, that the pre–1918 commuter is a significant figure in the developing discourse of urban modernity. Crossing twice daily the 'frontier' between suburb and city, moving between female- and male-dominated spaces via a journey that itself constitutes a separate dimension, and as an individual within a crowd that shares direction and purpose, the commuter's experience is distinct from the more familiar representatives of the modern city. Observed as part of an anonymous urban mass, he is also an observer of urban aspects otherwise hidden from the eye. Constructed by different writers as both comic and heroic object, as subject he adds a third spatial and temporal identity to the common binary of domesticity and labour, and engages in a daily negotiation of his three spheres. To commute may ideally mitigate some of the difficulties of urbanism; it undoubtedly adds complexity and interest to the experience of the modern city.

Notes

1. Dollie Radford, 'From the Suburbs', in *Songs and Other Verses*, London, 1895.
2. V.S. Pritchett, *A Cab at the Door*, London, 1968, 183.
3. Philip Davis, *The Oxford English Literary History, Volume 8. 1830–1880: The Victorians*, Oxford, 2002, 28.
4. Ana Parejo Vadillo, *Women Poets and Urban Aestheticism: Passengers of Modernity*, Basingstoke, 2005, 173.
5. 'City men who live in the distant suburbs of the metropolis are compelled to lose at least an hour each way in going to and from business every day.' *Building News*, no. 4 (1858): 1019. A horse-drawn omnibus would be expected to average six miles per hour; rail commuters, of course, could live much further out while still having no more than an hour's journey to work.
6. Charles Booth, *Improved Means of Locomotion as a First Step towards the Cure of the Housing Difficulties of London, being an Abstract of the Proceedings of two Conferences Convened by the Warden of Robert Browning Hall, Walworth, with a Paper on the Subject by Charles Booth*, London, 1901, 22.
7. According to the *Oxford English Dictionary*, the first usage of the word 'commuter' occurred in America in 1865, but did not become current in Britain until the 1930s.
8. Walter Besant, *South London*, London, 1899, 318.
9. Christian Wolmar, *The Subterranean Railway*, London, 2005, 14.
10. John Kellett, *The Impact of Railways on Victorian Cities*, London, 1969, 335.
11. J. Blundell Maple, *Cheap Trains for London Workers*, London, 1891, 30–31.
12. Wolmar, *The Subterranean Railway*, 108.
13. Frederick Willis, *101 Jubilee Road: A Book of London Yesterdays*, London, 1948, 42.
14. Donald J. Olsen, *The Growth of Victorian London*, London, 1976, 318.
15. Charles F.G. Masterman, *The Condition of England*, London, 1909, 70.
16. Thomas Burke, *The London Spy: A Book of Town Travels*, London, 1922, 14.
17. Thomas W.H. Crosland, *The Suburbans*, London, 1905, 24.
18. T.S. Eliot, *The Waste Land*, 1922, l. 62.
19. George Sala, *Twice Round the Clock; or, the Hours of the Day and Night in London*, London, 1859, 50–52.
20. Willis, *101 Jubilee Road*, 41.
21. William Pett Ridge, *Outside the Radius: Stories of a London Suburb*, London, 1899, 8.
22. Ibid., 16.
23. Charlotte Riddell, *The Race for Wealth*, London, vol. 1, 1866, 308–10.
24. Sidney Low, 'The Rise of the Suburbs: A Lesson of the Census,' *Contemporary Review*, LX (1891): 545–58.
25. According to Benjamin, the *flâneur* 'goes botanising on the asphalt' (Walter Benjamin, *Charles Baudelaire: A Lyric Poet in the Era of High Capitalism*, trans. Harry Zohn, London, 1983, 36).
26. John Stilgoe, *Borderland: Origins of the American Suburb, 1820–1914*, New Haven, CT, 1988, 5.
27. Shan F. Bullock, *Robert Thorne: The Story of a London Clerk*, London, 1907, 173.
28. Edwin Pugh, *A Street in Suburbia*, London, 1895, 71.

29. George and Weedon Grossmith, *The Diary of a Nobody*, London, 1965, 213.
30. W.H. Hartley, *In a London Suburb*, London, 1885, vol. 1, 4.
31. Willis, *101 Jubilee Road*, 42.
32. Grossmith, *The Diary of a Nobody*, 67.
33. Arthur Conan Doyle, *The Great Shadow and Beyond the City*, Bristol, 1893, 195.
34. Pritchett, *A Cab at the Door*, 186.
35. Conan Doyle, *The Great Shadow and Beyond the City*, 213.
36. Charles Dickens, *Great Expectations*, London, 1996, 206.
37. Ibid., 291.
38. Ibid., 210.
39. Conan Doyle, *The Great Shadow and Beyond the City*, 211.
40. Ibid., 212–13.
41. Ibid., 320.
42. Kellett, *The Impact of Railways on Victorian Cities*, chs 6 and 20.
43. Charles Dickens, *Dombey and Son*, London, 2002, 312.
44. Masterman, *The Condition of England*, 72.
45. Lucy Clifford, 'The End of Her Journey,' in Kate Flint, ed., *Victorian Love Stories*, Oxford, 1996, 222. Clifford's protagonist is not strictly a commuter, though as she is travelling to Clapham Junction, one of the major suburban commuting stations, I have taken her experience to be relevant.
46. Charlotte Riddell, *City and Suburb*, London, 1861, vol. 1, 285–86.
47. Grossmith, *The Diary of a Nobody*, 63.
48. Burke, *The London Spy*, 17.
49. Pritchett, *A Cab at the Door*, 184–86.
50. Kathryn Hughes, *The Short Life and Long Times of Mrs Beeton*, London, 2006, 312.
51. H.G. Wells, *Ann Veronica*, London, 1980, 16–17.
52. Burke, *The London Spy*, 42.
53. Bullock, *Robert Thorne*, 89.
54. See note 5.

JOHN THOMSON'S LONDON IN PHOTOGRAPHS

Lindsay Smith

The year is 1851. At 4 a.m. in London's Farringdon-Market, an eight year old girl shuffles along in carpet slippers too large for her feet. Wrapped in a threadbare shawl and cotton dress she is there to bargain for watercress. It is wintry and the price of the commodity she buys to sell has risen from a half penny to a penny. Having bought what she can afford, sixpence worth or as many as can be crammed into her basket, she will arrange the cress into bunches and wash them with numbed hands under the pump. Her street cry: 'creases, four bunches a penny, creases!' will be heard late into the evening.[1]

Twenty-five years on and a handsome though somewhat disheveled man sits indoors in his overcoat painting a sign or 'ticket' upon which may be read the words 'choice fruits'. His gaze is averted and emphasis falls upon his hands, those of a non-manual worker. A polyanthus is positioned for observational drawing on the table beside him, while an out of focus hat occupies the background. 'Tickets' the card dealer, as the man is commonly known in the neighbourhood, is a French refugee with a colourful past now struggling to make a living among the slums of London.[2]

These two poor workers come respectively from Henry Mayhew's *London Labour and the London Poor* (1851–52) and John Thomson's *Street Life in London* (1877), both of which were initially published in serial form.[3] The case studies, 'the watercress girl' and 'Tickets the card dealer', are separated by two and a half decades, by their age, gender and the vagaries of personal circumstance, but they are linked by the fact that they both eke out an existence in London, a capital city undergoing immense physical change during the period. These changes are singularly apparent in a cultural revolution in visual representation that is played out in both texts. Indeed, the popularization and development of technologies of photography occurring in the period between the publication dates of *London Labour and the London Poor* and *Street Life in London* distinguishes the two volumes in a way perhaps less palpable but nonetheless as significant as the more obvious legislative changes, represented in their pages, that affected metropolitan life of the time. While photography is already present in Mayhew in the mediated form of twenty-eight wood engravings taken from Richard Beard's daguerreotypes that accompany the text, it is more overtly evident in Thomson's volume in twenty-three photographs produced by the Woodburytype process.[4] Both authors were turning their attention to life on the streets of London precisely at the historical moment at which photography was making its presence felt in the city in all sorts of distinct ways. When in 1877 Thomson chose to present Victorian London in photographs it is the photographs themselves 'taken from life expressly for [the] publication' that form the kernel of the text. Those photographs are, in the words of the author, designed to lend to his book an 'authority' in supplementing Mayhew's original findings with fresh and unrivalled insight.

The first volume of Mayhew's *London Labour and the London Poor* features 'the watercress girl' as one of many poor subjects classified according to the 'type' of his or her labour. Evolving from a series of articles he wrote for the *Morning Chronicle*, Mayhew's voluminous work broadly categorizes the urban poor as belonging to three groups: 'those who work, can't work, won't work'. Each one of those groups burgeons into a myriad of subgroups between which the author forges a series of highly complex connections. As Mayhew writes: 'among the street-folk there are … people differing as widely from each in tastes, habits, thoughts and creed, as one nation from another'. At the top of the hierarchy are the 'patterers', or 'the men who cry the last dying-speeches', generally an educated class who despise the largest and 'most broadly marked class' of costermongers directly below them. Mayhew identifies the language of the costermongers exhibited in the beerhouses as dependent upon slang 'unintelligible even to the partially initiated'.[5] At the bottom of the Darwinian heap, by contrast, are the mud-larks, who scavenge through mud left by the retiring tide of the River Thames, and are represented by their extreme physical degradation. The equally pitiful class of crawlers tells its own dramatic stories through distinguishing dialect.

As an example of his first broad category, 'those who work', Mayhew represents the watercress girl largely through her own words. Her dialect is distinguished by its touching and repeated deduction of the limits of her knowledge: 'I can't read or write, but I knows how many pennies goes to a shilling … I don't know nothing about what I earns during the year, I only know how many pennies goes to a shilling'.[6] With a Dickensian proportion of self-revealed pathos, Mayhew has the child characterize herself as much by her language

Figure 2.1: '"Tickets" the card dealer'. Courtesy of the Trustees of the National Library of Scotland.

as by her appearance. Thomson's 1877 account of 'Tickets the card Dealer', by comparison, contains no direct or reported speech, as if the accompanying photographic portrait renders redundant the necessity of his own words. However, we are provided with his entire life story, in all its trials, as mediated through the self-assured omniscient narrative voice of the journalist and Thomson's collaborator Adolphe Smith. Yet working to a large extent against that tale, the photographic presence of 'Tickets' commands attention at odds with the moralizing tenor of the life-story. Save for the shabby dress of the figure, the portrait could be that of an eminent individual. Indeed, in a manner distinct from the majority of photographs in the volume, the image approximates in impact a portrait by the Frenchman's famous contemporary countryman, Nadar. Yet, at the same time, 'Tickets' is without a proper name; he is simply offered to the reader as a respected citizen devoid of his identity, 'shipwreck[ed] amid the slums of London'.[7] As foreign and thereby exotic, 'Tickets' is presented for the reader to consume with that extra pleasure gained from the retrospective knowledge of his, and others', thwarted foresight. If only, the story goes, this unsuspecting Frenchman had known what hopelessness awaited him on the streets of London, he would never have come to the city.

During the mid-nineteenth century, developments in photographing the city of London form part of a large and complex history of representing the urban poor in the visual arts. Following the public announcement of the daguerreotype process in Paris in 1839, the first photographs of London were taken in the autumn of that year by the French photographer Monsieur de St Croix. But it was the introduction in 1841 of William Henry Fox Talbot's calotype, the first negative/positive process from which multiple copies of an original could be made, that generated some of the earliest surviving photographs of architectural views of the city.[8] By the 1850s, when Mayhew was conducting his interviews and compiling his study, there had been huge advancements in technologies of photography. In particular, the publication in 1851 of the wet collodion process, invented in 1848 by Frederick Scott Archer and free from patent restrictions, made photography more freely available and affordable.[9] It also quickened exposure times, which was a huge advance for photographers working outside the context of the studio.

Between the publication of Mayhew's and Thomson's texts, poverty and homelessness among the working-class population of London remained significant social problems. There were many major Parliamentary Acts during the period dealing with public health in London, but as Richard Ovenden has indicated, 'by 1876 many of the social problems evident on London's streets had failed to disappear'.[10] While Thomson's photographs were not the first to record British streets they were novel in their attempt to influence public opinion on the matter. Thomson's photograph entitled 'Public Disinfectors' cuts to the heart of issues of public health. The two men posed pulling their 'hermetically closed' wagon and dressed in white protective clothing take on the uncanny look of pierrots, owing to the strong contrast of the woodburytype process by which the white of the cloth and the rim of the wheel, together with the right shoe of the left-hand figure, shine out from the image. At the same time, the formal incongruity of the uniformed men set against the black hole of a broken pane of glass in the background conveys the weight of Smith's accompanying narrative. This narrative stresses the thanklessness of the men's task, exposed as they regularly are to infectious diseases, but also the levelling power of disease: the 'public disinfectors alike

Figure 2.2: 'Public Disinfectors'. Courtesy of the Trustees of the National Library of Scotland.

disinfect the houses of the poor and rich; one day destroying the rubbish in a rag merchant's shop, and the next handling the delicate damask and superfine linen which shade and cover the bed in some Belgravian mansion',[11] just as throughout the volume Thomson employs photography to expose the type of common humanity that endures in spite of class differences. In 'Public Disinfectors', as in 'The Old Clothes of St. Giles', we are reminded not only that the threat of contagion circulates invisibly throughout all walks of society but, more specifically, that 'the germs of scarlet fever can live in woolen materials for several years'.[12] Both Mayhew and Thomson reflect upon the fact that the cloth of a new coat may be 'made from the cast-off garment of some street beggar!' Thomson incorporates, in particular, the metaphor of diseased clothing, as explored in both Charles Kingsley's *Alton Locke*, in which the sartorial fruits of sweated labour wreak their revenge upon the upper classes in the form of a pestilent coat, and Charles Dickens's *Bleak House*, in which a handkerchief becomes the offending article. In each the imperceptible cycle by which old clothing also serves to fertilize the land is present; old rags used to grow hops become beer for street folk.

When in his preface Thomson acknowledges his debt to Mayhew, it is primarily to register the need to update the 'facts and figures' of the earlier narrative. In turn, Thomson maintains, it is the visual accuracy of his photographs that provides the novel authority of his own unique account of London. For Thomson assuredly claims to have brought to bear upon contemporary London life 'the precision of photography in illustration of [the] subject: the unquestionable accuracy of this testimony will enable us to present true types of the London Poor and shield us from the accusation of either underrating or exaggerating individual peculiarities of appearance'.[13]

Thomson's is a popular claim for photography and one that was made repeatedly from its inception. However, it is also a contention that was challenged from the medium's very beginnings. Indeed, it was by no means news in the 1870s that the camera might lie. But, clearly, the relative ability of the medium to approximate 'truth' was entirely contingent upon context. In the shift from Mayhew to Thomson, from covert mediated use of photographic representation to the overt use of photographs, an emphasis upon the speech of depicted subjects gives way to an emphasis upon their appearance. While it is by no means simply the case that the relatively novel medium of photography in Thomson's book replaces direct speech earlier found in Mayhew's, Thomson's realization of particular visual types alters the role of speech in the textual context in which his photographs appear. For once it has become possible, as it is for Thomson, to photograph people *in situ* on the streets, there no longer exists the same requirement to disclose aspects of character through direct speech. Moreover, in Thomson's text, the photograph, by means of its physical and metaphysical distinctiveness from earlier forms of visual representation, recasts that which might have told us something about London life in Mayhew's 'speech'. And although, following Mayhew's lead, Thomson claims to have recorded a fair amount of dialect in his study, he moves away from a focus upon verbal idiosyncrasies of individual figures to an emphasis upon interaction among individuals and groups. Apart from Thomson's most well-known photograph, entitled 'The Crawlers' – a striking image of an old destitute woman huddled on a doorstep minding an infant – there are only two other photographs in *Street Life in London* in which a single person commands the frame: 'The London Boardmen' and 'The Watercart Man'; the remainder focus upon groups of subjects.

Although one might argue that Thomson's photographed groups of subjects are equally as staged as Mayhew's earlier engravings, the photographic medium harbours the potential to suggest otherwise. Such is the case, in part because photography appears to resist editing by way of its unique temporal existence, but also because it impacts in new ways upon that age-old philosophical category of mimesis. Photographs operate as parts of a larger whole petrified in time. Moreover, distinct from Mayhew's cameos of London life that function with the distilled impact of an emblem, Thomson's depictions operate as if in *medias res* as indiscriminate interruptions in a larger ongoing narrative of life on the streets. This difference owes both to the particular assault upon temporality that the photographic medium performs, and also to those ways in which Thomson's earlier China project subsequently affects his representation of people at 'home'. Thomson was 'the first professional photographer well-documented in Beijing after 1860'.[14] After first visiting Cambodia, he spent time in Formosa and mainland China between 1868 and 1872. The photographs that accompanied *Illustrations of China and Its People* are considered to portray cultural and ethnic differences with considerable insight.[15] Thomson's China photographs were unique in situating Chinese subjects in context, and the same is true of those subjects in *Street Life in London*. At one level the China experience subsequently makes newly strange the viewing of familiar subjects ('types') on the streets of London. Moreover, *Illustrations of China and Its People* explicitly required the photographer to ponder the construction of visual types and to explore the ways in which the photographic medium might newly realize processes of typification.

Throughout the nineteenth century, 'types' of the urban poor emerge in diverse fields of representation. The camera's record of 'street Arabs', for example, a term coined in Thomas Guthrie's 'First Plea for Ragged Schools' of 1847, was already underway by the early 1850s.[16] By the time of Thomson's publication in 1877 there were established precedents for photographing street urchins with archetypal images such as Oscar Rejlander's 'Night in Town' (1860) determining particular ways of realizing child poverty. Rejlander's lyrical image of a small white boy with dirt-blackened feet aestheticizes the figure of the child in a manner well rehearsed in painting. One only has to recall Bartolome Murrillo's earlier compositions of the ragged boys and 'flower girls' of Seville to find powerful parallels that influenced in British painting, for example, Joshua Reynolds's child portraits. But Rejlander's urchin, highly lit so as to accentuate the white shoulders, knee and calf protruding through the boy's torn clothing, poses not on the street but upon steps in the photographer's studio, mocked up to appear as an external doorstep. The photograph was adopted by the Shaftesbury Society for their publicity campaigns and influenced the later systematic production of Thomas Barnardo's 'Before and After' pictures.[17] These images, which used the photographic companion format to promote the transformative power of Barnardo's charitable work, were sold to gain revenue for the children's homes. However, the images were from the first controversial, not least owing to their capacity to fabricate relative degrees of poverty as displayed in the 'before' shot, which depicted the once-ragged child, and in the 'after' shot, a clean and civilized one.

Thomson's *Victorian London Street Life* is contemporary with Barnardo's more familiar 'Before and After' pictures and it is likely that the very difference between Barnardo's images and Thomson's photographs was in part 'responsible for making contemporary nineteenth-century viewers question the integrity of Barnardo's photographs'.[18] For Thomson's contextualization of his photographic subjects among those streets from which they came meant he avoided the charges of falsehood that were levelled at Barnardo's studio constructions. And while Thomson's London photographs undoubtedly owe much to his earlier recording of Chinese subjects, they share formal qualities, which acquire a profound metaphysical effect, with photographs by other contemporary British practitioners, most notably Thomas Annan's photographs of the slums of Glasgow.

Annan's thirty-one photographs, commissioned by Glasgow City Improvement Trust in the 1860s, show the destitution of working-class subjects by depicting them in the context of their inadequate housing.[19] The photographs have been regarded as aspiring to 'picturesque effect',[20] or as emphasizing 'the physical structures' of the British streets 'over the people who inhabited them', since, according to Richard Ovenden, those people 'register only as fleeting ghosts, the photographer allowing them to wander in and out of the camera's range at will'.[21] However, Annan's emphasis upon the physical fabric of the streets, haunted by the ethereal presence of their inhabitants, not only connects them with Thomson's work but also marks as distinctive this emergent form of social documentary. It is not simply the narrow alleyways of the Glasgow slums strewn across with washing, but also that pervasive sense of the buildings having been emptied into the streets, those flats regularly teeming with poor subjects having been turned out, that give Annan's photographs a cramped, claustrophobic feel. This type of physical exposure of the secret filth and squalor of inadequate housing is what the emergent genre of documentary photography sought to reveal. However, such an ability to dispel discrimination among objects submitted to the camera eye, such that a building is rendered with the same degree of verisimilitude as a human subject, is also a quality correlative with that larger indiscriminate nature of the photographic medium more generally.

During the period in question the concept of a documentary function for photography, as we now understand it, was in the process of being conceptualized. Annan followed a written brief when documenting Glasgow slums, but there existed few photographic precedents for his resulting work, just as there existed few for Thomson's London project. Yet in a manner that anticipates Thomson's *Street Life in London*, Annan's photographs summon a concept coined by the philosopher Walter Benjamin as 'the spark of contingency' at the heart of the photographic medium.[22] For those Glasgow images invite the viewer to search 'the here and now' among their apparently unselective visual field for that which might hold a key to the future. Indeed, they invite us to locate precisely that which, as a consequence of Thomson's text, will designate an authentic quality of 'documentary' photography. Yet, if Annan's photographs possess in the 1860s a version of Benjamin's 'spark of contingency', it exists not in the carefully composed architectural record but rather in the randomness of those human inhabitants who peer into a frame, who, as critics have remarked, 'give themselves over so easily to the camera'.[23] To what extent, however, may these figures captive on the photographic plate be said to have 'given' themselves as potential likenesses, rather than simply taking a look, wanting to look? For the other side of having one's likeness taken, of submitting to the lens, is actively taking a look back at the photographer and his elaborate set-up. Consequently, the presence of those subjects caught by Annan's camera need not be read as an act of submission at all and it is telling that we read complicity in such images that need not have required consent. For a 'likeness' in the form of Annan's documentary photography is simply 'taken'; there is not yet in the act of collective exposure to a camera an understanding of the act of conscious surrender as belonging to the medium of photography.

In the context of nineteenth-century realism Carol Armstrong has remarked upon the fact that since Annan's 'images were supposed to be historical records pure and simple, we might expect them to adhere most closely to the doctrine of realism', yet the status of what he was recording as 'a place and a whole way of life marked for obsolescence seems to endow these images with a fantastic quality that puts them at the opposite pole from realism'.[24] Clearly, as Armstrong notes, Annan's photographs contribute to a visual history of depicting urban poverty, 'rework[ing] conventions established when Frederich Engels and James Kay Shutttleworth described the condition of the working classes and Dickens, Elizabeth Gaskell, and Benjamin Disraeli, along with the popular engraver Gustave Doré turned these scenes of misery into popular entertainment'.[25] But what Armstrong perceives as 'an idealization' in Annan's representation of 'human misery, filth and disease' is perpetually undercut by the photographic medium itself.[26]

For the blurred life shown in the dark alleyways works against such idealization and against Armstrong's notion of the photographs' 'evacuation' of life from the streets. The human presence, in its translation from the captured stasis required of a traditional portrait to the streak of moving life is, in Annan, endowed with a new quality via the indiscriminate or 'documentary' potential of the medium. Rather than, as Armstrong states, the camera bringing recognizable 'principles of the picturesque into the city streets and [breaking] down the complex and fluid social life transacted there into purely visual components',[27] photography aspires to arrest such social life precisely as fluidity. Those resulting images, in the case of both Annan and Thomson, are distinguished by visually disruptive physical markers of flux, such as the blur, to the extent that the medium cannot be said to simply replicate a preexistent aesthetic of looking and representing.

The dilemma of how to arrest 'movement' was of course, along with that of polychrome, one of the key challenges to early photography. Throughout the nineteenth century, movement regularly disrupts the stasis of a photographic image, captured as an occasional blur on the plate. Yet such an element exists in a certain sense 'unseen' by the photographer at the time of taking the photograph; that which has moved is only really experienced as such in the past tense of viewing the perpetual present tense of a photograph. Yet by focusing on that flux – by its very nature inimical to the 'still' photographic – those blurs that register a photographer's presence, Thomson's photographs generate a relentless assault upon temporality. Characteristically, in Thomson we find this phenomenon in the smudged trace of a child's head turned during the exposure, as in 'The Old Clothes of St. Giles', or in a yet more unwitting presence such as that of a dog not cognizant of the strictures of exposure in 'A Convict's Home'. The function of these blurs is to fix retrospectively the photographs at a historical moment prior to instantaneous photography, to seal their existence as early photographs. But in disrupting the seamlessness of the unitary image these visual smears also haunt its apparently perfect surface, thereby impressing the power of a photograph's causal connection to its referent.

More significantly, Thomson's blurs also convey that metaphysical sense in which photographs capture the presence of the unseen as a larger kind of anti-editing or obliviousness to selectivity as the very lot, or nature, of the mechanical process itself. Such a capacity is congruent with attempts to record the plenitude of the metropolis together with that eternal sense of the impossibility of recording 'accurately' life on the streets. Such 'life' frequently takes the form of images that record social and economic transaction: the buying of fish, ices, coffee or the surveying of 'fancy ware'. Or they capture workers prior to or in between business such as 'the convent garden flower women' or 'the mush fakers and ginger beer makers'. At one level Thomson aspires to record 'life' as it is found on the streets rather than selecting individual representatives from it. In the photograph entitled 'the Cheap Fish of St Giles's' he provides the reader with a detailed account of those present. We learn of 'Joseph Carney' the costermonger who is seen regularly in the street market between

Figure 2.3: 'The Cheap Fish of St Giles's'. Courtesy of the Trustees of the National Library of Scotland.

'Seven Dials' and 'Five Dials', and of the 'German pal', shown on his left, who helps him. We look to pick out the unfortunately named 'Ugly', the homeless boy supported by the market, and have little trouble identifying the iconic figure of 'Little Mic-Mac Gosling', the very small seventeen-year-old who, clutching the graceful jug of a Dutch still life, frames the image on the right. We are told nothing, however, of the arguably more interesting throng of people who, to get into the picture, crowd behind the display of fish. They lean and poke out from behind each other to catch a look at and into the camera.

In Thomson's *Street Life in London* we thereby witness the emergence of that form of conscious surrender detectable only in embryonic form in Annan. Some figures in 'The Cheap Fish of St Giles's' remain as blurred faces that bear uncanny resemblance to portraits by Francis Bacon or, as in the case of a figure on the left, present only by virtue of the likeness of his hat that floats above the herring barrel, they are caught as something different from a likeness. They are captured, that is, by a certain unlikeness to an original, which is reciprocally a 'likeness', a visible mark of the flux of the street prior to a perfect petrification by photography. Moreover, the human forms appear as amorphous as those transactions occurring between the individuals on the streets themselves. Such is the movement that early film will subsequently come to capture. But it is not sufficient to describe as a pre-cinematic quality that which persists here as the 'still' camera's record of fluctuation. For something else is going on that pertains to a notion of willing participation on the part of the crowd. It is a distinguishing factor in Thomson and one quite different from that which film will become when it preserves the moving image as 'moving'. As Susan Sontag has remarked, 'the very muteness of what is hypothetically comprehensible in photographs is what constitutes their attraction and provocativeness'.[28] And in Thomson's photographs there exists an authenticity in the blurs, accidents inherent in the inability of the medium to capture movement.

The earlier engravings of Mayhew's *London Labour* could not by definition have this quality, evident in 'the Cheap Fish of St Giles's', of what is effectively consent, of subjects insinuating themselves in the picture, faces inscribed on the surface of the photograph simply as temporal marks. Nor could the engravings manifest such a sense of crowding into the temporally delineated frame that photography records. But in Thomson there occur additional differences from Mayhew when he creates in photographs his documentary of London life. At the same time, however, in subtle ways Thomson's later text remains dependent upon Mayhew's earlier one. For example, Thomson shares with Mayhew forms of expressing a concept of documentary accuracy; he uses the word 'unvarnished' in referring to his account of the nomads, the very word that Mayhew uses in the preface to describe the first-hand accounts of the poor that he brings before the public. And Thomson also begins his text with an example of nomadic people just as Mayhew firstly offers a discussion of 'the nomadic races of England'.[29] But, at a visual level, Thomson accentuates the ways in which his work is distinct from his predecessor; certain qualities that Thomson captures escape the engravings in Mayhew. For an engraver may edit out superfluous detail, and through different qualities of line and tonal variation achieve relative points of emphasis in a composition. Thus, for example, a gesture may be thrown into relief, made central to an image by strong chiaroscuro dwindling to a fine, barely discernable line in the background. Such a technique, familiar to contemporary readers of illustrated journals such as *Punch* or the *Cornhill Magazine*, is present in volume 2 of

Figure 2.4: 'The Dramatic Shoe-Black'. Courtesy of the Trustees of the National Library of Scotland.

London Labour in the engraving 'the Boy Crossing Sweepers', in which the gesture of the central child's interaction with the gentleman is dramatically offset by the cab drivers and those architectural elements of the background, which, by way of their tonal lightness and absence of dense cross-hatching, in no way compete for visual prominence with the foreground elements.[30]

Consider by comparison Thomson's 'The Dramatic Shoeblack', taken in strong sunlight as evidenced by the clear whites and deep shadows, which achieves a certain compositional equity. Like Mayhew, Thomson here depicts a dramatic moment, to which he refers self-consciously in his caption. We encounter an apparent street *tableau vivant* in which theatrical gesture, such as the elder shoeblack's pointing with his index finger, refers back to the scenarios of the earlier text. However, the surroundings and accoutrements of the shoeblack's trade are not here subordinated to the three adults and single child figure present. Signs advertising 'Lucifers by Bryant and May' and 'blacking' are clearly visible within the image. And one is additionally drawn to the carpet slippers of the shoeblack, which acquire a punctum-like function here along with the pipe belonging to the bearded gentleman on the right, which protrudes as a sparkling white shape from his mouth. Thomson's accompanying narrative that relates the life history of 'Jacobus Parker, Dramatic

Reader, Shoe Black and Pedlar' comprises almost entirely the 'hero's' own words, or 'quotations' that the author claims were 'jotted down as they were uttered'.[31] Parker turns out to be a remarkable man owing to his atypicality; he has a penchant for Shakespearian acting. And although he is allowed to articulate his tale as the central character in a fiction, the photograph tells a different story.

Like the earlier example of 'the Cheap Fish of St Giles's', 'The Dramatic Shoeblack' questions the distinction between the typical and the atypical poor subject. The viewer is able to pick out the Jacobus Parker of Thomson's story, both because of the way he stands over his wares and also because those textual allusions to failing sight may be read from his image. But who are these other figures present? We assume they are here to chat and trade with Parker. But the possibility of a simple dramatic moment played out in familiar bodily gestures is not available to the viewer in the way that it is in the previous example from Mayhew. Furthermore, there is a sense in which the photographic image and text work against each other. This is the case in part because that which should serve as the dramatic gesture of the protagonist of the text is diffused by the presence of other – not only animate – surfaces in the photograph. Indeed, within the photographic composition the texture of the face of the stone pillar on the right is rendered as visually present as the male figure that leans against it. But such a compromised reading is precisely occasioned by that photographic condition of which Roland Barthes reminds us,[32] that indiscriminate nature of photographic representation which must render the brightly lit railings and the creases in the clothing of the figures as faithfully as it does the 'important' parts of the composition. Thus, while the photograph is highly staged and edited in the manner of the earlier engraving 'The Boy Crossing Sweepers', the camera does not confer, in the manner of the hand-transcribed medium, a subordinate status to certain areas of the composition.

Critics have remarked upon Thomson's preference in *Street Life in London* for a portrayal of types over individuals. However, there is a fundamental sense in which, in such a context, the very medium of photography works against a notion of typicality. Mayhew was very interested in the a-typical poor subject, delineating a textual history that demonstrates 'how often the poor boys reared in the gutters are thieves, merely because society forbids them being honest lads'.[33] But Thomson, with the comparatively novel facility of photography, has only to photograph those poor subjects he encounters to realize their atypicality, since that quality of rendering remarkable is present in the very nature of photography. The medium performs this distinction by way of its unique relationship to analogy. For, possessing residual qualities that work against typification, photographs involve different kinds of causal connections to their referents from earlier forms of representation; the crease of a sleeve that is not any old sleeve. Such qualities that resist the ordering necessary for typification have been differently described by key theorists of photography. For Benjamin it is the prophetic look – the presentiment of fate – present in the eyes of the wife of the photographer Carl Dauthenday;[34] for Barthes it is a photograph of Alexander Paine prior to his execution in which he simultaneously exists as he who is 'dead' and is 'going to die'[35] that generates new conceptual possibilities that refresh the meaning of the word 'type'. Such a notion of the photograph capturing that which exceeds the visible realm is explored in the profession of the photographer as it is differently inflected in Mayhew and Thomson. Mayhew has an extended account of the differing fortunes of the photographer and his covert means (dodging and faking), of making a living. In his 'statement of a photographic man', photography as a miraculous medium is very much present in the discussion of the photographer's relationship to his sitters. Learning on the job, and having produced as a consequence a completely black image, the photographer's ruse is to claim to the unsuspecting client that it will become more distinct once taken away from the premises:

> The very next day I had the camera, I had a customer before I had even tried it, so I tried it on him, and gave him a black picture (for I didn't know how to make the portrait, and it was all black when I took the glass out), and told him that it would come out bright as it dried, and he went away quite delighted.[36]

An equally blatant 'dodge' involves:

> always tak[ing] the portrait on a shilling size; and after they are done, I show them what they can have for a shilling – the full size, with the knees; and table and vase on it – and let them understand that for sixpence they have all the background and legs cut off; so as many take the shilling portraits as sixpenny ones.[37]

In this early phase of photographic studio portraiture the greatest value for money equates with cutting off the fewest bits of the person photographed while including the greatest number of studio props. The more you cram into the image in terms of content, the greater the value for money. And quantity in terms of the portrait here relates again to plenitude, which the endemic selectivity of painting simply cannot record. It is equivalent to that phenomenon we witnessed above of the crowd putting itself in the picture. But, by the same token, where photography is concerned, that which is lost or thought of as lost, does not simply inhabit the conscious realm. So it is not simply the case that those obvious exclusions in a photograph – for example, the severing of a head or feet – register a sense of loss. At an equally fundamental level, photographs register the unseen.

Perhaps the most blatant 'dodge' Mayhew relates is that of the photographer substituting the client's image with that of someone else, not infrequently a person bearing little resemblance to the original. Thus we have for example the occasion of a childless woman being persuaded of the likeness of the image produced even when she appears in the photograph with a child. On another occasion we are told:

> Once a sailor came in, and as he was in haste, I shoved on to him a picture of a carpenter, who was to call in the afternoon for his portrait. The jacket was dark, but there was a white waistcoat; still I persuaded him that it was his blue Guernsey which had come up very light, and he was so pleased that he gave us 9d. instead of 6d. The fact is, people don't know their own faces. Half of 'em have never looked in a glass half a dozen times in their life, and directly they see a pair of eyes and a nose, they fancy they are their own.[38]

This incident dramatizes the mythic relationship of a photographic 'likeness' to an original. Clearly those photographic subjects cited here by Mayhew do not identify themselves by the accoutrements of their trades: the sailor reads as his own both the clothes and demeanor of the carpenter. And Mayhew voices a deceptively insightful reference to the power of misrecognition, and the way in which a photograph refashions a subject's relationship to his or her mirror image or 'likeness' in the glass.

In Thomson's portrayal of the photographer there is by comparison a shift from a stress upon the alchemy of the medium to its promotion as a lucrative commodity; a shift from success through relative incompetence of Mayhew, to success via a slick professionalism of Thomson. Photography appears in *Street Life in London* two-thirds of the way into the text in the section entitled 'Clapham Common Industries', as an itinerant 'industry' especially successful during holidays and festivals.

> Nurses with babies and perambulators are easily lured within the charmed focus of the camera. They are particularly fond of taking home to their mistresses a photograph of the child entrusted to their care; and the portrait rarely fails to excite the interest of the parents. Nor does the matter rest here. The parents are often so satisfied that the nurse is commissioned to obtain one or more likenesses on her next visit to the common. Thus practically she becomes an advertising medium, and the photographer generally relies on receiving more orders when he has once secured the custom of a nurse-girl.[39]

Thomson writes very little about the image of the photographer he includes in the text, other than to identify him as a 'faithful frequenter of the Common', but the image is significant not least because it portrays that quality of indiscrimination with which we have been concerned. The act of photographing as itself represented within a photograph is by this point historically a well-rehearsed conceit. Here we find the photographer in action, together with his portable dark room, wagon with exhibits, and the eager sitters including the baby in perambulator. However, in less than sharp focus leaning on a tree to the left background is a young errand boy who surveys the scene surreptitiously. He is not meant to be in either of the photographs we are here witness to, or certainly that is the effect conjured by his presence. But he is rendered visible by the medium nonetheless; a figure who believes he remains unseen or unobtrusive in the shadow but is captured anyway by that indiscriminate photographic agency.

Thomson himself marvels at such an indiscriminate capacity peculiar to the photograph when writing in *Science for All*, 1877: 'What occult science confers on this mystic apparatus the power of picturing objects placed before it, producing an image so perfect that alike no point of beauty, no spot or blemish, escapes its microscopic observation?'[40] The occult power of this 'black art from France' guarantees that nothing is lost to the camera eye. For the photograph, by definition, bears qualities distinct from those of written narrative, ones that require us to question how we might define the incidental or superfluous. Of course, 'extraneousness', that sense of the nonessential, or incidental, is conceptually vital to an understanding of documentary photography. And to an extent Thomson's wish to avoid claims of 'over-' or 'underrating accuracy' is bolstered by an understanding of photography as that medium which evades selection and is therefore supremely mimetic. Yet, in *Street Life in London*, the indiscriminate nature of the photograph by definition sometimes works against the strong documentary message that Thomson wishes to convey. In giving all that is visible, the photograph also renders the invisible, that is, those aspects which were more than were bargained for by the photographer. This claim is not to disregard the highly constructed nature of photographic images, nor the editing involved in taking a photograph, but rather to register the enduring quality of what Benjamin so artfully referred to as the 'optical unconscious' of the medium. Unconscious, that is, in the sense of a residue that resists conscious ordering and selectivity, but persists as a type of temporal disjunction, as it has done even in the seemingly most mundane photograph of nineteenth-century street life in London.

Notes

1. Henry Mayhew, *London Labour and the London Poor: a Cyclopaedia of the Condition and Earnings of those that will Work, those that cannot Work and those that will not Work*, London, 1865; new edition 1967, London, 4 vols, vol. 1, 151.
2. John Thomson and Adolphe Smith, *Street Life in London*, London, 1877, reproduced in John Thomson and Adolphe Smith, *Victorian London Street Life in Historic Photographs*, New York, 1994, 50–54.

3. Mayhew's book grew out of articles he wrote for *The Morning Chronicle*. The first of these, 'A Visit to the Cholera Districts of Bermondsey', was published in its columns on Monday 24 September 1840. Between 19 October 1849 and 31 October 1850 Mayhew's contribution consisted of seventy–six letters averaging 3,500 words each; subsequently they were issued in twopenny parts by George Woodfall (Henry Mayhew, *London Labour and the London Poor*, introduced by Victor Neuburg, London, 1985, xix–xx). Each serialized part of Thomson's *Street Life in London* sold for 1s 6d which, as Richard Ovenden has pointed out, was a competitive price, the same cost as 'other illustrated periodicals issued by Sampson Low, such as *Men of Mark … and The Picture Gallery*' (Richard Ovenden, *John Thomson (1837–1921) Photographer*, Edinburgh, 1997, 37).

4. Thomson's choice of the Woodburytype process to render images photochemically from his dry-plate process held advantages over other processes. Not only did it produce distinct contrasts, retaining detail in the shadows, but it ensured uniformity of image across print runs.

5. Mayhew, *London Labour and the London Poor*, 18.

6. Ibid., 67.

7. Thomson, *Street Life in London*, 54.

8. For a fuller discussion of the impact of William Henry Fox Talbot's calotype process see Larry J. Schaaf, *Out of the Shadows: Herschel, Talbot and the Invention of Photography*, New Haven and London, 1992.

9. Frederick Scott Archer's process was significant for its clarity (using glass as a base) but also for its reduction of exposure times, previously between five and fifteen minutes, to a matter of seconds.

10. Ovenden, *John Thomson (1837–1921) Photographer*, 79.

11. Thomson, *Street Life in London*, 22.

12. Ibid.

13. Ibid., preface.

14. Régine Thiriez, *Barbarian Lens: Western Photographers of the Qianlong Emperor's European Palaces*, Amsterdam, 1998, 13.

15. Ibid., 14.

16. Thomas Guthrie, 'First Plea for Ragged Schools', in Thomas Guthrie, *Seed Time & Harvest of Ragged Schools or a Third Plea with New Editions of the First and Second Pleas*, Edinburgh, 1860, 25–30.

17. For further discussion of Thomas Barnardo's uses of photography see Lindsay Smith, *The Politics of Focus: Women and Children in Nineteenth Century Photography*, Manchester, 1998, 111–31.

18. Ovenden, *John Thomson (1837–1921) Photographer*, 124.

19. After working as a copperplate engraver, Thomas Annan (1829–87) acquired patent rights in the photogravure process of Talbot and set up a studio in Glasgow. His commission for the city 'Improvement Trust' to record streets prior to urban renewal resulted in the series of photographs *Old Closes and Streets of Glasgow* published between 1868 and 1877.

20. Alan Thomas, *The Expanding Eye: Photography and the Nineteenth Century Mind*, London, 1977, 136.

21. Ovenden, *John Thomson (1837–1921) Photographer*, 82.

22. Walter Benjamin, 'A Small History of Photography', in *One Way Street and Other Writings*, trans. by Edmund Jephcott and Kingsley Shorter, London, 1985, 240–57.

23. Ovenden, *John Thomson (1837–1921) Photographer*, 82.

24. Nancy Armstrong, *Fiction in the Age of Photography: the Legacy of British Realism*, Cambridge, MA, 1999, 91.
25. Ibid., 93.
26. Ibid.
27. Ibid., 95.
28. Susan Sontag, *On Photography*, London, 1978, 24.
29. Thomson, *Street Life in London*, 1.
30. Mayhew, *London Labour and the London Poor*, 283.
31. Thomson, *Street Life in London*, 47.
32. Roland Barthes, *Camera Lucida: Reflections on Photography*, New York, 1981.
33. Mayhew, *London Labour and the London Poor*, 218.
34. Benjamin, 'A Small History of Photography', 243.
35. Barthes, *Camera Lucida*, 96.
36. Mayhew, *London Labour and the London Poor*, 336.
37. Ibid., 339.
38. Ibid., 341.
39. Thomson, *Street Life in London*, 31.
40. Ovenden, *John Thomson (1837–1921) Photographer*, 82.

CHAPTER 3

DISPLACING URBAN MAN: SHERLOCK HOLMES'S LONDON

Andrew Smith

Sherlock Holmes's association with an abstracted, instrumental and superior gaze has suggested to critics the presence of a specifically masculine intellect, one which is contrasted, in the tales, with images of feminine irrationality.[1] In *Sherlock's Men: Masculinity, Conan Doyle, and Cultural History*, Joseph A. Kestner suggests that rationality was 'strongly gendered masculine in the culture, so Holmes's initial appearance [in a scientific laboratory] and early demonstrations of "deduction" signal not only rationality but also masculinity'.[2] However (and as Kestner acknowledges), Doyle's tales often challenge the idea of rationality and consequently examine the expectations and limitations associated with dominant masculine scripts. Holmes is, as we shall see, at his most interesting when his claims for rationality become compromised by encounters with seemingly unconventional forms of masculine conduct. Such unconventionality is witnessed by how the tales represent male figures in disguise and how this raises often unresolved questions about the stability of gender scripts. This is in part to endorse Kestner's wider claim that 'the Holmes texts ... often present conflict which remains unresolved, resolutions which remain inconclusive, and masculinity which remains under siege rather than secure'.[3] However, although these are important associations, we will move beyond simply addressing the link between rationality and masculinity in order to explore an alternative but related drama that concerns the status and function of London.

London has often been treated merely as a backdrop to Holmes's mysteries, as the place where crime is committed and solved. In one way this suggests that the social tensions and complexities that exist between competing social classes are responsible for an urban criminality, which can be simply resolved by the application of the superior (masculine) rationality identified by Kestner. To argue in this way is to overlook the role that London possessed during the period in defining certain gender expectations. An examination of this role suggests that the ability to decode urban mysteries is dependent upon a reading of an already gendered space. This is not to claim that London is an exclusively masculine or feminine space, but rather to suggest that it becomes a site within which gender debates are determined by a form of political geography. London is not neutral in Doyle's tales because its complexities, mysteries and seeming social and political instabilities suggest that it too generates a discourse about gender that has not been properly accounted for, hitherto, in analyses of the tales. In other words, we should move beyond solely reading Holmes's rationality in gender-specific terms in order to explore how the city contributed to debates about masculinity.

At this stage it is important to debunk a myth about Holmes. Doyle's London with its fogs and alleyways has a place in a populist understanding of the tales. However, very few of the tales are actually set in London, and this chapter will account for why Holmes is typically sent to investigate crime a day's train journey away from London. This is not to say that Holmes's mentality is anything other than metropolitan; rather, the reasons for this displacement indicate changes in attitudes towards masculinity in the period because they represent a feminine displacement of a metropolitan, masculine consciousness.[4]

Displacing Urban Man

Franco Moretti in his *Atlas of the European Novel 1800–1900* maps (literally) the scenes of crime and Holmes's movements across London in the first two novels, *A Study in Scarlet* (1887) and *The Sign of Four* (1890). Moretti notes that most of the criminal activity takes place in the West End rather than in the more crime-ridden East End of the city. Moretti also acknowledges that much of the action of the other tales does not take place in London. However, he dismisses this by supporting the claim of Loïc Ravenel[5] that because of the Home Counties' proximity to London, 'the countryside is for all practical purposes a mere appendix of the urban context'. Thus, for Moretti, 'Doyle's favourite counties ... Surrey, Kent, Sussex' are merely 'code words for a weekend in the country'.[6] However, the displacement of this admittedly urban consciousness cannot be explained simply by suggesting that the Home Counties really function as some kind of outer London. Holmes is also quite explicit about this, telling Watson in 'The Adventure of the Copper Beeches' (whilst on a journey through Hampshire) that 'it is my belief, Watson, founded upon my experience, that the lowest and vilest alleys in London do not present a more dreadful record of sin than does the smiling and beautiful countryside'.[7] In response to Watson's protestations Holmes responds by saying that in London:

> There is no lane so vile that the scream of a tortured child, or the thud of a drunkard's blow, does not beget sympathy and indignation among the neighbours, and then the whole machinery of justice is ever so close that a word of complaint can set it going, and there is but a step between the crime and the dock. But look at these lonely houses, each in its own fields, filled for the most part with poor ignorant folk who know little of the law. Think of the deeds of hellish cruelty, the hidden wickedness which may go on, year in, year out, in such places, and none the wiser.[8]

The country is therefore a place where crime is less easily prosecutable and this explains why so many of the tales are set in the country. Also, although here Holmes is referring to 'poor ignorant folk', elsewhere in the tales the Home Counties' associations with wealth link them to a world of potentially sophisticated middle-class crime. It is therefore in the country that a greater degree of criminal ingenuity is to be found, whereas in the city 'Man, or at least criminal man, has lost all enterprise and originality'.[9] Although Moretti's literal mapping of the narratives does not duck the issue of East End crime, it overlooks how the tales symbolically represent issues about power. Holmes is not being perverse when he argues for the existence of a superior – that is, more sophisticated – criminal activity in the country. It is in the country that Holmes can reassert (although not unproblematically) a model of masculine rationality that was becoming increasingly squeezed out of the city in the nineteenth century. To appreciate this we need to return to Moretti's idea concerning the significance of locale.

Holmes's lodgings in Baker Street mean that he resides close to the areas of Paddington, Oxford Street, Bayswater and Edgware. This was an area over which, between the mid-nineteenth century and the 1920s, there was considerable gender contestation (the Holmes tales which were published between 1887 and 1927 also cover this period). Erika Diane Rappaport has examined how the growth of department stores in the area meant that it became progressively colonized as a space of female leisure. The growth in markets catering for female, middle-class shoppers might well indicate that the market had found a new group to exploit, but as Rappaport contends, 'although shopping was imagined as connected to a woman's domestic responsibilities, it was primarily conceived as a public pleasure'.[10] In this way the link between the private world of the home and the public world of the marketplace was broken down.

There has been some disagreement about how far one can plausibly claim that female shoppers were empowered. Judith R. Walkowitz argues that 'shopping emerged as a newly elaborated female activity in the 1870s, but it reinforced a public role traditionally performed by ladies as decorous indicators of social distance, visible signs of the social system. As consumers, ladies served as status symbols of their husbands' wealth'.[11] However, Walkowitz also argues that the female shopper challenged prevailing notions of feminine propriety because she confounded dominant notions of decency by being out in public at all, despite her associations with middle-class respectability. All this suggests the complex renegotiation required in order to make sense of this new semantic shift. It is Holmes who, by virtue of his location, is caught up in these new problems concerning gender identity.

Holmes's location in this area goes some way to explain how his own figuring as a metropolitan man comes to be associated with misogyny. The situating of Holmes's consulting room on Baker Street can be read as a gesture of defiance against this encroaching female colonization. As Barsham notes, '221B Baker Street became a magical site at which deformed, anxious and estranged masculinities encountered the corrective resymbolizations of ... manhood'.[12] This is important to note because the area was not simply one associated with female shopping; it was also an area associated with the emergence of women's clubs.[13] Rappaport notes that from the 1870s the area around Baker Street (specifically around the areas of Piccadilly and Berkeley Square) 'became the heart of female clubland'.[14] Also, Holmes's proximity to Langham Place locates him close to the 'center of the mid-Victorian women's movement'.[15]

For Rappaport the real issue at the time concerned a masculine anxiety that the distinction between pure and impure women had become threatened. These new female shoppers were frequently accosted as prostitutes. In 1880 Mark Twain noted that 'if a lady unattended walks abroad in the streets ... even at noonday she will be pretty likely to be accosted and insulted – and not by drunken sailors but by men who carry the look and wear of a gentleman'.[16] Twain's comment identifies the 'respectable' gentleman as the real source of corruption.

The notion that one could not distinguish between 'proper' and 'improper' women because of a strictly male (mis)perception of the performance of femininity is also obliquely addressed by Doyle. The idea of streetwalkers in disguise is central to 'A Scandal in Bohemia' from *The Adventures* (1892), a tale in which Holmes is outwitted by an actress.

Role Play and Gender Performance

In 'A Scandal in Bohemia' Holmes is approached by the King of Bohemia who, on the eve of announcing his marriage, believes he is about to be blackmailed by a spurned ex-lover, Irene Adler, who intends to reveal their affair by making public a photograph of her and the King taken at the time. Holmes is employed to retrieve the photograph and so save the King's reputation (the King states that he could not have married Adler, an opera singer, as she was not of his social rank).

The drama relating to the retrieval of the photograph takes place against a backdrop in which everyone is in disguise, where there are fundamental misconceptions (Adler has no intention of blackmailing the King) and a suggested, potential relationship between Holmes and Adler. Ultimately the tale suggests that Adler is a deeply disturbing presence for Holmes because she confounds his preconception that women are not able to think rationally and so challenges his own claims for the dominance of a superior, masculine and rational gaze. Watson acknowledges at the start that Holmes respects Adler precisely because she did not behave like women in general: 'To Sherlock Holmes she is always *the* woman. I have seldom heard him mention her under any other name. In his eyes she eclipses and predominates the whole of her sex.'[17] And although Watson is at pains to emphasize that Holmes is not in love with her, because he is incapable of love – 'he never spoke of the softer passions, save with a gibe and a sneer'[18] – nevertheless by a subtle process of doubling Holmes is drawn into the narrative in a personal way.

It transpires that Adler has fallen in love with a lawyer called Godfrey Norton, whom she subsequently marries. She only intends to keep the photograph in order to protect herself should the King ever attempt to harm her. In this way the plot unravels as no crime (blackmail) has taken place. If anyone it is Holmes and Watson who intend to break the law in conspiring to steal the photograph. Holmes asks Watson:

> 'You don't mind breaking the law?'
> 'Not in the least.'
> 'Nor running a chance of arrest?'
> 'Not in a good cause.'[19]

Not only are they positioned on the side of illegality, but the 'scandal' in Bohemia is imaginary in its connection with the King (because there is no blackmail) but symbolically real in its relationship to Holmes. It is a connection which also underlines Holmes's social position as outside prevailing cultural norms, which is reemphasized in the later suggestions of illegality. At the start of the tale, Watson acknowledges that his being happily married and living in contended domesticity contrasts with Holmes, 'who loathed society with his whole Bohemian soul'.[20] It is Holmes's cultural Bohemia which is disturbed by Adler as she challenges his sense of intellectual superiority.

The tale also constructs implicit parallels between Holmes and Norton; the latter is described as 'dark, aquiline',[21] which suggests Holmes. Also, both are first represented in the same attitude, seen through windows, pacing up and down, Holmes in thought and Norton in discussion with Adler. When Holmes pursues Norton and Adler he is surprised to find them in a church, and is then drawn into their wedding ceremony as a witness. Holmes at this point is in disguise as a stable-hand, but the claim that he is also a would-be 'groom' at a symbolic level is also implied. Watson notes that Holmes looked like 'a drunken-looking groom, ill-kempt and side-whiskered, with an inflamed face and disreputable clothes',[22] which in the context of the implied love narrative makes him look like a failed, manifestly working-class love rival.

The key issue here is that of performance. Holmes plays a variety of roles: a groom, and later, in order to gain access to Adler's house, 'an amiable and simple-minded Nonconformist clergyman'.[23] Watson says of Holmes that 'the stage lost a fine actor, even as science lost an acute reasoner, when he became a specialist in crime'.[24] However, Holmes is not the only actor: the King of Bohemia is wearing a mask when Holmes and Watson first meet him, although he soon discards it as Holmes, cunningly, has already worked out who he is. The King, at another level, also performs a particular model of masculinity, something which is foregrounded in Watson's initial description of him before his identity has been revealed. As a result, the King's identity is initially defined by Watson as:

> A man entered who could hardly have been less than six feet six inches in height, with the chest and limbs of a Hercules ... From the lower part of the face he appeared to be a man of strong character, with a thick, hanging lip, and a long, straight chin suggestive of resolution pushed to the length of obstinacy.[25]

No wonder that Adler keeps the photograph, as she states, 'only to safeguard myself, and to preserve a weapon which will always secure me from any steps which he might take in the future'.[26] Adler's intent is to control, rather than destroy. Nevertheless the tale is fundamentally concerned with the idea of displacing such male authority figures, to which the image of Holmes as a metaphorical rejected suitor also refers. Additionally, much of the important action concerns ownership of the street. Holmes, for example, stages a small riot in the street in which, in the guise of the clergyman, he is 'wounded' and taken into Adler's house. Watson then throws a flare through the open window and raises the alarm that a fire has been started, an alarm designed to provoke Adler into trying to secure the safety of the photograph and, in so doing, revealing its whereabouts to Holmes. This all-male street theatre is one which performs different kinds of class-bound masculinities, including 'loafers', 'guardsmen' and Holmes as the 'clergyman'. However, although Adler is initially duped she ultimately sees through this drama and, as she had been previously warned about Holmes, sees who is responsible for it.

That ownership of the street is related to these notions of masculine authority is emphasized by the final encounter that takes place in the street. When Holmes and Watson return to Baker Street in the evening, they have the following encounter:

> We had reached Baker Street and had stopped at the door. [Holmes] was searching his pockets for the key when someone passing said:
> 'Good-night, Mister Sherlock Holmes.'
> There were several people on the pavement at the time, but the greeting appeared to come from a slim youth in an Ulster who had hurried by.
> 'I've heard that voice before,' said Holmes, staring down the dimly lit street.
> 'Now, I wonder who the deuce that could have been.'[27]

The following day, when they return to Adler's house to retrieve the photograph, they find that she has disappeared, and where the photograph should be there is a photograph of her and a letter for Holmes. The letter reveals that the youth was Adler in disguise: 'I have trained as an actress myself. Male costume is nothing new to me. I often take advantage of the freedom which it gives.'[28] And so Holmes is beaten by a women in disguise who has stalked him in the streets, teasing him with her presence. The street is also owned through a parodic male performance, a woman in disguise, which at one level relocates the contemporary anxiety about distinguishing between women in disguise (prostitutes) and the proper woman. At another level Adler becomes a streetwalker who can infiltrate the streets without fear of being molested because her male costume gives her 'the freedom' to do so. In this way the streets become owned through stealth and subversion as parts of the city (the parts inhabited by Holmes) became progressively redefined as female owned (economically, culturally and intellectually) during the period.[29]

Rationality and the Country

The Holmes tales contrast the city with the country through the representation of crime. However, the city is never completely separable from the country because the latter is the place where predominantly urban debates about gender become staged. Nevertheless the tales represent this displacement into the country as if it were a disempowering of the masculine subject. It is in the country that rationality can seemingly be reasserted, but this process is often compromised by images of damaged masculinity which suggest that any such reassertion can only partially succeed. Its failures are ultimately related to the failure of gender.

A reading of the tale 'The Adventure of the Engineer's Thumb', also from *The Adventures*, helpfully illuminates this issue of confounded gender expectations, and their subsequent displacement into the country. Watson describes Victor Hatherley, the principal protagonist, as: 'young, not more than five-and-twenty, I should say, with a strong, masculine face; but he was exceedingly pale and gave me the impression of a man who was suffering from some strong agitation, which it took all his strength of mind to control'.[30] This struggle between masculine appearance and emotional agitation is subsequently underlined in Hatherley's hysterical response when he contemplates the mysterious events that have prompted him to consult Holmes. Watson attempts to quell the hysterical outburst by telling Hatherley to 'Stop it! ... pull yourself together!'[31] Such advice proves 'useless' and Watson notes that Hatherley 'was off in one of those hysterical outbursts which come upon a strong nature when some great crisis is over and gone'.[32] One of the principal reasons for this is because Hatherley requires medical attention – unusual in the Holmes tales – as well as professional advice. He removes a handkerchief which was wound round his hand. Watson relates that 'it gave even my hardened nerves a shudder to look at it. There were four protruding fingers and a horrid red, spongy surface where the thumb should have been. It had been hacked or torn right out from the roots'.[33] Kestner has argued that the tale represents a clear castration anxiety. It is an anxiety about disempowerment which is associated not only with Hatherley but also with Holmes, who is unable to catch the criminals, and Watson, who is recuperating from a wound inflicted during his time as an army physician in the Afghan war.[34] These three images of damaged masculinity are confronted by a mystery which concerns the identity of the group who had hired Hatherley (a hydraulic engineer) to inspect a hydraulic press. Hatherley was to be well paid for this work because of the need for secrecy, but after becoming suspicious he was attacked during his escape and lost his thumb. The criminal significance of the hydraulic press is that it was used to counterfeit money. The ostensible problem is locating the scene of the crime because Hatherley, after arriving at a small rural railway station, was transported in the dark for what he estimates to be twelve miles to the house where the hydraulic press was kept.

The tale is therefore about money, secrecy and identity. It is also about how counterfeiting works at a series of levels relating to the crime and to notions of gender. For Kestner, 'This anxiety about the self is reflected in the manifest subject of the tale, counterfeiting, which alludes to the true project of the narrative, to query whether masculinity is a counterfeit.'[35] According to Kestner, this is indicated by how the German villain, using the false name of Colonel Lysander Stark, represents contemporary anxieties about the possibility of a German invasion, a concern which is here associated with fears about a superior German masculinity which castrates the English Hatherley.[36] However, the tale also illustrates a failure on the part of Holmes because the criminals go undetected. Whilst Holmes is able to reconstruct what has happened to Hatherley and to discover the motivation of Stark and his associates, he is unable to locate them. The gang have disappeared by the time Holmes arrives although he has been able to determine the location of the house by deducing that it was near the station and that the carriage had merely travelled six miles out and then six miles back. This image of a departure which is really a return indicates a fascination with the symbolic representation of proximity.

Location is freighted with ambiguity because the question of where a crime has been committed constitutes the initial mystery. This emphasizes how place is bound up with the wider symbolic drama concerning castration, a drama which is also reflected in the displacement of Holmes from Baker Street into what turns out to be an equally threatening, castrating environment. The point is that it is the very displacement which enacts this castration. As we saw in 'A Scandal in Bohemia' Holmes is defeated in the city by a woman dressed as a man, and this effects a displacement of 'accepted' gender performances. Also, on a symbolic level, the issue of disguise points towards an implicit truth; for example, that Holmes is a pretend 'groom' at Adler's wedding suggests that he is drawn to her in a personal way. However, the tale also implies that Adler is more of a 'man' than either Holmes or the six-foot-six Herculean King of Bohemia. As a consequence normative masculine scripts (arguably parodically developed in the case of the King) are disrupted.

In 'The Engineer's Thumb' the ostensible point of the case, the mystery to be solved, concerns the whereabouts of the gang; the failure to locate them suggests that Holmes has been beaten. The tale also closes on an image of the despairing Hatherley, who did not even get paid for his work on the press. He complains that 'Well ... it has been a pretty business for me! I have lost my thumb and I have lost a fifty-guinea fee, and what have I gained!' Holmes's consoling words seem to fall short of providing any real recompense for the loss of both money and (symbolically) manhood. He tells Hatherley that what he has gained is 'experience ... Indirectly it may be of value, you know; you have only to put it into words to gain the reputation of being excellent company for the remainder of your existence'.[37] Hatherley is left with words rather than things which suggests an estrangement from the 'real' world. This final image is thus in accord with the idea of displacing, and so disempowering, the masculine. This is also clear in the inference that the storyteller is more likely to be Watson than Hatherley.

The tale works through a series of displacements: from the city to the country, from real to unreal (counterfeiting), from masculinity to symbolic castration. It is these displacements which figure Holmes's own displacement within the city. Debates about power are therefore developed and expressed beyond their site of origin, even as Holmes asserts his grip on a specifically rationalistic metropolitan consciousness. Holmes is thus of the city, but the reasons for his displacement from it can be related to the complex gender issues of the time relating to the changes in London and the emergence of female public spaces.

At one level it is important to note that Holmes, mentally, seems to personify the city. Watson, for example, notes in 'The Resident Patient', published in the *Memoirs of Sherlock Holmes* (1894), that Holmes 'loved to lie in the very centre of five millions of people, with his filaments stretching out and running through them, responsive to every rumour or suspicion of unsolved crime'.[38] The problem with this image of a consciousness situated in the centre of London is that it is one of a spider policing its web which, elsewhere in the *Memoirs*, is associated with Professor Moriarty. In 'The Final Problem', Holmes says of Moriarty: 'he has a brain of the first order. He sits motionless, like a spider in the centre of its web, but that web has a thousand radiations, and he knows well every quiver of each of them'.[39] It is Moriarty who challenges Holmes for control of London, a battle which pits the athletic Holmes against the unathletic Moriarty who:

> is extremely tall and thin, his forehead domes out in a white curve, and his two eyes are deeply sunken in his head. He is clean-shaven, pale, and ascetic-looking, retaining something of the professor in his features. His shoulders are rounded from much study, and his face protrudes forward and is forever slowly oscillating from side to side in a curiously reptilian fashion.[40]

Yet, famously, this was Doyle's image of Holmes's intended nemesis. The tale suggests a doubling between Holmes and Moriarty and this distorted image of a degenerate masculinity physically represents Holmes's own decline as his authority becomes progressively eroded. Like Moriarty, the danger is that Holmes 'pervades London, [but] no one has heard of him'.[41]

Moriarty is explicitly associated with degeneration. Holmes informs Watson that Moriarty's mental (and moral) decline was because 'the man had hereditary tendencies of the most diabolical kind. A criminal strain ran in his blood, which, instead of being modified, was increased and rendered infinitely more dangerous by his extraordinary mental powers'.[42] However, Holmes also operates beyond the normal moral constraints, which is in part suggested by his Bohemian lifestyle, though in this tale he also acknowledges that 'My horror at his [Moriarty's] crimes was lost in my admiration at his skill'.[43] Also, he evidences a sense that his own powers are in decline. He leaves a note for Watson written just before his final encounter with Moriarty, an encounter which he realizes is likely to lead to his own death. In the note he claims that 'my career had in any case reached its crisis, and ... no possible conclusion to it could be more congenial than this'.[44]

Ultimately the displacement of Holmes symbolically represents the marginalization of a particular model of a masculine metropolitan consciousness. This is indicated by Holmes's defeat in London in 'A Scandal in Bohemia'. 'The Engineer's Thumb' also illustrates this displacement through images of symbolic castration and Holmes's failure to apprehend the culprits. In the end Holmes cannot always 'master' the city or its crimes, and this failure is related to the gendered political geography of the area around Baker Street at the time.

Notes

1. Recent studies which explore this link include Joesph A. Kestner, *Sherlock's Men: Masculinity, Conan Doyle, and Cultural History*, Aldershot, 1997, and Dana Barsham, *Arthur Conan Doyle and the Meaning of Masculinity*, Aldershot, 2000. Barsham's book is also an exploration of how language use in the texts works to either challenge or enshrine certain gender scripts. All subsequent references are to these editions, and are given in the text.
2. Kestner, *Sherlock's Men*, 43.
3. Ibid., 45.
4. For an interesting discussion of the construction of a rationalistic metropolitan consciousness which bears on the period, see Georg Simmel's discussion of London in 'The Metropolis and Mental Life', in Donald Levine, ed., *Georg Simmel on Individuality and Social Forms*, Chicago, 1971, 324–39.
5. Loïc Ravenel, *Les Aventures géographiques de Sherlock Holmes*, Paris, 1994, 202–3, quoted in Franco Moretti, *Atlas of the European Novel 1800–1900*, London, 1998, 137.
6. Loïc Moretti, *Atlas of the European Novel 1800–1900*.
7. Arthur Conan Doyle, 'The Copper Beeches', in *The Penguin Complete Sherlock Holmes*, Harmondsworth, 1981, 323.
8. Ibid.
9. Ibid., 317.
10. Erika D. Rappaport, *Shopping for Pleasure: Women in the Making of London's West End*, Princeton, 2002, 5.
11. Judith R. Walkowitz, *City of Dreadful Delight: Narratives of Sexual Danger in Late-Victorian London*, London, 1992, 47.
12. Barsham, *Arthur Conan Doyle and the Meaning of Masculinity*, 1.
13. There has been a tendency to see London as dominated by the masculine mood of men-only clubs. Roy Porter, for example, has claimed that, 'clubs helped keep London a masculine city' (Roy Porter, *London: A Social History*, Harmondsworth, 2000, 342). Work such as Rappaport's *Shopping for Pleasure* provides an important corrective to this.
14. Rappaport, *Shopping for Pleasure*, 9.
15. Ibid.

16. Quoted in Rappaport, *Shopping for Pleasure*, 45.
17. Conan Doyle, 'A Scandal in Bohemia', in *The Penguin Complete Sherlock Holmes*, 162.
18. Ibid.
19. Ibid., 170.
20. Ibid., 161.
21. Ibid., 168.
22. Ibid., 167.
23. Ibid., 170.
24. Ibid.
25. Ibid., 164.
26. Ibid., 175.
27. Ibid., 173.
28. Ibid., 174–75.
29. It could be argued that, as Adler is only able to effect this by taking on a masculine guise, the streets exclude women. However, I am interested in how the performance suggests an infiltration of such masculine scripts, one which symbolically represents the taking over of the 'masculine' streets.
30. Conan Doyle, 'The Adventure of the Engineer's Thumb', in *The Penguin Complete Sherlock Holmes*, 274.
31. Ibid., 275.
32. Ibid.
33. Ibid.
34. Kestner, *Sherlock's Men*, 79.
35. Ibid., 80.
36. Ibid.
37. Conan Doyle, 'The Adventure of the Engineer's Thumb', 287.
38. Conan Doyle, 'The Resident Patient', in *The Penguin Complete Sherlock Holmes*, 423.
39. Conan Doyle, 'The Final Problem', in *The Penguin Complete Sherlock Holmes*, 471.
40. Ibid., 472.
41. Ibid., 470.
42. Ibid., 470–71.
43. Ibid., 471.
44. Ibid., 480.

Chapter 4

Aestheticism 'At Home' in London: A. Mary F. Robinson and the Aesthetic Sect

Ana Parejo Vadillo

I think that might be the test of poetry which professes to be modern –
its capacity for dealing with London, with what one sees or might see
there, indoors and out.

Arthur Symons[1]

This evening is a great tertulla at the R's [Robinsons's], so great that the
whole family is uninterruptedly engaged pushing furniture out of the
way and cutting up cakes – for 36 hours.

Vernon Lee[2]

I love this [Robinson's] salon! ... These walls of greenish blue set off my
yellow hair.

George Moore[3]

London and the Rise of Aestheticist Poetry

In 1882 Edmund Clarence Stedman, the American poet and critic
who coined the term 'Victorian Poetry', noted in his perceptive essay
'Some London Poets' that 'London has always been a city of song.' 'A
generation comes and goes,' he added, 'poetry is in and out of
fashion; but London at no season is without its poets.'[4] Written for the
periodical *Harper's New Monthly Magazine* and with the purpose of
keeping American readers abreast of London's modern schools of
poetry, the essay focuses on the life and work of renowned and well-
published poets and (often overlapping) poetic schools ranging from

verse de societé that celebrated the spirit of London (Austin Dobson, Andrew Lang and Frederick Locker-Lampson) and the prominent dramatic genre (Richard H. Horne and Augusta Webster), to the Pre-Raphaelite school (most notably Christina Rossetti and Algernon Charles Swinburne). To highlight the work of contemporary women poets such as Webster and Rossetti, it set out a lineage of women's poetry beginning with Letitia E. Landon and Elizabeth Barrett Browning, and placed a newcomer to the world of poetry, A. Mary F. Robinson, at the front of both women's modern verse and a new generation of London-based (post-Pre-Raphaelite) aestheticist poets – most notably Arthur O'Shaughnessy, Philip Bourke Marston, Edmund Gosse and Swinburne – whose artistic sensibilities found inspiration, expression and publication in London.

The London of the 1880s, in poetic circles still the cultural centre of both Britain and the USA,[5] was at the height of aestheticism and Stedman's account offered a very precise genealogy of its poetic schools. And yet, it is curious to see how in 'Some London Poets' he redraws and plays with the boundaries established between the London home and the London street, indoors and outdoors, the private and the public, and the spoken and the written world of British aestheticism. Describing himself as an 'American author whose ancestral instinct' led him to England, Stedman was proud to belong to this literary world and added that he had 'gathered friendships and memories which survive the international squabbles of provinces not Arcadian'. For it was his personal, first-hand knowledge of these poets and their circles that allowed him, as he put it, to read 'the writings of his welcomers, and [see] new meaning between the lines'.[6] Intimacy, Stedman suggested, opens up the world of the printed word. Accordingly, the article was an invitation to readers to get to know personally these coteries so that they, too, could read new meanings between the lines. If aestheticism, as a theory of art for art's sake, was understood as separated from everyday life, and if, as Regenia Gagnier puts it, 'its function [was] to negate the meansend rationality of bourgeois everyday life by theorizing art as an autonomous, "useless" realm', then, at the same time, it depended upon the public who consumed it.[7] And to appreciate, to consume such art, Stedman claimed, one needed to know this group in the intimacy of their homes.

Thus, thanking the camera 'for making life heartier for us', Stedman first made these poets visible to the reading public by documenting the article with his own personal photographs. Carefully selected and each with the author's personal signature (see figure 4.1),[8] the photographs not only gave the poets an exceptional degree of publicity and helped construct their celebrity image, but they also created, as Helen Groth has suggested, a sense of community in the reader by appealing 'directly to the desire of intimacy and presence that [Stedman] assumed would motivate his audience to read on'.[9]

Figure 4.1. 'A. Mary F. Robinson'. Photograph by Geruzet Frères, Brussels.

But, in addition, and more importantly for our purposes, Stedman interiorized the metropolitan aestheticism of the 1880s by revealing those streetwise omnibus-riding aesthetes and dandies in the privacy of their London homes. He told his readers where each of these poets resided in London: Horne in 'modest apartments near the York Gate of Regent's Park';[10] Locker in 'Belgravia';[11] Robinson in 'Gower Street';[12] Marston in Euston Road;[13] and Webster in 'a snug and semi-rustic house in Cheyne Walk, London, near the Chelsea Embankment, a region dear to the friends of Carlyle' (and an important aesthetic neighbourhood: D.G. Rossetti, George Meredith, Swinburne and Oscar Wilde all lived here).[14] Stedman opened up their homes and their London lifestyles to his readers: 'The Gosses live in a pleasant house in the northwestern part of London, near the abode of Robert Browning. ... Their home is attractive and on Sunday afternoons one who is welcome there is sure to meet a choice gathering of guests, many of whom are well known to the literary and artistic world'.[15] Or, with reference to the scholarly dramatist R. H. Horne: 'The room in which the old poet received us was his library, parlor, workshop, all combined, like a student's room in college. Here he lived alone amidst a bewildering collection of household treasures, the relics of years of pilgrimage and song'.[16] He revealed that Arthur W.E. O'Shaughnessy, who worked at the British Museum, was married to Marston's sister, with whom he wrote *Toyland* (1875), but that tragically she and their two children had died in 1879. Stedman also brought to light Dobson's family life, as well as his friendship with the elder poet Frederick Locker-Lampson, author of 'Piccadilly' (*London Lyrics*, 1857), and gossiped about Dobson's 'family crises':

> Personally, Mr. Dobson carries well his air of shyness and retirement, and is withal the best of good company. A married man, with a group of children to make home, 'like sudden spring,' he is found occasionally at the haunts of his brother craftsmen. One of his friends is Frederick Locker, that elder and favorite Piccadillian. It was pleasant to see the cordial relations between the two at a little breakfast in Mr. Locker's home in Belgravia, where Lord Houghton and Mr [Andrew] Lang were also among guests. ... Sometimes Mr. Dobson incontinentally takes flight from the round of home cares and office labors. At such a crisis I went down with him to Belvedere, where he had found a secret refuge in the rural home of a comrade, W. Cosmo Monkhouse, another London essayist and poet. (879)[17]

The revelation of such a private affair underlines the simultaneous power of home and street in the construction of London's urban aestheticism in the 1880s, demanding the interior to be publicly exteriorized. Knowing such details, Stedman argued, helped to contextualize Dobson's urban sensibility and explained the freedom Dobson's urban muse felt in the London street, a freedom later celebrated by Amy Levy in her own *A London Plane-Tree and Other Verse* (1889), which took as its opening paragraph these lines from Dobson's 'On London Stones' (1876): 'Mine is an urban Muse, and bound/By some strange law to paven ground.'

Furthermore, understanding the urban dynamics of these schools 'indoors and out', as Symons put it, shed light on the topographies of London poetries. 'Some London Poets', for example, publicizes the clique of poets clustered around the Savile Club, which is described as '[a] cozy and characteristic institution'.[18] A private, exclusive space situated in an extremely fashionable, upper-class shopping area (Savile Row), the Savile Club was a key network among male writers, one that excluded women poets.[19] Significantly, Stedman draws attention to the link between the social space of the club and London's contemporary poets by examining the networkings of the club in the context of T.H. Ward's *The English Poets* (1880), openly pointing out that the biographical and critical sketches that preceded the poetry selections were mostly written by members of the club:

Andrew Lang, Austin Dobson, George Saintsbury, Edmund W. Gosse and Arthur Symons amongst others.[20] But London's avant-garde poetics were not limited to the Savile Club, and Stedman continues his examination of 1880s poetic London by focusing on the clique of both male and female aesthetes surrounding the poet A. Mary F. Robinson. Thus he remarks that one of Ward's contributors to *English Poets* was A. Mary F. Robinson, a close friend of Edmund W. Gosse and Arthur Symons. Both were regular saloniers at her home in 84 Gower Street, which was well known among literary and artistic circles as *the* meeting place of London aesthetes, including Walter Pater, Vernon Lee and Oscar Wilde.

Stedman's photographic account of late-Victorian poetic circles offers therefore an interesting view of London's urban literary topography, one that will allow us to reconsider the bonds between the sphere of the private and the publicity of the street in the literary world of the *fin de siècle* capital. Curiously enough, in writing this piece, Stedman refused to adopt the position of literary critic. He remarks:

> I shall not be a critic, but a recounter: just for once giving venturing upon literary tea-gossip, half afraid by some awkwardness of speech to mar a good intent, yet hoping otherwise, and certainly meaning, in each instance, to offer nothing beyond the details which those who esteem a poet claim the traditional right to know of his walk and talk.[21]

Current studies of modern urban poetry, from Blake and Wordsworth to James Thomson and T.S. Eliot, have focused on the explorations of public street life to argue for an urban aesthetics of modernity.[22] In these accounts, the public lyricism of the street is presented in deep contrast to the aesthetic interiority of the home, a contrast invariably expressed in terms of gender. Though current critics have begun to question this gendered division of urban space by paying attention to the physical presence and the social and cultural practices of women in cities, in these accounts the doctrine of the separate spheres still defines the city within the dialectic street versus home, public versus private. In this context, Stedman's use of 'walk', 'literary tea-gossip' and 'talk' as an alternative form of literary criticism is noteworthy because it makes manifest the important link between the public, street-orientated world of letters and the private world of drawing-room conversations and tertulias, dislodging more academic critiques of the London literary world.

But more can be gleaned from this reorganization of private and public urban spaces. For, if for the London poets of the 1880s and 1890s London was synonymous with modernity in verse, then this urban sensibility was cultivated and fostered in London's 'at homes'. Indeed, what Stedman's article reveals is the pervasive power of London causeries and networks in the production and promotion of aestheticism. What I shall be arguing here is that the *fin de siècle* literary salon was a hybrid space, between the sphere of the public and that of the domestic, one which opened the privacy of the home to the publicity of the printed word, and hence a complex mediator between both. It created literary and personal opportunities and was the means of communication for *both* male and female aesthetes. As a result, it functioned as a space opened to public display and to the spectacle of the publishing industry, whilst still maintaining a façade of interiority associated with the enclosed world of aesthetes in general and women in particular. It was precisely this hybridity that was key for London female aesthetes. At a time when the 'angel in the house' had started to break through the frontiers of the private, and women's presence in the city was becoming more and more commonplace, London salons were, because of their hybrid nature, spaces that linked the private with the public, home and street, and the woman poet with the passenger and the flâneuse.[23]

Like their female counterparts, male aesthetes benefited equally from the social and professional networks promoted by London's salon culture. Recognizing that the *fin de siècle* London salon was a site of human and economic relations, male poets, intellectuals, artists and writers used its structure to express and discuss their ideas on poetics and aesthetics, to consolidate their own careers, and to establish contacts with publishers and editors of magazines and newspapers. To be sure, the periodical press played an important role in presenting London coteries to the late-Victorian reading public not only by printing, reviewing and publicizing their work, but also by making public and celebrating their socializing activities. The weekly literary and arts section of *The Lady's World* (later to be edited by Oscar Wilde under the new name of *Woman's World*),[24] for example, was called 'Five o'clock tea':

> I went to a tea-party yesterday where a little book-worm like yourself would have been in your element. All the poets and writers were there in full force, with a sprinkling of leaders of fashion. The ever-green and gay Lady Dorothy Neville looked in, accompanied by her daughter, and for the poets we had Mr. Robert Browning, Mr. Alfred Austin, and Miss Mary F. Robinson. Mr. Walter Pater, fresh from Oxford, was there; and I saw among the writers Mr. George Moore, Miss Mabel Robinson, and Mr. Justin Huntley McCarthy, M.P., also Miss Rosa Norreys.
>
> 'Amanda'[25]

The journal even included a series entitled 'London Drawing-Rooms and Their Châtelaines' with illustrated articles on well-known London female saloniers such as 'Lady Seton At Home' (June 1887) and 'Mrs. Joplin's' (August 1887), as Figure 4.2 shows.[26]

In other words, what I hope to show in this essay is that an examination of A. Mary F. Robinson's two London salons in the 1880s – first at 84 Gower Street, Bloomsbury (c. 1877–83), and later at 20

Figure 4.2 'Mrs Jopling at Home', from *The Lady's World*, August 1887. Courtesy of the Chris Brooks Collection, The Old Library, University of Exeter.

Earl's Terrace, Kensington (1883–88) – will provide us with a number of important examples about the different ways in which London's 'at homes' contributed to the formation of decadent aestheticism: that the greenish-blue walls of Robinson's salon 'set off' 'yellow' aestheticism.

A. Mary F. Robinson: London Poet and Aesthete

84 Gower Street. June 22, Thursday [1882] ... Yesterday was the grand tertulla, which has left me quite a rag. 70 people. ... I was fearfully tired & went to bed at 12 ½, the Maccarthys & [Philip] Marston staying till 2 ½. This morning a Mr. Fisher Unwin, a young publisher who is doing a book of H[elen] Zimmern's, called with an introduction from Dr. Allon: he wanted my advice about a life of Garibaldi.

Vernon Lee[27]

Tuesdays and Fridays. 4 – 7
Miss Robinson
20 Earls Terrace
Kensington W

A. Mary F. Robinson's card[28]

It is hard to imagine today that during the early 1880s the London poet and aesthete A. Mary F. Robinson (1857–1944) was just as famous as Oscar Wilde and more famous than Arthur Symons. Such are the fortunes of literary history. Robinson became a celebrity almost overnight with the publication of her first book of poems, *A Handful of Honeysuckle* (1878). The book was highly praised not only in 'Victorian' circles, most notably by Tennyson and Robert Browning (Robinson's close friend), but also by core members of the Pre-Raphaelite circle to which she belonged, including Dante Gabriel Rossetti, and by a newly emerging coterie of aesthetes which centred on her home in Gower Street.[29] Walter Pater, who borrowed Edmund Gosse's copy, wrote to Gosse to say that he 'and some others here' [in Oxford] had 'much enjoyed [*A Handful of Honeysuckle*] especially the "Ballad of Heroes."'[30] By 1879, Robinson's fame had extended beyond England. She was receiving constant letters from France and Germany asking permission to reprint her poems in anthologies of verse. News of the book got to John Addington Symonds's home in Switzerland. The poet, historian and sexual theorist thought so highly of it that he wrote to express his admiration for the book, thus beginning a lifelong friendship. Stedman was certainly right to note that to poets and critics alike she was 'thought to be possessed of that priceless faculty – a true gift of song'.[31]

After studying in Brussels, Robinson and her sister, the novelist and critic Frances Mabel Robinson, returned to England in 1874 to live with their parents, who had settled at 84 Gower Street, in the heart of Bloomsbury, London. Both sisters continued their education here. Mabel, the younger of the two and a fervent lover of the arts, joined the Slade School of Art, attended among others by Walter Sickert and Evelyn de Morgan, a friend of the Robinsons. At the Slade, which was located on Gower Street, she studied art under the direction of the impressionist Alphonse Legros, a former friend of Whistler.[32] William Michael Rossetti writes that Mary 'then still in her teens, was as bright as could be, and highly sympathetic in matters of art and literature.'[33] She joined University College, London (UCL) where she obtained a first in Greek, becoming the first woman to study Greek in a co-educational classroom.[34] During her five-year period at UCL, Mary gained a reputation for her extraordinary knowledge of Greek and for her poetry. As she wrote to John Addington Symonds: 'The Women's Debating Society at University College have [sic] elected me one of the Committee. I feel dreadfully out of place, a frivolous poet, among all the learned ladies in checked Ulsters. I suppose they elected me for the sake of the Greek.'[35] Significantly, her second collection of poems, *The Crowned Hippolytus: Translated from Euripides with New Poems* (1881) was a modern translation of Euripides' play that combined the modernisms of her poetry with her knowledge of the classics.

If, as Yopie Prins has argued, Robinson's identification with Greek defined her entry into the literary world (her command of the classics aligned her with Elizabeth Barrett Browning, Robert Browning and John Addington Symonds), then her career as an aestheticist poet had its roots in Bloomsbury as she became the centre of the aesthetic sect that met at her home at 84 Gower Street. Since the 1850s, Bloomsbury had been associated with the Pre-Raphaelite Brotherhood, which used to meet at 7 Gower Street. During the 1870s and early 1880s, although D.G. Rossetti had secluded himself in Chelsea, younger poets such as Marston kept the Pre-Raphaelite movement strong in Bloomsbury. Moreover, Ford Madox Brown still resided here, as did Christina and William Michael Rossetti. Mary was at the centre of this Pre-Raphaelite world, as George Moore discovered in his first visit to her home in Gower Street. Fresh from Paris, where Moore was known as 'l'anglais de Montmartre' because of his close links to Eduard Manet and the French impressionists, he quickly found out that Mary and her sister Mabel were followers of the aesthetic craze. They were dressed, to his immense surprise, in medieval costumes – those of the statues of the façade of Chartres Cathedral.[36] Indeed, as she explained to John Addington Symonds, dressing in such cultivated fashion was not just some kind of self-advertisement but a sign of belonging to the sect: 'I perfectly understand why you seem to think that we, the pre-Raphaelites, are affected and unnatural, that we support our opinions in the same way we carry our dress with strange colours because they are becoming.'[37]

The Robinsons were 'at home' on Tuesday and Friday afternoons, and their drawing rooms were 'almost an open house for the painters and writers of the pre-Raphaelite movement'.[38] Regular visitors included: Ford Madox Brown, through whom Robinson met the poet Mathilde Blind, also a regular at her 'at homes'; William Michael Rossetti and his wife the painter Lucy Rossetti (Madox Brown's daughter); Richard Garnett (keeper of printed books in the British Museum); William Sharp and Elizabeth Amelia Sharp; the publishers Kegan Paul and T. Fisher Unwin; Robert Browning; William Morris; Walter Pater; William Holman Hunt; Edward Burne-Jones; Oscar Wilde; James McNeill Whistler; Edmund Gosse; George Moore; Arthur O'Shaughnessy; Andrew Lang; Henry James; Arthur Symons; and, occasionally, James Thompson, to name but a few. But Robinson soon displaced her father and sister in these soirées, to become 'the shining and burning light among the Rossetti set', as the artist Joseph Pennell once observed.[39]

This aesthetic 'set' was influenced by the urban poetics of James Thompson and by French literature, most notably Villon and Marot, with Gautier and Baudelaire being their 'daily bread and butter'. And in relation to painting, Robinson noted that they all admired Whistler and Manet for their 'sincerity', and that the more advanced of the set (those 'who were over the Burne-Jones period'), including herself, thought that one could not see real art but in the impressionists' Parisian studios of La Rue Le Pelletier. The commitment of this group to the aesthetics of impressionism can be easily recognized in a particular 'aesthetic event' that Wilde arranged. Here is Robinson's own description of the occasion:

Yesterday my mother and we girls went to an afternoon-party at Mr Wilde's. ... He has two or three fine old state rooms in an old palace in Salisbury street. The rooms are large & queer octagonal shapes with carved ceilings and large windows looking over the Thames; it was evening then, outside the river lay an indefinite breath of blue mist & water; on the near side, the pure white lamps of electric light made luminous circles stretching faint haloes thro' the haze – of course everyone said it was 'quite a Whistler' – Inside was a dim aesthetic light, through which the large dingy old pictures on the wall (bad copies of foreign Christs, faded portraits of smooth-faced ladies, that suited the place better than more beautiful pictures) looked out scarcely less alive than the hushed guests. For we were very aesthetic.[40]

During the 1880s, poets, writers, novelists and dramatists used Robinson's salon to set up literary connections. For instance, it was at Robinson's house that William Sharp first encountered Walter Pater. Sharp, who was introduced to the circle by the blind poet Philip Bourke Marston, noted that he 'had no idea how much, and in how many ways, my entry into that friendly circle was to mean to me.' During Sharp's first visit, and unbeknown to him, he was approached by Pater, who told him: 'I am very glad to meet you. Your poetry has given me great pleasure.' Three days after this first meeting, Sharp received an invitation from the Robinsons to come to their drawing room 'to meet Mr. Walter Pater'.[41] In his autobiography, William Michael Rossetti explains in similar fashion how he met writers and artists at the Robinsons':

> Mr. George Moore the novelist, who has also been welcomed to our own house; Mr. Sargent the pre-eminent portrait painter (I was glad to find him a hearty admirer of my brother's work); Miss Violet Paget, who writes under the name of Vernon Lee, and whom I have pretty often re-encountered both in London and in Florence.[42]

Indeed, one of the key figures in this group was the aesthete Vernon Lee. Robinson met Lee in 1879, and they became almost inseparable companions and lovers (Lee lived with the Robinsons during her periods in London). Robinson's poem 'Wild Cherry Branches', from *The Crowned Hippolytus* (1881), is a loving reflection on Lee's influence on her salon:

> Lithe sprays of freshness and faint perfume,
> You are strange in a London room;
> Sweet foreigners come to the dull, close city,
> Your flowers are memories, clear in the gloom,
> That sigh with regret and are fragrant with pity.[43]

As critics have often pointed out, Lee used Robinson's salon to place herself at the centre of London's literary life. There she met Walter Pater, Arthur Symonds and Henry James (to whom she dedicated her 1883 novel *Miss Brown*) and publishers like T. Fisher Unwin and Kegan

Paul. But in addition, Lee and Robinson expanded this circle by nourishing a community of London female aesthetes. Such authors included Louisa S. Bevington, Mathilde Blind, Elizabeth Chapman, Bella Duffy, the American poet Louise Chandler Moulton, Margaret Veley, Emily Pfeiffer, Bertha Thomas, Augusta Webster and Amy Levy.[44]

The death of D.G. Rossetti on 9 April 1882, however, deeply affected this Pre-Raphaelite clique. As Vernon Lee wrote to her mother: 'All that little literary society which seems, in pre-Raphaelite days, to have met at 84 Gower Street, seems dispersed or melted away, & 84 is getting more & more commonplace & languid … All life is ebbing out of that house, & Mary would be left high & dry but for us.'[45] And, in 1883, as Pre-Raphaelitism was waning into aestheticism, and London was blossoming into the aesthetes' Arcadia, the Robinsons took the important decision to move from Bloomsbury to Kensington. Leaving Gower Street was an astute move. The new location, as Lee put it, was 'a great improvement'[46] and a huge social success. Kensington revitalized Robinson's salon, attracting star writers and poets to the drawing rooms of the new house, and reactivating her literary career and fame.[47] She was indeed in good company. Other celebrities living in Kensington were Robert Browning, a great admirer of Robinson's work, who lived next door to John Millais; Henry James, who lived at 34 De Vere Gardens, in the same street as Browning, and of course Walter Pater who lived at 12 Earl's Terrace, very close to Frederick Leighton and in the same street as Robinson.[48] Here is an illuminating description of Robinson's parties at Kensington by the art critic Elizabeth Robins Pennell:

> Tuesday, December 22nd. [1885]. In the afternoon to the Robinsons, found the house crowded, up stairs and down. Met Miss Prestor and Miss Dodge just going away. Dr. Garnett came in almost at the same time and, as usual began the conversation by asking me if there was nothing he could do for me at the Museum … Mrs. Oscar Wilde in olive plush lined with red and blowsy hair sat in the middle of the room talking to a young man with a bang and violets in his buttonhole & inexpressible eyes. George Moore talked most of the time to young ladies. Saw the Glazebrooks, Lemons, Sharps, Miss Dunn and her friend Miss Osborn. W.M. Rossetti there and Mrs. Francillon and the Paters, the Stillmans.[49]

In 1888, however, the aesthetic circle that congregated at the Robinsons' home in Kensington disintegrated when, to everyone's surprise, Robinson decided to marry the French orientalist James Darmester, whom she had met at William Michael Rossetti's. Her sudden marriage took place on the eve of the publication of *Songs, Ballads and A Garden Play* (1888), which she dedicated to her sister, Mabel. This turn of events marked a drastic change in Robinson's career. She notoriously broke up with Lee and, perhaps more crucially, left London for Paris, where she remained until her death in 1944.

It was fitting that her last two London volumes of poetry, especially *An Italian Garden*, were emblematic of the cosmopolitan aestheticism of 1880s London. This avant-garde volume was an inspiring dialogue between impressionist and symbolist aestheticism *avant la lettre*. The collection begins with a section entitled 'Nocturnes', deeply indebted to Whistler, and includes 'Venetian Nocturne', a favourite of John Addington Symonds:

> Down in the narrow Calle where the moonlight cannot enter
> > The houses are so high;
> Silent and alone we pierced the night's dim core and centre –
> > Only you and I
>
> Clear and sad our footsteps rang along the hollow pavement,
> > Sounding like a bell;
> Sounding like a voice that cries to souls in Life's enslavement,
> > 'There is Death as well'!
>
> Down the narrow dark we went, until a sudden whiteness
> > Made us hold our breath;
> All the white Salute towers and domes in moonlight brightness, –
> > Ah! Could this be death?

Aestheticizing the city through the moonlight effect (a common element in Whistler's work, see for example his *Nocturne: Blue and Gold or Nocturne in Black and Gold*) and stressing the subjective element of perception, 'Venetian Nocturne' was a poetic expression of the Venetian street. But halfway through the poem, the city's street (*calle*) becomes an imaginative space in which the *flâneuse* can evoke an emotional mood. The poem thus points towards symbolism in its use of an abstract, yet atmospheric, consciousness that emphasizes the ornamental (figurative) aspect of the city.

Even more impressive are the last poems of the collection: 'In Memoriam (Dante Gabriel Rossetti)', 'Arts and Life', 'Personality' and 'Pulvis et Umbra'. They read as Robinson's own poetic development first as a Pre-Raphaelite, then as an aesthete, and finally as a decadent (impressionist and a symbolist) poet. But, perhaps more importantly, the poems present the genealogy of London's aestheticist poetry. In 'In Memoriam,' she mourns the death of Rossetti and of Pre-Raphaelitism. 'Arts and Life', her aesthetic manifesto, suggests that the artist must reject materialism and opt for the unsatisfied pleasures of beauty. Hungered, she argues, the poet must go on gazing and singing. Finally, in both 'Personality' and 'Pulvis et Umbra', Robinson explores lyrically the transformation of impressionism into symbolism as the enchanting London street comes to be not an aesthetic object, but a door through which to understand the subjective experience:

As one who goes between high garden walls,
Along a road that never has an end,
With still the empty way behind, in front,
Which he must pace for evermore alone –
So even so, is Life to every soul.
Walled in with barriers that no Love can break.

The poem ends, fittingly, by linking the public street (the life on the other side of high garden walls, where the road never ends) and the interior space of the home, where the poet sings: 'I trust the end and sing within my walls,/Sing all alone, to bid some listening soul/Wait till the day break, watch for me in front!'.

Robinson, like the later Symons, understood that modern poetry dealt with London, with the city, with what one might see indoors and out, and in her poetry she houses the street in an attempt at locating the subjective reality of the urban self.

Intimate Publicity

I would like to finish this examination of Robinson's London coterie by examining how Robinson's London salon promoted its own intellectual and poetic circle. We might begin by pointing out that the literary connections established within this network were often used to help other poets, offering both personal and, when possible, even financial support. William Sharp, for instance, noted that '[a]mong the many avocations into which Miss Mary Robinson allowed herself to be allured from her true vocation was that of *soror consolatrix* to all young fellow poets in difficulty or distress'.[50] This was case for the blind poet Philip Bourke Marston. It was Robinson who first wrote to her friend the painter Madox Brown asking him to participate in a three-year fund that she and Sharp were creating to help Marston, who was going through a particularly difficult period, as his sight was failing.[51]

It should be obvious by now how important was one of the members of the coterie, the publisher T. Fisher Unwin, in bringing the works of this circle into print. Another important visitor was the editor of the journal the *Athenaeum*, Norman MacColl – whom many believed to be Hamlin in Lee's *Miss Brown*. To be sure, the role of the periodical press in bringing this circle to public attention was crucial. In her important work on women reviewers of the journal the *Athenaeum*, Marysa Demoor has paid particular attention to some of the members of this group, including Mathilde Blind, Augusta Webster and A. Mary F. Robinson. She writes that Robinson began her career at the *Athenaeum* with the publication of two poems in 1880 and that she remained a 'regular contributor of poems and reviews to the *Athenaeum* until 1900'.[52] The following illustration from *Punch* in

Figure 4.3: 'Valuable Collection in the Reading-Room, British Museum.' 28 March 1885. *Punch.* Courtesy of the Chris Brooks Collection, The Old Library, University of Exeter.

Figure 4.3 shows Robinson in the middle of the British Museum reading her own book of poems, *A Handful of Honeysuckle*. To the left one can see Swinburne and behind her is Norman MacColl. Observing that in Lee's *Miss Brown* one of the characters notes how this pre-Raphelite clique 'always read the "Athenaeum"', Demoor is right in noting 'the monopoly' this journal 'enjoyed in the Robinsons' circle of friends and acquaintances'.[53]

Equally arresting is her essay on 'Elihu Vedder', an artist whose importance lies, she writes, in that 'his pictures enrich the poet's world within us rather than the painter's world without' because he possesses 'in addition to his symbolic mind, a real sense of beauty.'[54] Between 1884 and 1885, and coinciding with her move to Kensington, she also wrote a section on 'Profiles from the French Renaissance', much in keeping with the works of Pater, Symonds and Vernon Lee, but, unlike them, focusing on France and not Italy. More extraordinary are the poems she submitted to the *Art Magazine*, which were included in a new section of the journal provocatively entitled 'Poems and Pictures'. See, for example, 'A Tuscan May-Day', which was designed by W. J. Hennessy (1884–85) and, especially, 'A Venetian Nocturne', which was designed by Clara Montalba (1886)

Figure 4.4: A. Mary F. Robinson, 'A Venetian Nocturne', designed by Clara Montalba. From *The Magazine of Art*, vol. 9 (1886), 256. Courtesy of The Old Library, University of Exeter.

(see Figure 4.4). The latter was printed among Henley's 'Ballade of Dead Actors' (designed by Elihu Vedder), Andrew Lang's 'Ballade of a Choice of Ghosts' (designed by Harry Furniss), Austin Dobson's 'The Screen in the Lumber Room' (designed by Randolph Caldecott), Cosmo Monkhouse's 'With a Drawing by Boucher' (designed by T. Blake Wirgman), Robert Louis Stevenson's 'To a Gardener' (designed by H. Gillard Glindonin), and May Kendall's 'A Long Goodbye' (designed by Arthur Hopkins).

The commission of articles was an important part of the literary world of the 1880s and 1890s because it helped financially, allowing one to live by the pen while generating publicity. As Mary Robinson wrote to her fiancé James Darmester:

> When I had written to you I wrote to Oscar Wilde. I sent him an article after all; firstly it seemed rather snobbish to refuse so old a friend; secondly the resulting £10 or so will furnish several table clothes for a certain flat in Paris (I want to spin all the house-linen out of my own head); & thirdly the illustrations for it will afford employment to a poor lame girl with a turn for etching.[55]

But even more important was the process of reviewing, because it would guarantee visibility and sales, and Robinson's salon had all those connections. Thus for instance, after receiving a lukewarm response in the press for her second book of poems, *The Crowned Hippolytus*, Robinson was eager to obtain good reviews:

> Mary has had only three reviews as yet, including the *Academy*; and all three most unsatisfactory. ... The *Athenaeum* one, supposed to be by [Andrew] Lang, is most stupid & faint praised. She was a little depressed, poor little woman; but I think she cares less now about reviewers' opinions. She thinks & they all do, with me, that there may be a certain reaction against the success of her first book; that the reviewers may have been called to task & accused of favouritism about it, and are now rather afraid of saying anything that they might have to unsay. But I hear that [Edmund] Gosse & Austin Dobson have reviews coming out.[56]

And indeed, more good reviews finally came through from two other members of her circle. As Lee wrote to her mother: 'Mary has got her only two good reviews – the *Saturday & Daily News* – one from Gosse, the other from Marston'.[57] Notice how Lee equally took full advantage of the influential position of this network to promote *Euphorion*. 'Dearest Mamma,' she writes on 8 July 1884, 'The review I sent you is by W[illia]m Rossetti. I hear there is one, long & good, in the *British Quarterly*, but no one reads that; also in the *Graphic & Pall Mall*'.[58] Even more interesting is the entry for 11 July of the same year:

> The afternoon tea was a great success; the Wards, Rossettis, Madox Brown, Theo. Watts, Henry James, John [Sargent], Paters [Walter, Clara and Hester], Sharps [Elizabeth and William], Stillmans, Pennells [Joseph and Elizabeth] & Mme. Villari. Theo. Watts was most charming & friendly and regretted he had not had the doing of my review, as he said Wm. Rossetti's was not near good enough. But Henry James was even nicer: he takes the most paternal interest in me as a novelist, says that *Miss Brown* is a very good title, and that he will do all in his power to push it on.[59]

These personal, aesthetic and socioeconomic relations worked especially well for women writers, who used the salon's hybrid structure to build personal and professional ties. An interesting example is the famous Eminent Women Writers Series, a collection of biographical and critical books on famous women authors, edited by J.H. Ingram. Notice for example the extensive number of volumes whose contributors were regular saloniers: Mathilde Blind's *George Eliot* and *Madame Roland* in 1883 and 1886 respectively; Bella Duffy's *Madame de Staël* (1887); Helen Zimmern's *Maria Edgeworth* (1883); Elizabeth Robins Pennell's *Life of Mary Wollstonecraft* (1885); Lucy Madox Rossetti's *Mrs. Shelley* (1890); Bertha Thomas' *George Sand* (1883); Vernon Lee's *The Countess of Albany* (1883); and Mary Robinson's *Emily Brontë* (1883) and *Margaret of Angoulême, Queen of Navarre* (1886).[60] This is an example of how personal relations were transformed into professional relations, because indeed knowledge of the commercial interests of publishers helped not only to obtain those desirable book contracts, but to negotiate a good deal, as the following letter of 2 September 1884 from Lee to her mother illustrates: 'I have applied to do *Mme d'Arblay* in the same series for which Mary has done her Emily.' Three days later, she wrote again to confirm that she had 'received an offer to do a volume of *Css. of Albany* uniform with Mary's *Emily* for £50 & have accepted'.[61]

Finally, Robinson and the fellow poets of her circle were also promoted and publicized in William Sharp's *Sonnets of this Century* (1886) and in Elizabeth Amelia Sharp's two anthologies of women poets, *Women Voices* (1887) and *Women Poets of the Victorian Era* (1890).[62] In her first anthology, for instance, Elizabeth Amelia Sharp acknowledged her debt to the culture of the salon by arguing that she had been 'fortunately placed' within coteries of women poets. Furthermore, the collection was very favourably reviewed by Oscar Wilde, who both commissioned and reviewed much of the literature published by this coterie as editor of *The Woman's World*.[63]

To conclude, by having examined the complex web of networks taking place at Robinson's 'at homes' what I hope to have shown here is the crucial significance of 1880s London's drawing rooms in the production and cultivation of aestheticism.

Notes

1. Arthur Symons, 'Mr. Henley's Poetry', *Fortnightly Review*, vol. 52 (1982), 184.
2. Vernon Lee, *Vernon Lee's Letters. With a Preface by Her Executor*, privately printed, 1937, 122.
3. (My translation) '"J'aime ce salon!" dit-il. C'était gentil, mais il va tout gâter par son inconcevable naïveté. "J'aime ce salon" fit-il. "Ces murs

d'un bleu verdi font valoir le jaune de mes cheveux" (*set off my yellow hair*)'. See Mary Duclaux, 'Souvenirs sur George Moore', *La Revue de Paris* XV, no. 2, 1 March (1933), 121.

4. Edmund Clarence Stedman, 'Some London Poets', *Harper's New Monthly Magazine*, vol. 64, no. 384 (1882), 874. A later account of the 1880s world of art, poetry and science in London is R.R. Bowker, 'London as a Literary Centre', *Harper's New Monthly Magazine*, vol. 76, no. 456 (1888), 815–44.

5. See David Perkins, *A History of Modern Poetry From the 1890s to the High Modernist Mode*, Cambridge, MA, 1976, 4.

6. Stedman, 'Some London Poets', 874–75.

7. Regenia Gagnier, *Idylls of the Marketplace: Oscar Wilde and the Victorian Public*, Stanford, CA, 1986, 6.

8. Reproduced in Stedman, 'Some London Poets', 885.

9. Helen Groth, *Victorian Photography and Literary Nostalgia*, Oxford, 2003, 186.

10. Stedman, 'Some London Poets', 887.

11. Ibid., 879.

12. Ibid., 886.

13. Ibid., 881.

14. Ibid., 886.

15. Ibid., 878.

16. Ibid., 887.

17. Ibid., 879.

18. Ibid., 875.

19. Writing of London's female club culture, Amy Levy notes that 'Not long ago, indeed, a motion was brought forward for the admission of women to the Savile Club. Its rejection must be a matter of regret to all women engaged in literature and education.' (Amy Levy, 'Women and Club Life', *Woman's World*, ed. Oscar Wilde, no. 1 (1882), 366). The best known male and female club was the Albermarle, which was founded in 1881. Women-only clubs included the Alexandra Club (funded in 1884) and the University Club for Women (in 1887).

20. T.H. Ward, ed., *The English Poets: Selections* (with critical introductions by various writers, and a general introduction by Matthew Arnold), 4 vols, London, 1880.

21. Stedman, 'Some London Poets', 875.

22. See for example Raymond Williams, *The Country and the City*, London, 1973, and William B. Thesing, *The London Muse: Victorian Poetic Responses to the City*, Athens, GA, 1982.

23. However, it is particularly important to bear in mind that socialist 'at homes', unlike aesthetic ones like Mary Robinson's, were gender biased, as Ruth Livesey has recently argued in her study of the clique of poets surrounding William Morris and Dollie Radford. (Ruth Livesey, 'Dollie Radford and the Ethical Aesthetics of *Fin-de-Siècle* Poetry', *Journal of Victorian Literature and Culture* (special issue: *Fin-de-Siècle Women Poets and Literary Culture*, ed. M. Thain and A. Vadillo), vol. 34, no. 2 (2006), 508.)

24. Wilde was an inveterate networker in London's drawing-room culture, preferring 'at homes' to other social gatherings. W.B. Yeats, for example, tells of how it was only when the Rhymers met at private homes that Wilde would show up: 'Sometimes if we meet in a private house, which we occasionally did, Oscar Wilde came. It had been useless to invite him

to the Cheshire Cheese for he hated Bohemia' (Bruce Gardiner, *The Rhymers' Club: A Social and Intellectual History*, New York and London, 1988, 71).

25. Amanda, 'Five o'clock tea', *The Lady's World. A Magazine of Fashion and Society*. London, (January 1887), 103.

26. From *The Lady's World*, (August 1887), 341.

27. Lee, *Letters*, 89.

28. A. Mary F. Robinson's card.

29. For more details on Robinson's early reception see Ana Parejo Vadillo, 'Immaterial Poetics: A. Mary F. Robinson and the Fin-de-Siècle Poem', in Joseph Bristow, ed., *The Fin-de-Siècle Poem: English Literary Culture and the 1890s*, Athens, OH, 2005, 236–39.

30. Walter Pater to Edmund Gosse, 29 January 1881, in *Letters of Walter Pater*, ed. Lawrence Evans, Oxford, 1970, 61.

31. Stedman, 'Some London Poets', 886.

32. Sylvaine Marandon, *L'Oeuvre Poétique de Mary Robinson, 1857–1944*, Bordeaux, 1967, 22.

33. William Michael Rossetti, *Some Reminiscences*, vol. 2, New York, 1970, 488.

34. For a particularly insightful examination of Robinson's early poetry and her use of Greek see Yopie Prins, '"Lady's Greek" (with the Accents): A Metrical Translation of Euripides by A. Mary F. Robinson', *Victorian Literature and Culture*, vol. 34, no. 2 (2006), 571–81.

35. Quoted in ibid., 596.

36. See Duclaux, 'Souvenirs sur George Moore', 116.

37. Marandon, *L'Oeuvre Poétique de Mary Robinson, 1857–1944*, 24.

38. Ruth Van Zuyle Holmes, 'Mary Duclaux (1856–1944): Primary and Secondary Checklists', *English Literature in Transition (1880–1920)*, vol. 10 (1967), 27.

39. Elizabeth Robins Pennell, *The Life and Letters of Joseph Pennell* (2 vols), vol. 1, 1929, 94.

40. Robinson to John Addington Symonds, Fonds Anglais 248 ff.84–84B. I wish to thank Yopie Prins for sharing this letter with me.

41. William Sharp, 'Some Personal Reminiscences of Walter Pater', *The Atlantic Monthly*, vol. 74, no. 446 (1894), 801, 802 and *passim*.

42. Rossetti, *Some Reminiscences*, 489–90.

43. A. Mary F. Robinson, *The Crowned Hippolytus: Translated from Euripides with New Poems*, London, 1881, 179.

44. For further discussion see Ana Parejo Vadillo, 'New Woman Poets and the Culture of the *Salon* at the fin de siècle', *Women: A Cultural Review*, vol. 10, no. 1 (1999), 22–34.

45. Lee, *Letters*, 104.

46. Ibid., 119.

47. Elizabeth Robins Pennell writes thus of Robinson's renewed fame in Kensington: 'I remember hearing [disabled poet W.E. Henley] announced once at the Robinson's Earl's Terrace but Miss Mary Robinson, as she was then ... left everybody in the drawing-room while she went to see him downstairs, because of his lameness she said, but partly, I fancied, because she wanted to discuss a new series of articles.' Indeed that year she increased the number of her contributions to Henley's new journal, *The Magazine of Art* (Elizabeth Robins Pennell, *Nights: Rome, Venice, London, Paris*, Philadelphia and London, 1916, 129).

48. See Rayburn Moore, *The Correspondence of Henry James and the House of Macmillan, 1877–1914*, London, 1993, 120, n. 1 (letter 147), and 122, n. 1 (letter 151).

49. John Lawrence Waltman, 'The Early London Journals of Elizabeth Robbins Pennell', unpublished doctoral thesis, University of Texas at Austin, 1975, 251.

50. Sharp, 'Some Personal Reminiscences of Walter Pater', 801.

51. V&A, MSL/1995/14/88/1.

52. See Marysa Demoor, *Their Fair Share: Women, Power and Criticism in the Athenaeum, from Millicent Garett Fawcett to Katherine Mansfield, 1870–1920*, Aldershot, 2000, 51.

53. Ibid., 52.

54. A. Mary F. Robinson, 'The Art of Seeing', *The Magazine of Art*, Vol. 4 (1882), 462–63.

55. FNL Fonds Anglais 249 ff. 16–17.

56. Lee, *Letters*, 71.

57. Ibid., 82.

58. Ibid., 153.

59. Ibid., 155.

60. The poem was later published in *Apollo and Marsyas, and Other Poems*, London, 1884, 108–13.

61. Lee, *Letters*, 141.

62. William Sharp, *Sonnets of this Century*, London, 1886; Elizabeth Amelia Sharp, ed., *Women's Voices: An Anthology of the Most Characteristic Poems by English, Scotch, and Irish Women*, London, 1887; and Elizabeth Amelia Sharp, ed., *Women Poets of the Victorian Era*, London, 1890.

63. See 'Literary and Other Notes' by the Editor, *Woman's World*, (1888), 36–37. He refers again to Sharp's anthology in the next number, December 1888, 82.

CHAPTER 5

'THERE'S MORE SPACE WITHIN THAN WITHOUT': AGORAPHOBIA AND THE *BILDUNGSROMAN* IN DOROTHY RICHARDSON'S *PILGRIMAGE*

Deborah Parsons

'At times we think we know ourselves in time,' Gaston Bachelard writes in *The Poetics of Space* (1958), 'when all we know is a sequence of fixations in the spaces of the being's stability – a being who does not want to melt away.'[1] Bachelard's project, he declares, is 'the systematic psychological study of the sites of our intimate lives', an investigation into not only the emotional or affective experience of space and place, but also the manner in which this relates to the ways in which we imagine and represent them.[2] Focused on man's relationship with the 'felicitous space' of the home and interior, it nevertheless prompts comparison with, and indeed is arguably symptomatic of, his more typically phobic experience of the indifferent or abstract space of the street and marketplace.[3] Perhaps the most influential motif for recent readings of the production, experience and representation of urban space has been the figure of the leisured *flâneur*, the strolling dandy of the boulevards and arcades of 1830s Paris whom a century later Walter Benjamin would employ as a model for thinking the psychological topography of capitalist modernity. For the *flâneur*, Charles Baudelaire declares in his essay 'The Painter of Modern Life', it was 'an immense joy to set up house in the middle of the multitude'.[4] The *flâneur* 'sought his asylum in the crowd', Benjamin observed in turn in his study of Baudelaire.[5] The growing city might threaten him with alienation, but it had not yet overwhelmed him. 'The crowd was the veil from behind which the familiar city as phantasmagoria beckoned to the *flâneur*', Benjamin argued; 'in it, the city was now landscape, now a room.'[6]

If the *flâneur* turned space inside-out, making the arcade and the street a felicitous interior, by the end of the century he was being succeeded by the neurasthenic urban-dweller, who was pathologically attuned to the seemingly disintegrating boundaries of self and world, and fearful that amidst the 'vertigo and whirl' of an increasingly unfamiliar and indifferent metropolis he or she might indeed 'melt away'.[7] Beginning with an outline of clinical accounts and cultural conceptualizations of agoraphobia from the 1880s and 1890s, this essay explores the projection of anxieties of selfhood and embodiment onto physical spaces of the modern city that are experienced as disorienting or threatening. Where Bachelard argues for the familiar and homely as sites of contrasting reassurance, however, recognition of the dialectic of agoraphobic and claustrophobic experience blurs such boundaries of public versus private space, open versus enclosed and exterior versus interior. Just such a nuanced hypersensitivity to the phenomenological experience of space, I argue, is articulated in Dorothy Richardson's thirteen-volume novel *Pilgrimage* (1915–67), in which the *Bildungsroman* of its quasi-autobiographical protagonist Miriam Henderson is played out against the social, physical but also psychological geography of her life in London in the 1890s.[8]

'Recently a unique nervous disorder has been diagnosed – "agoraphobia",' the Viennese architect Camillo Sitte declared in 1889, 'numerous people are said to suffer from it, always experiencing a certain anxiety or discomfort whenever they have to walk across a vast empty space.'[9] Enlisting agoraphobia to the cause of his attack on the ordered yet homogenizing formalism of modern urban planning, Sitte complains that the spatially rationalized metropolis was losing any individual identity or relation to human scale, its buildings becoming anonymous and repellent. 'On our modern gigantic plazas,' he declares, 'with their yawning emptiness and oppressive ennui, the inhabitants of snug old towns suffer attacks of this fashionable agoraphobia.'[10] Georg Simmel would make a similar claim in his essay 'The Metropolis and Mental Life' (1903), arguing that the structures and rhythms of the modern city were markedly different from those of small-town life, and threatened to disorientate and overwhelm the mind that could not evolve some form of protection against, or means of evasion from, its bewildering rush of external stimuli.[11]

The condition of agoraphobia had first been identified some twenty years before Sitte's critique by the German neurologist Carl Otto Westphal, whose analysis of three male patients suffering from disabling anxiety when in large open spaces was published in the journal *Archiv für Psychiatrie und Nervenkrankheiten* in 1871.[12] Similar symptoms were in fact recorded the previous year by Moritz Benedikt, who had attributed them to sudden attacks of vertigo caused by a disorder of the eyes, which he called *platzschwindels* or 'place dizziness'. As ophthalmic tests revealed no evidence of sight problems, however, Westphal dismissed this conclusion, although he was also reluctant to diagnose the condition as a purely psychological disorder because its aetiology did seem to lie in external environmental factors. Noting that Benedikt's account reported the attacks occurring in enclosed, crowded spaces (such as public transport) as well as vast, open ones, he coined the term agoraphobia from the Greek word *agora*, meaning 'marketplace', arguing that the condition was a fear of specifically *public* space rather than *open* space. Westphal's study was influential, and over the following decade the clinical definition of the new 'space anxiety' became something of a preoccupation amongst neurologists and psychologists. While the symptoms of agoraphobia were generally agreed upon, typically including dizziness, paraesthesia, a sense of de-realization and fears of madness or losing control, its aetiology was less certain. Suggestions for its cause ranged from nervous exhaustion to epilepsy to various kinds of moral debauchery; in women it was most commonly put down to excessive child-bearing or a disorder of the reproductive system.[13]

Whilst exploring agoraphobia as part of his early studies on the neuroses, Sigmund Freud rejected both physiological and sociological definitions for the disorder. For Freud, it was not the aspect of a particular space that induced anxiety, but rather an earlier psychological trauma that had become associated with that space through the mental processes of repression and projection. Therapy for such phobias, he argued, involved facing the spaces where anxiety was experienced, and the associations and memories that they contained. Freud makes only passing explicit reference to agoraphobia in his writings, and indeed would later turn away from the trauma theory for the aetiology of neuroses more generally. Noting that Freud himself suffered from occasional agoraphobia as a young man, however, his pupil-analyst Theodor Reik suggested that it was in part this experience that prompted the self-analysis which would lead to the Oedipal narrative of his mature thought.[14] As early as 1896 Freud was in fact already writing to Wilhelm Fleiss of a suspicion about agoraphobia in women that anticipates his mature psychoanalytic thought. 'You will guess it if you think of prostitutes,' he states; 'it is the repression of the impulse to take the first comer on the streets – envy of the prostitute and identification with her.'[15] The fear of public space is here attributed to the fear of a woman's own repressed sexual desire, the fear that by walking in the street alone she might not only be taken for but herself identify with the sexualized figure of the streetwalker. By projecting this desire onto the street, which she then avoids, the agoraphobic is able to escape it.[16]

One of Freud's most pertinent allusions to his own agoraphobia, which significantly focuses on the dialectic of the homely and the disorienting or threatening, is his account of spatial dis-ease that begins his essay on 'The Uncanny' (1919). 'Strolling one hot summer afternoon through the empty and to me unfamiliar streets of a small Italian town,' Freud recalls, 'I found myself in a district about whose character I could no longer remain in doubt':

> Only heavily made-up women were to be seen at the windows of the little houses, and I hastily left the narrow street at the next turning. However, after wandering about for some time without asking the way, I suddenly found myself back in the same street, where my presence began to attract attention. Once more I hurried away, only to return there again by a different route. I was now seized by a feeling that I can only describe as uncanny, and I was glad to find my way back to the piazza that I had recently left and refrain from any further voyages of discovery.[17]

The repeated, involuntary return to a place that he is consciously attempting to avoid is identified by Freud as an example of the 'uncanny'. Referring to a previous study of the phenomenon of the uncanny by E. Jentsch, in which he notes that 'the essential condition for the emergence of a sense of the uncanny is intellectual uncertainty', Freud comments that, 'one would suppose, then, that the uncanny would always be an area in which a person was unsure of his way around: the better orientated he was in the world around him, the less likely he would be to find the objects and occurrences in it uncanny'.[18] Uncertainty is here accorded a metaphorical spatiality and locatedness; the uncanny is the result of disorientation. Freud ultimately rejects this view, however. His subsequent analysis is based in a lengthy corpus study of the term 'uncanny' or *unheimlich*. The heimlich, he argues, has two main meanings, 'the one relating to what is familiar and comfortable, the other to what is concealed and hidden'.[19] In the former heimlich and unheimlich operate as formal opposites, but in the second, less common, heimlich 'becomes increasingly ambivalent, until it finally merges with its antonym unheimlich'. Freud thus concludes that 'the uncanny (*das Unheimliche*, 'the unhomely') is in some way a species of the familiar (*das Heimliche*, 'the homely')'.[20] Translated into spatial terms, in the first usage space is experienced psychologically on a spectrum between the homely and nurturing, and the unfamiliar, disorienting and threatening. In the second, ambivalence and anxiety stem from the place of the home itself.

When asked, in an article for *Little Review*, 'what would you most like to do, to know, to be?', Dorothy Richardson replies, 'how to be perfectly in two places at once'. Although narrated entirely through the 'stream of consciousness' of Miriam Henderson, *Pilgrimage* is dominated by sets of spatial oppositions: the city and the suburb, north of the Euston Road and south of the Euston Road, the street and the interior, and so on. What is so idiosyncratic about Miriam, and so distinctive of Richardson's treatment of her consciousness, is her ultra-heightened awareness of the space around her and her relation to it. This is particularly the case in the middle books ('The Tunnel', 'Interim', 'Deadlock', 'Revolving Lights', 'The Trap'), in which Miriam's journey to identity is initially dependent on the mapping out of a clearly delimited London landscape, as she attempts to fix herself in relation to space for fear of melting away.

'The Tunnel' opens with Miriam embarking upon an independent life as an urban working woman. With her one pound a week as a dental assistant just enough to cover her rent and frugal meals, she ardently claims her place within the traditionally male preserve of the public life of the city, revelling in her new social freedoms: smoking, learning to cycle, and wandering at midnight through the Bloomsbury squares, certain that 'no one who had never been alone in London was quite alive'.[21] Yet this embrace of her new life belies the unspoken traumatic event that has precipitated it, the suicide of her mother at the close of the previous book 'Honeycomb', who slit her throat with a kitchen knife while on a short holiday with her daughter, as Richardson's own mother had done. The horror of this event is represented so obliquely in the final paragraphs, and so disassociated by Miriam's numb mind, that readers with no awareness of the autobiographical nature of *Pilgrimage* are likely to miss it. Its silenced yet haunting trauma, however, breaks through in occasional moments of paralysing anxiety, and also in Richardson's fragmentary and elliptical typography. The first instance occurs in the half-page, single paragraph that constitutes chapter seven:

> Why must I always think of her in this place? ... It is always worst just along here. ... Why do I always forget there's this piece ... always be hurrying along seeing nothing and then, suddenly, Teetgen's Teas and this row of shops? I can't bear it. I don't know what it is. It's always the same. I always feel the same. It is sending me mad. One day it will be worse. If it gets any worse I shall be mad. Just here. Certainly. Something is wearing out of me. I am meant to go mad. If not, I should not always be coming along this piece without knowing it, which ever street I take. Other people would know the streets apart. I don't know where this street is or how I get to it. I come every day because I am meant to go mad here. Something that knows me brings me here and is making me go mad because I am myself and nothing changes me.[22]

Despite the focus of the narrative on Miriam's consciousness, there is no such explicit allusion to Mrs Henderson's death until this point, and indeed rarely afterwards. Miriam's repeated but involuntary return to the street, with its distinctive teashop sign, compares strikingly with Freud's description of finding himself again and again in the red-light area of the small Italian town. As with Freud, the more Miriam attempts to evade the street, the more she seems to be inevitably drawn to it, as in the kind of unlikely recurrence that Freud identifies with the uncanny. Overwhelmed by a sense of physical and psychological disorientation, and the suppressed trauma of Mrs Henderson's nervous illness, she fears madness, the spatial recurrence of the uncanny street reflecting the potential repetition of hereditary insanity. Miriam will battle against this street, with its insistence on her identification with the memory of her mother, again and again through the years of her urban life. As Richardson later wrote to a friend who had herself recently lost a friend through suicide, 'I know how you must feel, knowing you could have kept her alive if only she stayed with you. She is planted in your memory, & will recur.'[23]

The psychoanalyst Ernest Jones notes in his article 'Fear, Guilt and Hate' (1929): 'If we have a patient suffering from any form of fear neurosis, of bound or unbound "morbid anxiety", we know from our experience that guilt must surely be present also. ... Clinically observed fear, a neurosis in which fear is one of the symptoms, always has guilt behind it.' Jones goes on to argue that guilt is a highly defensive emotion, typically suppressing its object through projection: 'the evoking of external punishment, a disguised form of the original one, [protects] the personality from the severity of the self-punishing tendencies'.[24] Miriam's guilt too is projected onto the external scene of her forbidden urban life. Immediately prior to the first phobic attack outside Teetgen's Teas, she rebuffed a tentative hint of marriage. Her repressed feelings of guilt at both her mother's death and her rejection of the domestic life her mother embodied, I suggest, surface in spatial anxiety, as when the London within which she rejoices in her new-found freedom suddenly appears alien and threatening rather than enabling. Significantly, contemporary feminist accounts of agoraphobia, which note that two-thirds of sufferers are female, of whom a high proportion are in their twenties and are developing the condition after marriage or childbirth, argue that female spatial anxiety results from ambivalence towards a suddenly accentuated domestic role. Agoraphobia, on this reading, results not so much from the guilty repression of sexual desire, as Freud implied, but the equally guilty repression of claustrophobia due to domestic responsibility, which then develops in turn into a pathological, self-imposed withdrawal from public space.[25] Miriam's ambivalence towards the social expectations of marriage, and her mother's own life of submissive dependence, similarly results in anxiety within the external space of the city.

Hypersensitive to the symbolic and affective boundaries of space and locale, Miriam's agoraphobia is notably paralleled by her much more common and violent expression of claustrophobia when faced with the monotonous landscape of the suburbs. Her fanatical hatred of suburban domesticity is first aroused during the engulfing stasis she feels working as a teacher in a north London girls' school in the second book of *Pilgrimage*, 'Backwater':

[She] sent her mind feeling out along the road they had just left. She considered its unbroken length, its shops, its treelessness. The wide thoroughfare, up which they now began to rumble, repeated it on a larger scale. The pavements were wide causeways reached from the roadway by stone steps, three deep. The people passing along them were unlike any she knew. There were no ladies, no gentlemen, no girls or young men such as she knew. They were all alike.[26]

The northern suburbs signal for Miriam stasis and imprisonment. In the streets of narrow terraced houses, she believes 'dreams for the future faded' and that life would become ever more restricted and restricting: 'All the space was behind. Things would grow less and less'.[27] Indeed just crossing the Euston Road is enough to provoke phobic distress. 'Why is it that no one seems to know what north London is?', she thinks to herself in 'The Tunnel':

They say it is healthy and open. Perhaps I shall meet someone who feels like I do about it, and would get ill and die there. It is not imagination. It is a real feeling that comes upon me. ...
    The north London omnibus reached the tide of the Euston Road and pulled up at Portland Road station. Miriam got out, weak and ill. The first breath of central air revived her. Standing there, the omnibus looked like any other omnibus. She crossed the road, averting her eyes from the north-going roads on either side of the church, and got into the inmost corner of another bus. She wanted to ride about, getting from bus to bus, inside London until her misery had passed.[28]

Miriam's feeling of sickness and oppressive confinement in the northern suburbs might be put down to an instinctive class superiority, were it not for the fact that she suffers a similarly phobic reaction as a governess for the wealthy Corries of Surrey, in 'Honeycomb'. Mrs Corrie and her friend Mrs Craven appear to her as 'bright beautiful coloured birds, fading slowly year by year in the stifling atmosphere, the hard brutal laughing complacent atmosphere of men's minds'.[29] Her description of Mrs Corrie as 'Dead because of something she had never known', 'dead in ignorance and living bravely on', hints at the forthcoming death of Miriam's mother. 'Nearly all women were like that,' she thinks, 'living in a gloom where there were no thoughts ... no room for ideas'.[30] Shortly afterwards she is shocked by the abrupt realization that her mother's marriage has been similarly less than happy:

'My life has been so useless,' said Mrs Henderson suddenly.
    Here it was ... a jolt ... an awful physical shock, jarring her body. ... She braced herself and spoke quickly and blindly ... a network of feeling vibrated all over to and fro, painfully.
    'It only seems so to you,' she said, in a voice muffled by the beating of her heart. Anything might happen – she had no power. ... Mother – almost killed by things she could not control, having done her duty all

her life ... doing thing after thing had not satisfied her ... being happy and brave had not satisfied her. There was something she had always wanted, for herself ... even mother.[31]

It is ultimately the restrictions of the domestic home, Miriam comes to realize, that break her mother's spirit. Her persistent fear throughout *Pilgrimage* is of the same domestic fate within the social and mental suffocation of middle-class suburbia. The limit placed on marriage by the insurmountable divide of gendered consciousness seems an inevitability of womanly life that even Miriam's beloved friends Michael and Amabel, companions of her urban wanderings in her Tansley Street days, fail to overcome. Visiting them in their newly built suburban home in the final book, 'March Moonlight', she struggles against the familiarly 'oppressive sense, hanging so heavily over this sprawl of outer suburbia'. Of Michael, she notes, 'at last, child and man, he is at home'. Amabel, however, feels this home to be a prison: '"Be glad, Mira," her gravest tone from the furthest distance allowed by the small room, "that you can go *away*."'[32]

Of course, the reason that Miriam can escape is that she has jealously guarded her private physical and psychological space ever since her arrival at Mrs Bailey's boarding house in Tansley Street at the start of 'The Tunnel', where she will live for most of the next ten years:

> She closed the door and stood just inside it looking at the room. ... She was surprised now at her familiarity with the detail of the room ... that idea of visiting places in dreams. It was something more than that ... all the real part of your life has a real dream in it; some of the real dream part of you coming true. You know in advance when you are really following your life. These things are familiar because reality is here. ... I left home to get here. None of those things can touch me here.[33]

In possession of the all-important room of her own, Miriam shouts with joy as she eats her bread and butter to the sound of the St Pancras bells coming through the window on her first morning. The room signifies at once a return and an escape; a return in terms of a life path that Miriam senses she has always been meant to follow, but an escape from the unspeakable memories of a 'home' that has no place on this path. Home for Miriam is not the maternal, womb-like space that Bachelard suggests, but rather a space of suffocation, with release to be found only in the blade of the kitchen knife. Tansley Street provides Miriam for much of the novel with a liminal space, a place of restful contemplation away from her daily work, and yet without the demands of social femininity. If at times of weariness with secretarial drudgery she feels isolated within the four narrow walls, the awareness of the freedom of the vagabond life with which they are associated brings relief. Tansley Street is a haven precisely because of its collective and permeable seclusion. She finds the extra floor space of a shared rented apartment in Flaxman's Terrace to be worth less than the private, internal space of Tansley Street, to which she returns: 'In place of this large room … and the small sitting-room and huge attic, there would be one small, narrow room. But all round it, in place of the cooping and perpetual confrontations of Flaxman life, the high, spacious house.'[34] As Miriam's sense of her inner self strengthens, at Tansley Street she comes to feel at once independent and yet not isolated:

> In the house, but not, too much, of it. Supported and screened by the presence of the many rooms that made the large house; each one occupied by strangers who soon, just because she need establish with them no exacting personal relationship, would be richly and deeply her housemates, sharing the independent life of this particular house.[35]

Fundamental to Georg Simmel's writings on the city is the argument that the mental isolation of the urban environment is the cause of both alienation *and* freedom. While the metropolis offered the individual a private realm for reflection and contemplation, Simmel thought, autonomy yet required a rejection of accountability to any form of social, political or cultural system, which he regards as threatening to the creative dynamism of the individual. Simmel's theory is illuminating for an analysis of Miriam's effort towards self-identity, vacillating as she does between desire for freedom and fear of isolation. In Simmel's view the modern metropolitan consciousness is trapped in a struggle against both the excessive formal restrictions of the capitalist money economy and the formlessness of everyday mental life within it. What Simmel ultimately advocates is an act of self-definition on the part of the individual, which is to be achieved through a transcendence of the impersonal stimuli and objectifying demands of the external socio-spatial world, and a turn inward towards psychological independence. This transcendence is itself *dependent* on the diversity of the metropolitan environment; moreover, it is the anonymity and alienation caused by the nature of urban space that encourages individualism. The difficulty for the human consciousness is to achieve a unique and self-sufficient individuality as opposed to an exaggerated and self-serving individualism. Simmel argues that, in modern society:

> In the light of the unbelievable expansion of theoretical and practical horizons, it is understandable that the individual should ever more urgently seek a fixed point, but that he should be no longer capable of finding it in anything external to himself. … In the end, all relations to others are merely stations on the road on which the ego arrives at itself.[36]

By the second half of *Pilgrimage*, Miriam's *Bildungsroman* takes a new and more mature direction, as her locatedness becomes less dependent on external relations and develops increasingly from within. Significantly, the marker of this gradual process to the stability of internal identity is again the small street of her early uncanny experience. After learning to control her phobic response, her fear has disappeared when she comes across it again suddenly after a period of several years:

> She saw, narrow and gaslit, the little unlocated street that had haunted her first London years, herself flitting into it, always unknowingly, from a maze of surrounding streets, feeling uneasy, recognizing it, hurrying to pass its awful centre where she must read the name of a shop, and, dropped helplessly into the deepest pit of her memory, struggle on through thronging images threatening, each time more powerfully, to draw her willingly back and back through the intervening spaces of her life to some deserved destruction of mind and body. She had forgotten it; perhaps somehow learned to avoid it. Her imagined figure passed from the haunted scene, and from the vast spread of London the tide flowed through it, leaving it a daylit part of the whole, its spell broken and gone.[37]

In a final, although still involuntary, return to the street in the tenth book, 'Dawn's Left Hand', the memories and associations that she had earlier repressed and projected onto it have been accepted into her consciousness, so that the external environment no longer resonates their affect:

> Teetgens's Teas, she noted, in grimed, gilt lettering above a dark and dingy little shop. ...
> Teetgen's Teas. And behind, two turnings back, was a main thoroughfare. And just ahead was another. And the streets of this particular district arranged themselves in her mind, each stating its name, making a neat map.
> And this street, still foul and dust-filled, but full now also of the light flooding down upon and the air flowing through the larger streets with which in her mind it was clearly linked, was the place where in the early years she would suddenly find herself lost and helplessly aware of what was waiting for her eyes the moment before it appeared: the grimed gilt lettering that *forced me to gaze into the darkest moment of my life and to remember that I had forfeited my share in humanity for ever and must go quietly and alone until the end.*
> *And now their power has gone. They can bring back only the memory of darkness and horror, to which, then, something has happened, begun to happen?*
> She glanced back over her shoulder at the letters now away behind her and rejoiced in freedom that allowed her to note their peculiarities of shape and size.[38]

Retracing and reflecting upon the spaces and places of her first London years, Miriam has reached a new stage in her *Bildungsroman*. 'Miriam in her London is somehow different', observes Hypo Wilson, the fictional version of H.G. Wells with whom Richardson had a long intellectual friendship and short affair: 'she's ... pervasively at *home*.' 'There's more space within than without,' Miriam declares.[39]

Notes

1. Gaston Bachelard, *The Poetics of Space*, Boston, 1979, 8.
2. Ibid.
3. See David Frisby, *Fragments of Modernity: Social Theories of Modernity in the Works of Georg Simmel, Siegfried Kracauer and Walter Benjamin*, Cambridge, 1985; and David Frisby, *Cityscapes of Modernity: Critical Explorations*, Oxford, 2001.
4. Charles Baudelaire, *The Painter of Modern Life and Other Essays*, ed. and trans. Jonathan Mayne, London, 1986, 9.
5. Walter Benjamin, *Charles Baudelaire: A Lyric Poet in the Era of High Capitalism*, London, 1973, 170.
6. Ibid.
7. Max Nordau, *Degeneration*, London, 1913 [1895], 42. See also T.C. Allbutt, 'Nervous Diseases and Modern Life', *Contemporary Review*, no. 67, 1895, 210–31.
8. The first eleven books of *Pilgrimage* were published separately: *Pointed Roofs* (1915), *Backwater* (1916), *Honeycomb* (1917), *The Tunnel* (Feb. 1919), *Interim* (Dec. 1919; also serialized in the *Little Review*, June 1919–May 1920), *Deadlock* (1921), *Revolving Lights* (1923), *The Trap* (1925), *Oberland* (1927), *Dawn's Left Hand* (1931), *Clear Horizon* (1935). The twelfth, *Dimple Hill*, was added to the four-volume collected edition *Pilgrimage* (London, 1938, and New York, 1938). A thirteenth, *March Moonlight*, which Richardson had been working on up to her death, appeared in the revised edition published by Dent in 1967.
9. Camillo Sitte, *City Planning According to Artistic Principles*, trans. George and Christiane Collins, New York, 1985, 45.
10. Ibid.
11. Georg Simmel, 'The Metropolis and Mental Life', in Donald N. Levine, ed., *On Individuality and Social Forms*. Chicago, 1971.
12. Carl Otto Westphal, 'Die Agoraphobie', *Archiv für Psychiatrie und Nervenkrankheiten*, 1871.
13. For an analysis of the medical literature on agoraphobia published between 1871 and 1930, see Shelley Z. Reuter, 'Doing Agoraphobia(s): A Material-Discursive Understanding of Diseased Bodies', *Sociology of Health and Illness*, vol. 24, no. 6 (2002): 750–70.
14. Theodor Reik, *The Search Within*, New York, 1956, 260–62. See also Paul Carter, *Repressed Spaces: The Poetics of Agoraphobia*, London, 2001, 7–8 and 88–91.
15. Jeffrey Masson, trans. and ed., *The Complete Letters of Sigmund Freud to Wilhelm Fleiss*, Cambridge, MA, 1985, 217.
16. On the increased presence of single women in the public spaces of the modern city, and their consequent vulnerability to accusations of disrespectability, see Rachel Bowlby, *Just Looking: Consumer Culture in*

Dreiser, Gissing and Zola, New York, 1985; Elizabeth Wilson, *The Sphinx in the City: Urban Life, the Control of Disorder, and Women*, London, 1991; and Lynda Nead, *Victorian Babylon: People, Streets and Images in Nineteenth-Century London*, New Haven, CA, 2000.

17. Sigmund Freud, *On Metapsychology*, Penguin Freud Library, vol.11, Harmondsworth, 1984, 144.
18. Ibid., 125.
19. Ibid., 132.
20. Ibid., 134.
21. Dorothy Richardson, *Pilgrimage* (4 vols), London, vol. 2, 76.
22. Ibid., 136
23. Gloria G. Fromm, ed., *Windows on Modernism: Selected Letters of Dorothy Richardson*, Athens, GA, 1995.
24. Ernest Jones, 'Fear, Guilt, and Hate', *International Journal of Psychoanalysis*, 10 (1929), 387.
25. See Esther Da Costa Meyer, 'La Donna è Mobile: Agoraphobia, Women, and Urban Space', in Diana Agrest, Patricia Conway and Leslie Kanes Wesiman, eds, *The Sex of Architecture*, New York, 1996, 148–49.
26. Richardson, Pilgrimage, vol. 1, 194–95.
27. Ibid., 289.
28. Richardson, *Pilgrimage*, vol. 2, 144.
29. Richardson, *Pilgrimage*, vol. 1, 443.
30. Ibid., 404.
31. Ibid., 472.
32. Richardson, *Pilgrimage*, vol. 4, 80.
33. Richardson, *Pilgrimage*, vol. 2.
34. Richardson, *Pilgrimage*, vol. 4, 194.
35. Ibid., 196.
36. Georg Simmel, 'Freedom and the Individual', in Donald N. Levine, ed., *On Individuality and Social Forms*, Chicago, 1971, 223.
37. Richardson, *Pilgrimage*, vol. 3, 107.
38. Richardson, *Pilgrimage*, vol. 4, 156.
39. Ibid., 168.

CHAPTER 6

THE AESTHETICS OF WALKING: LITERARY AND FILMIC REPRESENTATIONS OF LONDON IN JOSEPH CONRAD'S *THE SECRET AGENT*

Roger Webster

Literary and cinematic depictions of 'London's topographic mysteries',[1] from those found in Dickens's novels to John Schlesinger's film *Sunday, Bloody Sunday* (1971), strive to convey the scale and incomprehensibility of the megalopolis through metaphorical or metonymical images which are suggestive of the random, fragmented, depersonalized and seemingly arbitrary nature of existence in the city – at least as constructed through a range of literary and cinematic discourses. T.S. Eliot's evocations of the metropolis in his 1917 collection *Prufrock and Other Observations* or in *The Waste Land* (1922) are indicative of the 'unreal city' and its 'broken images' – its incomprehensibility and inability to coalesce into a coherent, homogeneous, knowable whole. Their fragmented and disjointed representations of space produce a form of literary cubism analogous to the contemporaneous movement in modernist painting. Michel de Certeau, writing towards the end of the twentieth century, offers a view, now tragically lost, of New York from the World Trade Center:

> To be lifted to the summit of the World Trade Centre is to be lifted out of the city's grasp. One's body is no longer clasped by the streets that turn and return it according to an anonymous law ... When one goes up there, he leaves behind the mass that carries off and mixes up in itself any identity of authors or spectators. An Icarus flying above these waters, he can ignore the devices of Daedalus in mobile and endless labyrinths far below. ... It transforms the bewitching world by which

one was 'possessed' into a text that lies before one's eyes. It allows one to read it, to be a solar Eye, looking down like a god. The exaltation of a scopic and gnostic drive: the fiction of knowledge is related to this lust to be a viewpoint and nothing more.[2]

Slightly earlier, Robert Hughes in *The Shock of the New* argues that in the 1890s in Paris the 'most spectacular thing … was not the view of the [Eiffel] Tower from the ground. It was seeing the ground from the Tower'.[3] Opposed to such 'imaginary totalizations',[4] de Certeau positions the everyday activities which cannot surface, the 'ordinary practitioners' of the city who live 'down below', who are characterized as 'walkers':

> They walk – an elementary form of this experience of the city; they are the walkers, *Wandersmanner*, whose bodies follow the thick and thin of the urban 'text' they write about without being able to read it. These practitioners make use of spaces that cannot be seen; their knowledge of them is as blind as that of lovers in each other's arms. … The networks of these moving, intersecting writings compose a manifold story that has neither author nor spectator, shaped out of fragments of trajectories and alterations of spaces: in relation to representations, it remains daily and indefinitely other.[5]

For de Certeau then, the only totalizing possibilities through which the city might be knowable are imaginary, fictional: urban experience is characterized by 'walking' as an isolated integer, a blind fragment of a disconnected totality: a walker participates in the 'text' of the city without being able to decipher it, a character rather than a reader or perhaps a narrator. Walking in this context is opposed to Romantic conceptions of its significance: for Wordsworth or Coleridge in particular walking offered the possibility of being at one with the world, providing insights into the very essence of life, albeit in a rural environment.[6] Equally contrasting is the *fin de siècle* conception of the urban *flâneur* figure, frequently found in Charles Baudelaire's or Guillaume Apollinaire's poetry.[7]

Joseph Conrad's novel of 1907, *The Secret Agent*, offers no such bird's-eye view of the city of London: there is no sense of the scopic or panoramic; rather, the text is suffused with an all-pervasive aura of enclosure and fragmentation. Studies of the novel have drawn attention to its unusual spatial organization and the degree of animation in the physical world juxtaposed by a corresponding degree of detachment in the human with characters reduced to automatons.[8] Examples of this are the cracked bell in Verloc's shop, often anthropomorphized and appearing to lead a life independent of any human control, or the piano which starts and stops of its own accord, possessing a 'grumpy' psyche. The overall impression of the novel's cityscape is of a world of fragmented, random occurrences where the conventional connective relationships between people and the objects which surround them are lost and substituted by sequences of apparently disjointed and chaotic events. The only seemingly clear-cut actions and perceptions belong in the realms of deception and intrigue. Conrad's London, a vision of a 'monstrous town'[9] which achieves its fullest articulation in *The Secret Agent*, is announced in the 'Author's Note':

> Then the vision of an enormous town presented itself, of a monstrous town more populous than some continents and in its man-made might as if indifferent to heaven's frowns and smiles; a cruel devourer of the world's light. There was room enough to place any story, depth enough for any passions, variety enough there for any setting, darkness enough to bury five millions of lives.[10]

The 'monstrous town'[11] image is used earlier in Conrad's novella of 1902, *Heart of Darkness*, to describe London, along with the 'whited sepulchre'[12] metaphor applied to another capital city, Brussels. In both texts, the irony is that at 'the very centre of the Empire on which the sun never sets'[13] lies a corrupt darkness, whether it be a trading station in the Congo or Verloc's shop 'hidden in the shades of the sordid street seldom touched by the sun'.[14]

Peter Ackroyd, in *London: The Biography*, draws a connection between Conrad's London in *The Secret Agent* and that of Dickens: 'When Joseph Conrad described the city "half lost in night" ... he was echoing Charles Dickens's remark seventy years before in *Sketches by Boz* that "the streets of London, to be beheld in the very height of their glory, should be seen on a dark dull winter's night." The tone is ironic, but the meaning by no means so.'[15] The links between Dickens's and Conrad's depictions of London are significant, in particular their depictions of the River Thames as a complex image of the city's history, signifying its wealth but simultaneously inextricably linked with its decay and corruption – a potent source of metaphors for the contradictions of burgeoning capitalism and the growth of empire. The monstrosity and wildness of the city, with butchery and carnage never far beneath its surface, are shared in both novelists' visions. Stevie and his sister Winnie in *The Secret Agent* are linked to or associated with butchers and cannibalism in various ways in the text, and both attempt direct or unmediated action with a knife as a means of redressing what they perceive as injustices, cutting through layers of mediation and deception. Winnie was previously engaged to a butcher, but marries the apparently more respectable Verloc, who is revealed through the narrative as much more of a butcher with the carnage he wreaks. In an early encounter with London in *Great Expectations* (1860–1), Pip finds when walking through Smithfield market that 'the shameful place, being all asmear with filth and fat and blood and foam, seemed to stick to me'.[16] As Verloc sets off on his early morning walk, 'Carriages went bowling by ... with here and there a victoria with the skin of some wild beast inside and a woman's face and hat emerging above the folded hood.'[17] As Jeremy Hawthorn has persuasively argued, the term 'agent' signals the mechanism for widespread mediation and alienation whereby the origins and processes of wealth and refinement are disguised, masking cruelty, savage exploitation and maintaining the illusions of the status quo.[18] Verloc's walk takes him from his home and shop to the foreign embassy, where his identity shifts from purveyor or agent of pornography to political secret agent; the detached narrator articulates a shifting set of perspectives on the city constructed through metonymic and metaphoric detail, a form of literary montage.

> And a peculiarly London sun – against which nothing could be said except that it looked bloodshot – glorified all this by its stare. It hung at a moderate elevation above Hyde Park Corner with an air of punctual and benign vigilance. The very pavement under Mr Verloc's feet had an old-gold tinge in that diffused light, in which neither wall, nor tree, nor beast, nor man cast a shadow. Mr Verloc was going westward through a town without shadows in an atmosphere of powdered old gold. There were red coppery gleams on the roofs of houses, on the corners of walls, on the panels of carriages, on the very coats of the horses, and on the broad back of Mr Verloc's overcoat, where they produced a dull effect of rustiness.[19]

As Peter Ackroyd notes, London has often been apostrophized as the city of gold,[20] but the metallic effect here is of an inverted alchemy – from 'old gold' via 'copper' to 'rust' – a decay which envelopes the city. This miasmic patina combines with images of enclosure, of compartmentalization, and of barriers – people and scenes are frequently depicted via windows, railings and walls and enclosure of some kind seems to be a fundamental aspect of existence. Metaphors and similes of the jungle, ocean or the aquarium abound, suggestive of immanent savagery and the 'sprat-like' insignificance the city's inhabitants. Conrad's urban landscape concentrates the qualities of dehumanization and the oppressive environment of Dickens's grotesque realism, producing an urban landscape devoid of any unifying, cohesive features.

Conrad's portrayal of the urban landscape has links with Dickens's London in *Great Expectations* or *Our Mutual Friend* (1864/5) where characters become 'random integers'[21] surrounded by fog and filth. There are also examples in Dickens of anthropomorphism in the material setting which anticipate Verloc's cracked bell or the piano – Pip's night at the Hummums with a 'despotic monster of a four-poster bedstead, straddling over the whole place, putting one of his arbitrary legs into the fireplace and another into the doorway, squeezing the wretched little washing-stand in a quite Divinely Righteous manner'.[22] Dickens counterbalances bleakness and corruption with the potential of transcendent qualities of human nature and spirit, and of cohesive micro-communities such as Wemmick's home or the Joe's forge: no such alternatives exist in *The Secret Agent*. *Great Expectations* also has the additional cohesiveness of a reliable first-person narrator whereas the third-person narrative voice in *The Secret Agent* is primarily distinguishable through ironic detachment, possessing a supreme indifference to events which seem at some remove. At times the third-person narrator disclaims any omniscient position, for example claiming not to know what the expressions of 'the inventors of invigorating electric belts and ... the inventors of patent medicines'[23] might be in relation to Verloc. There is still a sense that Dickens's London is recognizable and to an extent knowable: there are glimpses of transcendent 'scopic' fiction articulated throughout the novel's moral vision, whereas in *The Secret Agent* no such unifying aesthetic exists – apart, perhaps, from Stevie's drawings:

> Drawing circles, innumerable circles, concentric, eccentric; a coruscating whirl of circles that by their tangled multitude of repeated curves, uniformity of form, and confusion of intersecting lines suggested a rendering of cosmic chaos, the symbolism of a mad art attempting the inconceivable.[24]

Ironically Stevie, a latter-day Wordsworthian 'Idiot Boy', comes closest to expressing the unknowability of the city and its workings as represented in his geometric forms. It is of course the symbol of the blue triangle which again randomly and ironically links Verloc (his secret sign as an agent being a triangle) and Stevie: the latter remains only identifiable or knowable by the triangular label in his coat which his sister Winnie had sewn in. Stevie also walks through the city but finds emotional connections with his surroundings, whereas Verloc seems oblivious and insensible to them:

> This detachment from the material world was so complete that, though the mortal envelope of Mr Verloc had not hastened unduly along the streets, that part of him to which it would be unwarrantably rude to refuse immortality, found itself at the shop door all at once, as borne from west to east on the wings of a great wind.[25]

Or:

> As to Mr Verloc, his intense meditation, like a sort of Chinese wall, isolated him completely from the phenomena of this world of vain effort and illusory appearances.[26]

Stevie, on the other hand, decides he must walk because of the cruelty shown by the cabman to his horse on the journey which he takes from the Verlocs' shop across London in a hackney carriage with his sister Winnie Verloc and their mother. He is made to get back into the cab, and journey through the muddy streets past 'steamy, greasy'[27] shops to a 'squalid and wide thoroughfare, whose poverty in all the amenities of life stood foolishly exposed by a mad profusion of gaslights'.[28] The driver has 'a hooked iron contrivance'[29] for a hand and his vehicle appears to Winnie as 'the Cab of Death itself'[30] with its macabre and grotesque appearance. Stevie lacks 'the power of connected speech',[31] but his singular monosyllabic utterances, 'No. No. Must walk',[32] 'Bad! Bad!',[33] 'Poor! Poor!',[34] 'Bad world for poor people'[35] ironically cut through the layers and nets of linguistic mediation and deception shared by establishment figures and revolutionaries alike in the novel. It is soon after this that Stevie takes his final walk. Sent by Verloc with an explosive charge to blow up Greenwich Observatory, he trips en route and is blown to pieces before reaching the target. As Verloc and Stevie set off on their fatal mission, Winnie ironically sees them in a sentimental and illusory light:

> Winnie, at the shop door, did not see this fatal attendant upon Mr Verloc's walks. She watched the two figures down the squalid street, one tall and burly, the other slight and short, with a thin neck, and the peaked shoulders raised slightly under the large semi-transparent ears. The material of their overcoats was the same, their hats were black and round in shape. Inspired by the similarity of wearing apparel, Mrs Verloc gave reign to her fancy.
> 'Might be father and son,' she said to herself.[36]

In Winnie's mind the two walking together suggests the possibility of sameness and unity, whereas the ironic narrator's urban perspective and subsequent events contradict and negate this illusory possibility. Winnie and Stevie are denied the relationships which seem to them natural – both are effectively destroyed by the world of butchery and deception which they cannot escape: Stevie is reduced to 'a heap of nameless fragments';[37] 'the by-products of a butcher's shop';[38] 'a sort of mound – a heap of rags, scorched and bloodstained, half-concealing what might have been an accumulation of raw material for a cannibal feast'.[39]

Any forms of connectivity in *The Secret Agent* are paradoxically arbitrary and random or disconnected. The thematic links are largely constructed around images of atomized urban existence, enclosure, teeming oceans, savage jungles and geometric forms. Inspector Heat's mission is with 'the teeming millions struggling upon the planet',[40] the Assistant Commissioner is 'chained to a desk in the midst of four millions of men',[41] Stevie's 'coruscations of innumerable circles suggesting chaos and eternity',[42] 'Mankind as numerous sands of the seashore'.[43] Heat's 'descent into the street was like the descent into a slimy aquarium from which the water had been run off'.[44] Brett Street's 'triangular space'[45] encloses Verloc's home and shop; Winnie finds herself alone in London 'and the whole town of marvels and mud, with its maze of streets and its mass of lights, was sunk in a hopeless night, rested at the bottom of a black abyss from which no unaided woman could hope to scramble out'.[46] The Professor sees 'an undergrowth tangle of table legs, a tall pier glass glimmered like a pool of water in a wood'.[47] Stevie 'prowled around the table like an excited animal in a cage',[48] and Verloc 'turned around the table in the parlour with his usual air of a large animal in a cage'.[49] Heat feels 'as though he had been ambushed all alone in a jungle',[50] Ossipon 'positively saw snakes now. He saw the woman twined around him like a snake, not to be shaken off'.[51] Chief Inspector Heat's visit to the Assistant Commissioner's claustrophobic office finds 'speaking tubes resembling snakes were tied by the heads to the back of the Assistant Commissioner's wooden armchair, and their gaping mouths seemed ready to bite his elbows'.[52] Verloc appears to have 'gills';[53] during the meeting between the Assistant Commissioner and the 'revolutionary Toodles'[54] the government is couched in sustained fish metaphors: 'sprat', 'dog-fish', 'whale', 'sardine-canneries'[55] and so on, pepper their conversation. The most comforting relationship Winnie experiences through the narrator's intercession is with the lamps' gas jets: 'one of the two gas burners, which being defective, first whistled as if astonished, and then went on purring comfortably like a cat'.[56] In Verloc's home after Stevie's disappearance, 'only the gas jet above the table went on purring equably in the brooding silence of the parlour'.[57] This denaturalized setting is overlaid with a discourse of foreignness, of the alien; nationality and identity appear uncertain or blurred, the characters' names contributing to this – Yundt, Verloc, Ossipon (an anagram of 'poisons'), Michaelis – or are known only as 'the Assistant Commissioner'. Terms such as 'paynim' and 'hyperborean'[58] are employed; the Assistant Commissioner recollects a conversation 'as the efforts at moral intercourse between the inhabitants of remote planets'.[59]

As suggested earlier, a very noticeable feature of the novel is the extent to which geometric forms permeate the text, accentuated either in the material setting or in the narrator's imagery. Stevie's drawings have already been mentioned, but triangles, circles and squares are continuously foregrounded throughout, creating a set of forms and structures into which characters are contorted. Ossipon's final walk through the city, after he has deceived Winnie and stolen the Verlocs' money, epitomizes the moral anarchy and self-interest of the city and of the character who most strongly represents the absence of any value system or human connectivity:

> And again Comrade Ossipon walked. His robust form was seen that night in distant parts of the enormous town slumbering monstrously on a carpet of mud under a veil of raw mist. It was seen crossing the streets without life and sound, or diminishing in the interminable straight perspectives of shadowy houses bordering empty roadways lined by strings of gas-lamps. He walked through squares, Places, Ovals, Commons, through monotonous streets with unknown names where the dust of humanity settles inert and hopeless out of the stream of life. He walked.[60]

Characters are delineated primarily in their materiality or by objects: Verloc is 'steady like a rock – a soft kind of rock';[61] his 'gross bulk'[62] is frequently referred to, his bowler hat appears to live on after Winnie has murdered him with the carving knife, itself a significant action which literally cuts through the layers of indirect mediated action and language which are the norm for Verloc and his accomplices. Michaelis is 'round like a distended balloon'[63] with 'thick legs similar to bolsters',[64] has a 'round and obese body',[65] and his back is 'vast and square'.[66] The Assistant Commissioner, 'vast in bulk and stature', has a face 'which appeared egg-shaped'.[67] The Professor is reduced to a pair of spectacles walking the streets on occasion; overcoats and boots and thickness of limbs, inertness or immobility, and possessing geometric forms are qualities associated with revolutionaries, politicians and Verloc alike.

Although I have suggested that the depiction of London in *The Secret Agent* has much in common with Dickens's portrayal of the city, there are significant differences, both aesthetic and ideological. The cityscapes in *Great Expectations* or *Our Mutual Friend*, though highly suggestive of meaning beyond the literal, always revert to realism, to a recognizable or conventional depiction within the fictional discourses which were available to and developed by Dickens. A visual parallel might be the urban landscapes of a Victorian painter such as John Atkinson Grimshaw,[68] whose works combine a strong realist dimension with underlying meanings suggested by their content and style: the all-pervasive fog and gloom offering a radical alternative to some of the more idealized paintings of city life or the mythical versions of society so fashionable in high-Victorian art towards the end of the nineteenth century. However, the painterly equivalents to the urban landscapes in *The Secret Agent* are closer to the modernist styles of art, in particular to the cubist works by Picasso, Braque, Gris, Delaunay or Fernand Léger, for example: Stevie's coruscating circles bring to mind Marcel Duchamp or Giacoma Balla.[69] The ways in which characters are reduced to automaton-like figures anticipate the mechanical portrayal of figures in works by Balla or Fernand Léger a few years later: 'Mr Verloc obeyed woodenly, stony-eyed, and like an automaton whose face had been painted red. And this resemblance to a mechanical figure went so far that he had an automaton's air of being aware of the machinery inside of him.'[70] Verloc as an agent cog in the wheels of state machinery has been reduced to pure mechanical function; the human, emotive, sentient dimension is completely absent and instead dominated by the 'machine aesthetic' found in the futurist forms of Marinetti.[71] The cabman's 'hooked iron contrivance'[72] substitute for a hand is similar to paintings by Léger or sculptures by Jacob Epstein where human and machine forms merge, or Francis Picabia's painting *La Fille Née Sans Mère* (1916–17) in which humans have become machines. The sustained emphasis throughout the novel on geometric forms, the city composed of arbitrary and randomly intersecting shapes with its 'stayed houses'[73] combined with the reduction in the colour spectrum correspond with the typical patternings of cubist painting: 'the conjuncture of light and dark planes and sharply broken lines, the alternate curves and angles, give rise to forms reminiscent of those proper to geometry and stereometry'.[74] The geometric forms cut across and blur the human and nonhuman elements of the text, producing an underlying set of structures and relations of which the humans themselves, with the possible exception of Stevie, remain unaware. Robert Hughes identifies one of the canonical images of modernism as Marcel Duchamp's *Nude Descending a Staircase No. 2* (1912),[75] which is a pertinent example, the human form broken down into constituent geometric forms to produce a mechanized and kinetic set of images with no recognizable human or emotional content. Cubism offers no fiction of a stable or scopic single point of perspective, breaking with the painterly convention dating from the Renaissance which offered an apparently accurate and fixed, if illusory, view of the world. Cubist art is characterized by intersecting and arbitrarily linked planes and surfaces. Georges Braque's *Chateau de La Roche-Guyon* (1909), for example, is a 'jumble of conical spires and triangular gables, vertically stacked',[76] a 'discontinuous geometry ... a geometry of allusion, incompletion, and frustration'.[77] There is an emphasis on the weight and solidity of material objects, often human and nonhuman intertwined or indistinguishable. Human forms and interaction are often reduced to mechanical components indistinguishable from their mechanical counterparts. In the text of the novel Verloc's codename – or rather symbol – is referred to as a triangle not by word, but by the geometric form: $\triangle$.[78]

The parallels between Cubist art and *The Secret Agent* are significant: the ironically detached anonymous narrative voice articulates this world largely indifferently, compounding the lack of a unified and coherent perspective or moral framework, unlike Dickens's narratives wherein forms of unity and moral vision are always discernible in spite of the surface anarchy or disintegration. As noted already, the emphasis on arbitrary geometric forms underpinning a chaotic and amoral urban setting, reduced to a homogenized colour spectrum in which people and material objects are at times indistinguishable or their relationships reversed, produces 'a mad art attempting the inconceivable'.[79]

In painterly terms, the visual distinctions between the naturalist style of Atkinson Grimshaw and that of the modernist cubist and futurist styles discussed above is a helpful framework in which to consider how different responses to and representations of *The Secret Agent* might be located, both as literary and cinematic texts. The 1963 Penguin edition, one of the Penguin 'Modern Classics' series which introduced a number of twentieth-century works – including many of Conrad's novels – to a wider audience, shows on its cover a detail

Figure 6.1: Cover of the
1963 Penguin edition of
The Secret Agent showing
detail from 'Hampstead
Hill' by Atkinson
Grimshaw. Courtesy of
Penguin Books.

from John Atkinson Grimshaw's painting *Hampstead Hill* (1883). The
Penguin Classics series was distinguished by its use of a range of fine
art images usually appropriate to the literary text in question – such
as the detail from F. Lens's *The Steamer Stanley* in the case of *Heart of
Darkness*.[80] The image on the cover of *The Secret Agent*, which shows a
number of darkly silhouetted figures walking and a horse-drawn cab
in a gloomy nocturnal setting, is typical of the atmosphere generated
in many of Atkinson Grimshaw's paintings and seems highly
appropriate to the novel. However, as I have suggested above, it
belongs much more to the nineteenth-century Victorian tradition and
conventions of realism rather than those of modernism, and arguably
is much more analogous to Victorian novelists such as Dickens or
Wilkie Collins. Although very evocative of urban anonymity and
squalor with a reduced colour spectrum and chiaroscuro lighting
effects, Grimshaw's paintings are still fundamentally naturalist
representations of the cityscape from a one-point perspective and do

not contain the effects of fracture or fragmentation which characterize the move to modernist painting, or the equivalent literary experimentation in Conrad's text. Grimshaw's painting still offers a coherent if un-idealized image of London, perhaps suggestive of class distinctions; in the context of *The Secret Agent* the viewer might infer a more sinister and exploitative set of relations.

The relationship between Grimshaw's painting and the novel, though, is coincidental. In the case of cinematic versions of *The Secret Agent*, there is an intentionality at work which seeks to translate the literary into the visual. The novel has lent itself to a series of cinematic and televized adaptations, and, as has been observed, 'adaptation is a two-way process, and the study of films can help us understand Conrad's literary works precisely because they are "unfaithful" to the latter'.[81] Conrad's novels and short stories do lend themselves to cinema, in terms of both their plot lines and settings; the exotic locations of *Lord Jim, Nostromo* or *Heart of Darkness* find powerful visual counterparts in their filmic versions.[82] Interestingly though, the domestic setting of London in *The Secret Agent* has inspired at least nine screen adaptations, including French and Italian versions. Some tend to reduce the narrative to a surface crime-thriller plot and dwell on the kind of images in the setting which might be associated with popular fiction such as Conan Doyle's Sherlock Holmes stories. One overriding characteristic of film adaptations of Conrad's novels, as with those of other novelists such as Thomas Hardy, is the inability to compensate in visual mode for the subtleties of literary narrators' voices, especially if there is a strongly ironic overlay as in *The Secret Agent*. The normally linear sequence of cinematic chronology is also a further simplification of the time shifts and dislocations in *The Secret Agent*, or layering effects in *Heart of Darkness*, although Coppola's *Apocalypse Now* (1979) does offer an equivalent filmic structure. Similarly some film versions resort to romantic interest and resolutions, which, although not faithful to the original plot, create more of a distortion in their shift of subject matter. These more general issues provide a useful approach to the cinematic and literary interface, but I want to turn now to examine specifically the representations of London in three screen versions of *The Secret Agent*, and to consider in particular to what extent they engage with the modernist and experimental portrayal of the urban landscape in the novel. The screen adaptations I have selected are Alfred Hitchcock's feature film of 1936 entitled *Sabotage*, which was retitled *The Woman Alone* for American distribution; David Drury's 1992 production for BBC Television, dramatized by Dusty Hughes, and Christopher Hampton's 1996 feature film, the last two both retaining the original title of the novel. For the purposes of the argument, I will consider the television version first.

The 1992 BBC television version broadcast in three episodes has high production values, with David Suchet as Verloc, Cheryl

Campbell as Winnie, Warren Clarke as Heat, Janet Suzman in a vignette role as Margaret, Duchess of Chester and Stratford Johns as the Home Secretary amongst the cast. It won the Prix Italia for Best Series, as did Cheryl Campbell for Best Supporting Actress. It was shot partly on location in Liverpool as well as in London studios. In several respects it is very faithful to the novel, following the plot quite closely and not deviating into popular romantic or crime-thriller territories – although David Drury has made his reputation directing crime productions such as *Prime Suspect* (1994) and *Messiah* (2004) as well as political thrillers such as *Defence of the Realm* (1985). Suchet makes a convincing Verloc, rotund and relatively immobile. The overall treatment of the setting is very much in keeping with the high-quality period feel which the BBC achieved with a number of historical and literary dramas from the 1980s onwards. It opens with a montage sequence, starting in an ornate interior which we are told is the Russian Embassy, where a letter is being addressed to Mr Adolf Verloc at 32 Brett Street, Soho, then switching to the interior of the Verloc household where we see Verloc examining photographs of naked women. The screen returns to the Embassy and then an exterior street scene; then via the deliverer the camera moves back to the interior of the Verloc household. The atmosphere generated in the house is consonant with the claustrophobic and dingy images in the novel, and generally juxtaposes the gloomy interior of the Verloc household and the grand interiors of the Embassy and the plushness of the Duchess of Chester's house where the irony of Michaelis's hypocritical role, first seen in the dark interior of the Verloc house with other 'revolutionaries' and then as the celebrity guest and pet revolutionary of Lady Chester in her opulent salon, is foregrounded.

London is evoked largely by street scenes which usually are interspersed between the interiors of the Verloc household and shop, drinking establishments and the grander settings of establishment offices such as the Embassy, a government ministry and so on. The backdrop is quite often a Georgian terraced street, as in the cab ride which Winnie, her mother and Stevie take. Shot in sombre tones which recall the style of Atkinson Grimshaw, this scene was in fact shot on location in Faulkner Street, Liverpool, and Grimshaw painted a number of scenes in Liverpool, mainly around the waterfront. The overall atmosphere generated through the setting is of an all-pervasive claustrophobia and unrelieved gloom, produced through shots of cab rides and gas-lit interiors – especially Verloc's shop and house, which also has sequences of doors, dingy patina-covered walls, opaque windows and a kind of counter, suggesting the layers of mediation and duplicity which Verloc as 'agent' performs. The scene in which Winnie stabs Verloc is notable in that the joint of very rare beef which has previously been foregrounded together with the long carving-knife is again in shot as Winnie prepares to go out following her discovery of Stevie's death and Verloc's role in it. The actual plunging of the knife into Verloc's chest is not seen on camera; the viewer only realizes what Winnie has done after she parts from embracing him as he slumbers in his chair, the effect being perhaps more shocking because of its initial concealment. Certainly, as in the novel, this unmediated direct action combined with the link of the rare beef to Stevie's remains, creates a very significant moment. However, the symbolic geometric patterning of triangles, circles, etc. is lost to an extent, the name-tag on Stevie's garment being square, not triangular. The screen version achieves a degree of faithfulness to the novel in terms of plot, character portrayal and historical period. However, its representation of the city of London is largely conventional and predictable, striving for a continuation of the Atkinson Grimshaw naturalist effects rather than a more radical or experimental approach; the urban disruptions and chaos of the novel are largely absent.

The 1996 feature film *The Secret Agent*, written and directed by Christopher Hampton, again has high production values, at least in terms of its cast with Bob Hoskins playing Verloc and Patricia Arquette as Winnie, Gerard Depardieu as Ossipon, Christian Bale as Stevie, Eddie Izzard as Vladimir and Robin Williams as the Professor. Denis Lenoir was responsible for the photography and Philip Glass provided the score. It was filmed in London at Ealing Studios. The title sequence, accompanied by Glass's Bach-like cello music score, is followed by the introductory statement:

> In the 1880s (unlike today) London was a haven for political refugees of all nationalities. They were kept under constant surveillance by their embassies as well as Scotland Yard. This was fertile soil for every kind of conspiracy and betrayal.

Apart from the presumably unintentional retrospective irony of this statement's '(unlike today)', it establishes the tone of the film, which presents London as a seething mass, albeit with a heritage aura. The ironic overlay of the novel's narration and its complex vision of international politics and law and order are, however, lost. London is reduced to a relatively simplistic historical positioning in the 1880s, as is the contemporary capital: the parenthesized 'unlike today' suggests a wish not to affect tourism and acknowledge such political forces as the IRA. The periodization issue is also of interest: as is commonly known, the novel's fictional bombing incident was based on an actual attempt to blow up Greenwich Observatory in 1894, and the evidence to suggest that the historical setting is earlier than this in the 1880s designation fixes the film more firmly in nineteenth-century Victorian London, which assists its construction of and emphasis on periodicity.[83] It also generates the kind of atmosphere associated with accounts of the Jack the Ripper murders, which took place in 1885.

figure 6.2: Image from the Christopher Hampton film version of *The Secret Agent* (1996).

The opening statement is followed by a long single-lens tracking shot which begins with very shadowy silhouettes; the main figure is then followed, Robin Williams as the Professor (who bears a very strong resemblance to the appearance of Alfred Lynch in the BBC production, although his role is not as strongly foregrounded) as he walks from a dark street scene passing a begging child. This shot moves from narrow dingy back streets and entries to a wide studio street scene which could as easily be a representation of a scene from a Dickens novel or one of Henry Mayhew's *London Children*, with its contrived sense of period detail and authenticity. At the centre of the scene a gratuitous coffin is being loaded onto a carriage – presumably to suggest that in Victorian England death was commonplace (perhaps more so than 'today'?). The Professor's walk is a cinematic addition, presumably to create atmosphere and establish the historical credentials of the film, and to an extent it does convey something of the immensity and anonymity of London, with members of the crowd blending into one another; however, the overriding sense is that this is constructing a very English Victorian scene, possibly with an American audience in mind. From the Professor and the panorama the camera lens moves to the window above Verloc's shop – and the viewer sees through the grimy lattice panes the revolutionaries lit by a gas lamp. The lens then moves seamlessly into the Verloc household where we are introduced to Winnie and her mother and Stevie, their cockney affectations suggestive of *EastEnders* (although Patricia Arquette struggles to maintain this; in the same vein Christian Bale's attempt at dialect is a dead ringer for Michael Crawford in the 1970s television series *Some Mothers Do Have Them*). We hear snatches of the revolutionaries' discussion regarding the imminent collapse of capitalism 'under the weight of its own contradictions', whilst Stevie, who has taken out his geometric drawings, begins to doodle. The background music meanwhile has been building to a portentous crescendo, suggesting presumably the importance and possibly revelatory nature of these events.

The interior of the Verlocs' household is more elaborately constructed than in the BBC version, floral Morris-style wallpaper replacing monotone hues and various attempts to emphasize period detail. The dialogue, however, does remain quite close to the novel, as do certain details such as the cabman's metal hook prosthesis in the cab ride to Winnie's mother's house. The cab ride also strives for the Atkinson-Grimshaw effect, shot mainly against a foggy Georgian street background with hazy lamps, as do a number of other scenes. The film oscillates between a form of constructed historical 'authenticity', and a degree of faithfulness to the text of the novel in the script and the events depicted. Details such as the 'mechanical piano' are used to significant effect, and the portrayal of Verloc's stabbing by Winnie is played out in gruesome detail, unlike the BBC version, as are also the numerous flashbacks to Stevie's disintegration – one which Winnie imagines just before murdering Verloc, in which, somewhat bizarrely, Stevie's decapitated head is perched on the branch of a tree in the Greenwich Observatory grounds. The film's treatment of chronology is to an extent in keeping with that of the novel in the use of flashback sequences around the attempt to blow up Greenwich Observatory and Stevie's death, but it is used as a crude psychological ploy rather than a structural narrative device. The most notable feature is the emphasis given to the role of Robin Williams's Professor: the film opens and closes with his walking through London's streets, the latter, of course, as in the novel: 'He passed on unsuspected and deadly, like a pest in the street full of men.'[84] In the novel the Professor is, like Verloc, frequently referred to as an 'agent' and in his own mind as a 'moral agent': [85]

> Lost in the crowd, miserable and undersized, he meditated confidently on his power, keeping his hand in the left pocket of his trousers, grasping lightly the indiarubber ball, the supreme guarantee of his sinister freedom: but after a while he became disagreeably affected by the sight of the roadway thronged with vehicles and the pavement crowded with men and women. He was in a long, straight street, peopled by a mere fraction of an immense multitude; but all around him, on and on, even to the limits of the horizon hidden by the enormous piles of bricks, he felt the mass of mankind mighty in its numbers. They swarmed numerous like locusts, industrious like ants, thoughtless like a natural force, pushing on blind and orderly and absorbed, impervious to sentiment, to logic, to terror, too, perhaps.[86]

The narrator's depiction of the Professor in the novel is entirely negative, presenting him as delusional with 'an astounding ignorance of worldly conditions' and possessing 'a frenzied Puritanism of ambition'.[87] The scene in the film which approximates to that in Chapter 5 in which Chief Inspector Heat meets the Professor on one of his missionary walks through London contains a significant amount of dialogue as the Professor tempts Heat to arrest him, and thus be blown to smithereens. He states, 'you'd do it if you knew how cruelly tempted I am every time I walk in a crowd'. Hampton's screenplay does bring out the anarchical and delusional character to an extent; ironically, the Professor is a kind of inverted Icarus in which he possesses a 'fiction of knowledge' that allows him his sense of moral superiority over the teeming crowd. Verloc's walk to the Embassy is also given considerable screen time, moving from the dank shop, then across Hyde Park and to the foreign embassy. His rotund inertness is contrasted with the opulent carriages, and then followed by an aerial camera shot emphasizing his diminutive status as he enters the Embassy set against vertical classical columns. The contrasting settings linked only via Verloc's walk do suggest the contradictions and compartmentalization of London as in the novel, and thereby Verloc's role as secret agent in maintaining the status quo as he moves between these normally discrete spheres. However, the film does not use the technique of montage as utilized in the opening sequences of the BBC version, in which these components of London's political scene are juxtaposed and their connections subsequently played out in the narrative. Both versions employ spatial relationships and perspective to suggest the insignificance of characters against the backdrop of international political conspiracy, the domestic interiors employing close-up shots but the exterior scenes reducing characters to a diminutive status. The camera lens is at times the equivalent of Conrad's detached ironic narrator in the overarching panoramic or aerial perspectives adopted, wherein the immensity of London swallows up individual human forms: Stevie's violent disintegration is a powerful metaphor for the more generalized fragmentation, alienation and depersonalization which these screen versions both emphasize.

The final version of *The Secret Agent* which I want to discuss is Alfred Hitchcock's film *Sabotage* (1936), subsequently released in America as *The Woman Alone*. The film was clearly produced with as wide an audience in mind as possible and the changes in title are indicative of this: *I Married a Murderer* was also considered as a possibility. Hitchcock also directed a film in the same year called *The Secret Agent* which has nothing to do with Conrad, the plot being a spy story set in the First World War, starring John Gielgud and Peter Lorre. Of the three screen versions considered here, *Sabotage* is the least faithful to the novel in terms of plot and historical setting. The narrative focus is not on the relationship between Verloc and Winnie,

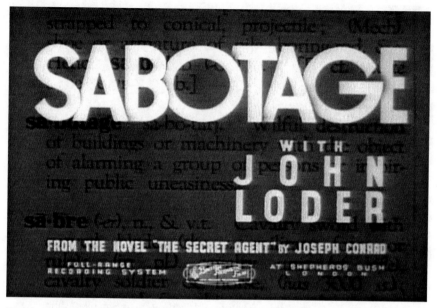

Figure 6.3: Title image from Alfred Hitchcock's feature film *Sabotage* (1936)

nor to the same extent on Verloc's relations with foreign embassies, politicians and the police, but largely on the developing romantic interest between Winnie and a character called Ted, a policeman who is sent by Scotland Yard to spy on Verloc. The film departs from the novel's ending in that Winnie and Ted are presumed to live on happily together; the only significant revolutionary figure is the Professor, who blows up all of the evidence which might have condemned Winnie for Verloc's murder (and it is not clear in the film in the struggle between Winnie and Verloc whether she does actually kill him) as well as himself. The setting is very strongly London, but London of the 1930s, a contemporaneous historical setting full of motorized buses and cars, advertisements and an all-pervasive sense of popular or plebeian culture. This combines with a certain prescient brooding atmosphere, undoubtedly reflecting the mood of the time with the rise of Nazism and the threat of impending war: it is in some respects similar to the imagery in George Orwell's novel of 1939, *Coming Up for Air*, which is shot through with imagery of immanent bombs. Plot and historical fidelity, then, are apparently compromised, but in several respects, because of this departure, *Sabotage* is the most interesting film if we judge it not as an unfaithful transcription of the literary text but rather as a version or imaginative reflection of certain aesthetic characteristics of the novel through a more cinematic approach. In particular, the depiction of London offers a much more complex vision, achieved by the use of a range of innovative and unsettling cinematic techniques.

Figure 6.4: Image from Hitchcock's *Sabotage* with Verloc (Oscar Homolka) silhouetted in front of Battersea Power Station after having sabotaged its generator.

The film's opening sequence, following a close-up of a dictionary definition of 'sabotage' and the title sequence which states that it is 'from the novel *The Secret Agent* by Joseph Conrad', is a montage of starkly outlined images beginning with a close-up of a light bulb in which the element glows and dims, followed by another of a dial which flickers as the electrical current fluctuates and then a panoramic view of Oxford Street at night with Selfridges' façade illuminated along with street lamps and traffic which are then plunged into darkness. This is followed by a sequence of powerful silhouetted and chiaroscuro images of London landmarks shot at acute angles reminiscent of Sergei Eisenstein's innovative techniques:[88] Big Ben and the Houses of Parliament, Nelson's Column, Piccadilly Circus and then, significantly, Gilbert Scott's very contemporaneous monolithic Battersea Power Station of 1933 symbolizing electricity and the power upon which the city's activity depends. Combined with the ominous music soundtrack suggesting suspense and horror, these images produce a dynamic and tense opening effect. The camera then shifts to the interior of Battersea Power Station and staff discover that the machinery has been tampered with by sand: the first staccato dialogue is 'Sand – Sabotage – Wrecking – Deliberate', followed by a sinister close-up shot of Verloc with the edifice behind him. This is followed by an image of the 'Underground' logo in its then modern Edward Johnston and Eric Gill sans serif typography and a scene in a tunnel with trains halted in darkness and passengers making their way on foot by candlelight.

The effect is of the city brought to a halt, which is then localized in what is probably intended to represent South London rather than the novel's Soho, the setting of Verloc's home and the cinema where Winnie in the box office is having to deal with irate customers who want refunds because the film show cannot continue with the power cut – a neat introductory irony in that Verloc has sabotaged his own income as well as the city as a whole.

The opening sequence foregrounds cinematic form and technique, in particular montage, a term which Eisenstein developed as the key formal feature of cinematic art in both his practice and subsequent theory. The rapid changes in pace of the juxtaposed scenes, shifts from close-up to long-shot and panorama, stark chiaroscuro effects, images of tradition and modernity, combine to produce a powerful effect on the viewer. In theoretical terms, the contrasts fit the popular Hegelian dialectical model which Eisenstein was drawn to, of antithetical forces. There is also a form of alienation effect here and throughout the film, in which the comfortable perspectives of traditional family and social life are contrasted with the acute perspectives of the modern, of the spectre of war and of disintegration and destruction. To an extent as well, there is a strand of cinematic self-consciousness or self-reflexivity in which the experimental is contrasted with the conventional: Hitchcock's innovative style set against Walt Disney's cartoon; although even this film-within-a-film is innovative. Two versions of London arise from this: that of the known, recognizable and familiar, and that of the unknown, complex and alien.

The depiction of Verloc's home and the 'Bijou Cinema', in which the two are interconnected as with the pornography shop and domestic premises in the novel, provides a powerful sense of popular and working-class culture in the 1930s: the film is redolent with images of advertising hoardings, bargain shops, cinema posters and also the showing of part of Walt Disney's cartoon *Who Killed Cock Robin?* Verloc, played by Oscar Homolka, has a strong middle-European, possibly German accent, and from the dialogue which takes place in Scotland Yard about the sabotage activity, is 'making trouble at home to take our minds off what's going on abroad'.

Verloc meets his foreign controller, who wears a monocle, in a scene set in London Zoo; another allusion to the novel's imagery of caged animals and forms of savagery. In the novel Verloc is described as a 'bear in a cage',[89] or having 'his usual air of a large animal in a cage',[90] and on exiting the zoo in the film he is temporarily caged in a turnstile until a passer-by assists him. They meet in the aquarium section in front of a tank which contains turtles swimming, bringing to mind the novel's characters' hands described as 'flippers' or 'paws'. We see them only from behind in silhouette form, as with many shots in the film, and after their coded introductions the controller takes his wallet out as if to pay Verloc but instead shows him in close-up a newspaper cutting in which 'London laughs at Blackout ... Comedies in the Dark'. The controller's response is that Verloc needs to 'pay a visit' to Piccadilly Circus, referred to in a sign he has seen as 'The Centre of the World'. He is instructed to leave a parcel containing 'fireworks' at Piccadilly Circus Underground Station. The scene in the aquarium is an allusion to the repeated aquatic imagery in the novel, in particular Heat's 'descent into the street was like the descent into a slimy aquarium ... he might have been but one more of the queer foreign fish that can be seen of an evening about there flitting round the dark corners'.[91] On departing the aquarium, a young arm-in-arm couple representative of innocent London working-class humour walk past Verloc and are heard saying, [man:] '... after laying a million eggs the female oyster changes sex'; [woman:] 'Hmm! I don't blame her.' Verloc is next seen looking at the window of an aquarium that becomes transposed into a cinema screen, depicting Piccadilly Circus with all its teeming activity which then slowly implodes accompanied by a volcanic sound track, following presumably a massive underground explosion. He is presented as reluctant to undertake this act, having told his controller that he doesn't want anything to do with any loss of life. The final part of this sequence returns to the aquarium teeming with hundreds of tiny fish, the symbolism again close to that in the novel, if more literally deployed.

Contemporaneous London mores are reflected in the scene in which Ted the police sergeant, who has been working undercover at a greengrocer's store adjacent to the Verlocs' cinema, apparently bumps into Winnie and Stevie feeding pigeons in Trafalgar Square and invites them to lunch, suggesting the relatively upmarket Simpsons in the Strand; Winnie protests and says they are going to a (Lyons) Cornerhouse or a teahouse, but Ted insists, feigning that he has never been to Simpsons before. Winnie and especially Stevie are made to look awkward in the upper-middle-class restaurant setting, Stevie upsetting the tablecloth and Winnie suggesting he just has a 'nice poached egg on toast', which has previously been mentioned by Winnie's box-office assistant at the cinema who struggled to eat the same during the power blackout, presumably intended to be typical of the staple fare for working-class households. In the end they have sirloin at Ted's behest, and the waiter recognizes him from previous dining, thus provoking an outburst of 'What's the game?!' from Winnie, who then later explains her American background.

The detailed London topography continues when Verloc goes to the Professor's shop in Liverpool Road, the street sign depicted in a close-up shot. The scene, like a number of others in the film, is initially a comic encounter similar to a music hall act, with a woman complaining that her recently purchased canary won't sing. Following this, Verloc is taken to the Professor's 'other department', where explosive chemicals sit on a shelf along with his illegitimate granddaughter's doll: the chiaroscuro effects in the film are not only visual but also foregrounded in the narrative in terms of class, family domesticity against international political intrigue, the comic and the tragic, which construct an ironic narrative mode and detached viewing frame parallel to that of Conrad's ironic narrator.

The central climactic scene in the film is Stevie's journey to plant the bomb, innocent of his mission as he is in the novel. Verloc, trapped in his house by the police with the bomb which he needs to take to Piccadilly Circus, seizes on Stevie and asks him to deliver the package together with two film cans containing *Bartholomew the Strangler*, warning him, 'You'll have to walk all the way!' Stevie's response is, 'Walk? What for?' and Verloc explains that he cannot take flammable film cans on public transport. Stevie sets off through street market scenes and is waylaid by a comical salesman purveying 'Salvodent' toothpaste and hair dressing, with Stevie being dragged into his chair and used as a demonstration model much to the amusement of the crowd. The pace and tension of Stevie's walk begin to quicken, and he is then stopped from crossing a street which appears to be at the Aldwych end of the Strand, with the Law Courts recognizable in the background: this would make sense if the Verlocs' home is in SE5, as he would most likely cross by Blackfriars Bridge and go down the Strand to Piccadilly.[92] Clutching his packages, restrained by a policeman, Stevie looks up to see a clock showing 1p.m.; prior to this, after the street-market scene the piece of paper which the Professor included with the bomb delivered in a birdcage saying 'the birds will sing at 1.45' is shown in close-up again, heightening the dramatic irony for the audience. The Lord Mayor's procession passes by (which is the correct route from the City of London to Westminster), the mayor's coach being followed by huge crowds. Stevie sees an omnibus (with the then modern London Transport logo prominent on its side) and tries to get on, the conductor initially refusing him entry because of the film cans but then relenting on seeing the title *Bartholomew the Strangler*, he says, 'ah well, as long as it's you Bartholomew old fella, you can stay as long as you promise not to set about me or any of the passengers'. The bus journey is a sequence of increasingly rapidly interposed images combined with a quickening music sound track reminiscent of Igor Stravinsky's mechanical turbine-like music; Stevie sits next to a lady with a small pet dog which he fondles, whilst we are shown images of traffic jams and more and more clocks in acute close-up angles as the time when the bomb will explode approaches; the clocks are very contemporaneous 1920s and 1930s art deco designs in most cases. The bus is also agonizingly held up by traffic lights, another symbol of detached electrical and mechanized modernity introduced from 1931 in London, juxtaposed against the image of the affectionate pet dog. The final clock image is an extreme close-up as the minute hand approaches the forty-five minute mark, followed by the crescendo of the explosion.

The depiction of London is both realist and radical. In terms of topographical sense, the delineation of geography is quite accurate, street signs providing a mapping dimension, except for the nonexistent 'Plouthorp Road' on Verloc's headed notepaper: the SE5 location would appear to be accurate both in terms of Stevie's walk and the general ambience created around the cinema, which is much more Kennington, Walworth or Camberwell than Soho as in the novel, although the distances walked by Stevie and Verloc are perhaps somewhat improbable. There is at times a documentary feel to the street scenes in particular, reminiscent of newsreel footage, which, combined with the soundtrack, give a feel of everyday life in the metropolis with all its hustle. The film's starkly accentuated monochrome qualities, especially around the images of electric power, are a strong link with the novel and although there is a historical time-shift, the sense of London's 'darkness enough to bury five million lives'[93] is frequently felt. The sabotage aspect of the film in particular employs the experimental and powerful imagery, providing alienation effects through acute camera angles, silhouettes, chiaroscuro emphasis, close-ups and quite often stasis as opposed to the very kinetic feel associated with general London life. These effects combine to evoke the imminent terrorist threat, and also perhaps a more immanent unspecified 'foreign' threat, that the normality and humour of everyday London life may be threatened by some cataclysmic event, as in the image Verloc imagines where Piccadilly Circus is destroyed. The romantic storyline between Ted and Winnie tends to dissolve against the much more haunting backdrop of the threat to London and its seemingly inevitable catastrophe as represented in Stevie's teleological journey. Significantly, the totalizing images of the city tend to arise from an external perspective, in contrast to the homely street scenes, suggesting some form of threat which London is in the grip of and unaware of, and possibly current anxieties about the growth and dangers of Nazism. The use of cinema within the film is also worthy of note, not only depicting popular culture and the working-in of *Who Killed Cock Robin?* at a crucial plot moment acting as the catalyst for Winnie's revenge on Verloc, but also providing a meta- and self-reflexive narrative within the more experimental dimension of the film, signifying that the filmic text works at different levels.

Conrad's novel articulates a radical and disturbing image of modern city life: its portrayal of social and political relations points to an underlying savagery and perhaps the first designation of the city as 'jungle', which is superficially masked by layers of mediation and deception. The depiction of the city as a network of mechanized processes in which the human and nonhuman become inseparable and indistinguishable, moulded into activities and relationships which are represented through the geometric forms in particular is an aesthetic which anticipates and to an extent coincides with the most powerful images of cubist painting. Of the three screen versions, Hitchcock's representation of London is an imaginative cinematic development, weaving the forms and artefacts of modernity into a conventional romantic story. In particular, both novel and film offer no sense of a totalizing and harmonizing perspective, but rather a disjointed and fragmented vision of London in which its citizens will always walk alone.

Notes

1. Joseph Conrad, *The Secret Agent*, Harmondsworth, 1965, 21.
2. Michel de Certeau, *The Practice of Everyday Life*, Berkeley, 1988, 92.
3. Robert Hughes, *The Shock of the New: Art and the Century of Change*, London, 1980, 14.
4. de Certeau, *The Practice of Everyday Life*, 93.
5. Ibid.
6. Numerous poems by Wordsworth and Coleridge revolve around the experience of walking, early examples being Wordsworth's 'I Wandered Lonely as a Cloud' (1804) or Coleridge's 'This Lime Tree Bower My Prison' (1800), in which the sick poet imagines his friends on a walk on which he cannot join them. Walking tends to suggest unity and insight, a means to knowledge.
7. The *flâneur* represents a figure who derives pleasure and delight from the city's hustle and bustle, promenading without purpose. For Walter Benjamin he is the 'heroic pedestrian', retaining his individuality and resisting incorporation into the milieu in which he moves (Walter Benjamin, *Charles Baudelaire: A Lyric Poet in the Era of High Capitalism*, London, 1983, 54).
8. See for example C.B. Cox, *Joseph Conrad: the Modern Imagination*, London, 1974, Chapter 5: '*The Secret Agent*: The Irresponsible Piano', 83–101; also Jeremy Hawthorn, *Joseph Conrad: Language and Fictional Self-Consciousness*, London, 1979, Chapter 4: '*The Secret Agent*: animism and alienation', 72–93.
9. Joseph Conrad, *Heart of Darkness*, Harmondsworth, 1973), 10.
10. Ibid., 10.
11. Ibid., 7.
12. Ibid., 14.
13. Ibid., 174.
14. Conrad, *The Secret Agent*, 40.
15. Peter Ackroyd, *London: The Biography*, London, 2000, 111.
16. Charles Dickens, *Great Expectations*, Harmondsworth, 1965, 189.
17. Conrad, *The Secret Agent*, 19.
18. Hawthorn, *Joseph Conrad*, 73–74.
19. Conrad, *The Secret Agent*, 19.
20. Ackroyd, *London*, 513.
21. The phrase is taken from Dorothy Van Ghent, 'The Dickens World: a View from the Todgers's', in George H. Ford and Lauriat Lane Jr., eds, *The Dickens Critics*, Ithaca, 1961. Van Ghent also identifies the animate/inanimate inversion in Dickens's portrayal of city life: 'The animate is

treated as if it is a thing. It is as if the life absorbed by things had been drained out of the people who have become incapable of their humanity' (ibid., 214).

22. Dickens, *Great Expectations*, 379.
23. Conrad, *The Secret Agent*, 21.
24. Ibid., 45–46.
25. Ibid., 39.
26. Ibid., 129.
27. Ibid., 136.
28. Ibid., 141–42.
29. Ibid., 130.
30. Ibid., 142.
31. Ibid., 132.
32. Ibid.
33. Ibid., 139.
34. Ibid., 139.
35. Ibid., 143.
36. Ibid., 154.
37. Ibid., 78.
38. Ibid., 79.
39. Ibid., 77.
40. Ibid., 85.
41. Ibid., 97–98.
42. Ibid., 92–93.
43. Ibid., 245.
44. Ibid., 124.
45. Ibid., 126.
46. Ibid., 218.
47. Ibid., 74.
48. Ibid., 53.
49. Ibid., 193.
50. Ibid., 126.
51. Ibid., 234.
52. Ibid., 86.
53. Ibid., 29.
54. Ibid., 174.
55. Ibid., 175–76.
56. Ibid., 157.
57. Ibid., 160.
58. Ibid., 181.
59. Ibid., 94.
60. Ibid., 241.
61. Ibid., 21.
62. Ibid., 29.
63. Ibid., 49.
64. Ibid., 44.
65. Ibid., 50.
66. Ibid., 94.
67. Ibid., 115.
68. John Atkinson Grimshaw (1836–93), a Victorian genre painter who has become increasingly popular in the twentieth century, with a number of

major exhibitions; best known for his sombre cityscapes such as *Liverpool Quay by Moonlight* (1887) and *Prince's Dock, Hull* (1887) which accentuate fog and pollution. Not to be confused with his son, Arthur E. Grimshaw, who painted similar scenes.

69. Many of the paintings of Pablo Picasso (1881–1973), Georges Braque (1882–1963), Juan Gris (1887–1927), Marcel Duchamp (1887–1968), Giacomo Balla (1871–1958), Fernand Léger (1881–1955) and Robert Delauney (1885–1941) are examples of cubist or futurist art in which experimental forms of perspective, colour, intersecting planes, spatial relations etc. are distorted as compared with conventional realist or natural painting techniques; in particular, human forms and material objects are sometimes blurred or indistinguishable and reduced to geometric shapes. A number of their works, such as Delauney's *The Red Tower* (1911–12), present radical images of cityscapes.

70. Conrad, *The Secret Agent*, 162.

71. Filippo Tommaso Marinetti (1876–1944), who became an impresario for 'Futurism'.

72. Conrad, *The Secret Agent*, 130.

73. Ibid., 22.

74. Maly and Dietfried Gerdhaus, *Cubism and Futurism: The Evolution of the Self-sufficient Picture*, Oxford, 1979, 11.

75. Hughes, *The Shock of the New*, 52.

76. Ibid., 27

77. Ibid., 32.

78. Conrad, *The Secret Agent*, 31, 149, 232.

79. Ibid., 46.

80. The art director at Penguin Books between 1961 and 1972 was Germano Facetti, who continued the ethos of his predecessor, the typographer Jan Tschichold. In particular, Facetti defined the look of the Modern Classics series, frequently using details of classic fine artworks.

81. Gene M. Moore, ed., *Conrad on Film*, Cambridge, 1997, 2.

82. See Moore's 'A Conrad Filmography', ibid., 224–49, for an excellent account of the many screen versions of Conrad's novels and short stories.

83. There is some debate about the precise historical setting of the novel. Although the attempted Greenwich bombing was in 1894, Spittles locates the novel in the 1880s in terms of both the number of riots and political unrest of the decade, and textual evidence in the form of the inscription on Winnie's wedding ring – engraved '24 June 1879' – and her speaking of being 'seven years a good wife', but he goes on to say, 'although the concerns of the novel are certainly those of 1907' (Brian Spittles, *Joseph Conrad*, Basingstoke, 1992, 118).

84. Conrad, *The Secret Agent*, 249.

85. Ibid., 73.

86. Ibid., 73–74.

87. Ibid., 73.

88. Sergei Eisenstein, the Russian revolutionary film director and theorist, is best known for *The Battleship Potemkin* (1925). He introduced in particular the cinematic technique which has become known as montage in order to maximize the radical potential of the camera lens via perspective and time-sequencing, combined with extremes of chiaroscuro.

89. Conrad, *The Secret Agent*, 147.

90. Ibid., 193.

91. Ibid., 124.

92. The location of Verloc's shop in the film has been questioned by Avrom Fleischman in his essay 'The Secret Agent Sabotaged?' (Moore, *Conrad on Film*, 48–60) as an 'implausible location' (ibid., 60), and takes the location to be Soho. However, although the street name 'Plouthorp Road' on the headed paper that Verloc uses is fictitious, it is clearly SE5, and, as I have argued, there is enough evidence in the film to suggest that Hitchcock indeed intended the more suburban south London to be the setting for the Verlocs' home and cinema, together with the lifestyle and class scenes depicted there.

93. Conrad, *The Secret Agent*, 10.

PART II

THE MODERN AGE:
LONDON IN IMAGE

Introduction

Stephen Barber

In this part of the book, the focus turns to film and London. But the filmic rendering of London remains always intimately interconnected with the literary representation of London, as these essays, in their different ways, will all propose; the construction of the urban and suburban film image uses many of the strategies of construction, temporal sequencing, framing and character delineation that are recognizable from the work of the city's novelists. Similarly, the act of writing on film and London is one inflected by literary approaches, as it has been throughout the history of cinema; this is why some of the most prominent novelists of London, such as H.G. Wells, Graham Greene and Will Self, have had close connections with film, as scriptwriters or as film journalists. Even the most dense film theory of the 1970s (one of whose principal concerns was to probe the power structures of urban space) retained elements of literary strategies, derived from a familiar fascination with the abyss between subject and object (in this case, the eye of the observer or spectator, and the surfaces of the city itself), as well as from French structuralist, semiotic and linguistic preoccupations. Films of London have always comprised an infinitely malleable medium of imageries and texts: a medium always vitally generated by oblique textures and undercurrents of the city, and which notably (like literature) projects memory, individual mappings of the city, urban fragility and eruptiveness, exile and sexual difference, and the intricate rapport between urban and suburban space. In contemporary London, as at the moment when the first film image of the city was made, in 1890, technology forms an engulfing preoccupation and an essential part of the spectatorial experience of the city; the evidence of that technology is now inscribed as a digital amalgam of text and image – a new and unprecedented kind of rapport between film and literature – upon the external visual surfaces and image-screens of the city.

In recent years, in writing on cinema, a new fascination (an obsessive fixation, almost) with the film image of London, especially that of London in past decades, such as the 1960s, has manifested itself. This, too, has emerged from new technologies of the word and image – particularly, for films of London, in the form of the DVD. In her book *Death Twenty-four Times a Second* (2005), the most influential English-language film theorist of the past three decades, Laura Mulvey, turns her attention to the way in which the time of the film, and also the time of the city, can literally be stopped dead through the medium of the DVD. Where film images of the city once shot past the spectator in the cinema space, always unseizable, the explorer of the city can now freeze exactly the image which requires special attention. It is then possible to explore, at will, for an indefinite time, all of the resonances, textures and meanings of the urban film image, like an unhurried stroller or *flâneur* moving leisurely through the space of the city; the film image, for that scanning eye, is simultaneously vividly alive and open, and dead. For writers on film and London, particular films have always served as especially revealing conduits into the city, and those key films have oscillated and changed according to the dynamics of the moment; for most of the writers in this part of the book, that seminal film has now become the Italian director Michelangelo Antonioni's 1966 film *Blow-Up*. Forty years after its making, *Blow-Up* has transformed itself into a uniquely determining and inexhaustible text of filmic London, able to seize both the in-flux perception of London, and also the capacity of the city (and of its perception) to vanish without trace. London has often been a space of exile (whether intentional or involuntary, permanent or momentary) for displaced filmmakers, and Antonioni is one example of the way in which London's space has been expertly dissected by such inhabitants; many of the city's newer arrivals, from such countries as Turkey and Japan, continue that project, using the new (low-cost) media of digital film cameras for their London imageries.

The essays in this part of the book examine and unravel a succession of moments from the entire history of London on film. My own essay surveys and provides an overview for that history, looking in particular at the originating work of Wordsworth Donisthorpe, who shot (but never worked out a way to project for audiences) the first-ever film image of London in 1890; drawing on the challenges which have always beset representers (in both image and text) of London, the essay also examines the new set of demands facing London filmmakers of the contemporary, digital city. Hugo Frey's essay goes on to group together a number of films by *auteur* filmmakers, each with distinctive perspectives on London, in order to assess the impact which filmic representations have had on both the material fabric and the imaginary conception of London. Roland-François Lack's exploratory essay looks more insistently at one of the 1960s films introduced in Frey's corpus, *Blow-Up*, and reveals its intricate topographical bluffs and oblique movements, as well as its enduring insights into the vanishing forms of London; Lack deploys a critical language of London that probes and embodies annotational commentary, thereby allying itself with the endless dead-ends and sudden through-ways in the perception of the city itself. Sara de Freitas assesses the prevalence of dystopic views of London in film, and interrogates the ways in which London has often been visualized in film (as in some of its most contemporary representations) as a destroyed or accursed city, subject to decimation from multiple sources, both natural and supernatural; she questions why London, on film, has often been a far more shadowy and forbidding place to inhabit than literary London. Martin Dines's essay examines the spatialized narrations of London in contemporary gay writing, focusing in particular on the way criss-crossing narrative trajectories between the suburbs and the city both confirm and complicate sexual identity, revealing an eroticized landscape that extends far beyond the environs of London's West End. Jeremy Reed, regarded by J.G. Ballard as London's finest contemporary writer and who, along with Aidan Dun and Iain Sinclair, is often acclaimed as the city's preeminent living poet, ends the book with a short walk through what he views as London's pivotal creative space, Soho, in the footsteps of the writer/filmmaker (and painter) Derek Jarman, the figure of recent decades who, from his Soho base, most extraordinarily welded together the literature and the filmmaking of London.

CHAPTER 7

AN INDESCRIBABLE BLUR:
FILM AND LONDON

Stephen Barber

London, over the twentieth century, gathered a layered network of resonant film imageries of itself that gradually formed a revealing screen, drawing the eye of the urban spectator into the city's transmutations, expansions and disasters. The literary creation of London and its spaces that had profoundly engaged and recast its inhabitants over the nineteenth century now shifted focus as literature began to work in alliance and in tension with a visual medium which, at its origins, appeared disreputable and unstable as a form for representing the city. Film reconfigured the city with such immediacy that it required a fundamental accommodation of perception and structure for literature to adapt itself to that medium. To some extent, the innovations generated by the modernist experience of the city, in literature and film – experienced throughout Europe's urban cultures to their maximal degree in the 1920s – allowed that welding-together of literature with cinema to take place, at the very moment when cinema itself was finally divesting itself of the aura of insalubriousness of its earliest decades, with its ascendance into London's urban life marked preeminently by the construction on the city's central and suburban avenues of a vast network of cinema palaces that, even in their contemporary destitution and absence, remain the prominent evidence of film's original seizure of the spaces of London.

In the first decades of the twentieth century, photography occupied a space of intermediation between literature and film in the rendering of London and its inhabitants. Over much of the Victorian era, photography had secured the representation of the city's public spaces and their great gestural events; in usurping the monopoly of painted portraiture, it had also formed an adhesive medium for consolidating family life, imperial grandeur and industrial dynastics through the demonstration of the human body as an emanation of power. The grouping of London's human figures within Victorian photographic portraiture had formed as intricate a narrative of collective authority or discord as the literary narratives of the period, and the trapping of time's evanescence within photography's capacity to record the rapport between the body and the city also echoed literature's ability to pinion the most intimate or powerful corporeal gestures at the very moment before they disappeared forever. Film was able to consolidate itself as the essential medium for representing such vanishings of power and the body in its early years through such events as the filming of Queen Victoria's cortège in its traversal of London in 1901, while photography focused on the individual manifestations of emotion among the spectators. Across Europe, in the twentieth century's first decades, film panoramically tracked the movements – both urban and human – of empires heading into historical transformation or oblivion, from Tsarist Russia to Imperial Austria. By the end of the First World War, photography had come to occupy another dimension of the city (often through the exploration of its subterranean or occluded human spaces) and the vital confrontation between film and literature as interlocking media of the city reinforced itself.

In the 1920s and 1930s, while generating narratives and imageries of the city's social and familial conflicts (often in the form of comedies or musicals) for the mass-audiences of its picture-palaces, film also reacted to London as an imperative entity that demanded experimentation with its own forms. Many of the filmmakers who became engaged with that visual exploration of the city's multiplicitous textures and infinite histories came to London as exiles or refugees from the upheavals and persecutions of central and eastern Europe, thereby strengthening the representation of London as a site of displacement and sensory flux that had already achieved a forceful presence in the literature of the Victorian era. In modernist London, the forms of the city needed to be radically disassembled or fragmented in order to meet the sensorial and perceptual requirements of their new literary and filmic architects. While diverse experiments in the forms of the city were being pursued across Europe in the 1920s, especially in Germany and the Soviet Union, to instigate the seminal genre of the 'city-film', London possessed an exceptional status in that reinvention of the city, its imageries carrying disquieting resonances of exile rather than the more habitual textures of urban exhilaration. The imageries created by London's displaced filmmakers of the 1920s and 1930s would acquire new significance in the 1960s and 1970s, when the city again became a focus for interrogative experiments into both its spatial forms and its political stasis.

The destruction of large areas of London by German bombing during the Second World War formed a crucial puncture point in the city's filmic representation, just as it did in all other creative media of the city. But film secured a distinctive status for itself in its depiction of the impact of cancelled urban space and of the human response to that calamity. In a sense, the films of London's conflagrations – both the often-surreal documentary films of Humphrey Jennings and the anonymous newsreels projected nightly to vast wartime audiences in the city as a prelude to the main evening feature – operated with the same strategy of generating airless vacuums and voided space as the fire-bombing itself: in their ferocity and vivid splendour, the film images of London in flames largely supplanted and preempted any other medium's effective representation of the city in meltdown, including that of literature. London had experienced a prescient film imagery of that threat to its existence several years earlier, with the newsreels of the Crystal Palace's destruction by fire in 1936. And ultimately, the films of London's conflagration – inassimilable as events in their moment – would be set against film documents of the more engulfing decimation inflicted upon Germany's cities in the subsequent war years, so that London's own opaque inferno would be transformed into the determining element of a transparent narrative of resilience and triumph.

In the postwar filmic London of furtive dealings and fragile affluence, with its subterranean Soho drinking clubs and neon-illuminated central spaces, the austerity of the urban landscape lacked the sense of mutation and crisis that had allowed film to encompass the representation of the city in the previous decades. While literature of the postwar years crystallized the slow-burning atmosphere of a stultified, encrusted city, photography was able to resurge again as a visual medium of London, scanning and excavating the human impact of the war's residue more acutely than film, in facial portraits and streetscapes such as those of John Deakin. Filmmakers often abandoned London in those postwar decades to locate the raw material for their urban imageries, heading for the industrial North and its insurgent manifestations of social unrest or ambition. As in the prewar decades of filmic experimentation with the city, it was often the transitory inhabitants of the city, such as the Italian director Michelangelo Antonioni, who created the most sensitized filmic representations of London's abrupt sensory and topographical upheavals as the city passed through the 1960s.

London again disintegrated as a filmic city during the 1980s as the city underwent its corporate and technological envelopment within a political culture that existed at extreme variance with the factors that had made London a compelling filmic and literary space over the previous century; that political period was retrospectively anatomized as one of violent urban nullification in Patrick Keiller's unique film-essay of the city, *London*. But in contemporary London, the powerful form of the digital city, with its corporate screens and surface homogeneity, conceals vast zones of peripheral spaces and image-seamed layers which carry the open potential to inspire and incite urban filmmakers, just as they do for literary explorers of the city.

In tracing the existence of London on film, the determining moment and space is undoubtedly that of the very first image, together with the motivation for its recording and the responses of its original spectators. In the particular historical situation of London at the beginning of the 1890s, that formative image – once recorded – lacked spectators, for both technological and financial factors; it was never a cinematic image. For over a century, it remained a virtual image, lost in the interstices of London's swarming visual histories, before the innovation of contemporary digital animation and the internet abruptly enabled that image's surviving elements to be resuscitated and made viewable, instantaneously and worldwide. Every first image and first language of the city (from the cities of Mesopotamia onwards) constitutes a precarious and unsettling form; it may risk effacement or even obliteration, and in its survival it carries all of the imperative demands that the city transmits to those who attempt to represent it.

The origination of film imageries of cities developed historically over the final two decades of the nineteenth century from the convergence of the many, disparate technologies which finally enabled the registration upon celluloid of urban surfaces and human figures in movement, and the projection of those images to spectators. In that process, many filmmakers' inventions and innovations were cast aside and their instigators forgotten. In the representation on film of London, the seminal figure is the inventor Wordsworth Donisthorpe, who began to develop his ideas for a film camera from the end of the 1870s. As with many film pioneers, he took his inspiration from industrial technology, in his case that of the Yorkshire-based textile industry in which his father had worked as an inventor of wool-combing machinery. The French-born inventor Louis Le Prince, who took the very first image in film history, in October 1888, also emerged from the same industrial milieu, and one of his first films – of figures crossing Leeds Bridge, in Yorkshire – records the urban heartland of that then-thriving industrial axis. Unlike Le Prince (who disappeared without trace on a journey to France in September 1890), Donisthorpe based himself in London, and by the end of the 1880s he had developed a film camera which he called the 'Kinesigraph': a device which used unperforated celluloid film, pulled across the lens through a mechanism derived from textile-machinery. It was with this camera that Donisthorpe captured the first film image of London, probably in 1890. Significantly, he chose the central and immediately recognizable area of Trafalgar Square as the subject of his experiment, with the dome of the National Gallery clearly visible above two slowly moving horse-drawn omnibuses and the figures of many pedestrians. Donisthorpe shot his film over several seconds from a darkened room above now-vanished shops located at 1–4 Charing Cross. Although only ten frames of Donisthorpe's original film have survived, it is often through such abbreviated fragments of images or texts that the forms and historical layers of London have most evocatively been rendered. Donisthorpe appears to have conducted his work in film in large part for reasons of political activism. Professionally, Donisthorpe worked as a libertarian barrister whose political activities – with their anarchistic emphasis on anti-socialist 'individualism' – aimed to combat the moment's worldwide rise of emergent socialist and communist movements; the surviving evidence of his activities suggests that his aim in attempting to develop the means to project his films to audiences was to instil in them a sense of their capacity to impose their own imaginative vision upon the city and to thereby reformulate it for 'individualist' political ends. Although Donisthorpe attempted to generate the resources necessary to extend his filmic experiments into the area of projection, his applications for funding to 'learned societies' in London were always refused; one justification for these refusals reads: 'The idea is wild, visionary and ridiculous, and the only result of attempting to photograph motion would be an indescribable blur.'[1]

Donisthorpe's film of Trafalgar Square was never projected during his lifetime and spent many decades in total obscurity; a number of its frames became irretrievably lost. Donisthorpe died in 1914 and his reputation fell into oblivion until a new engagement with the history of early cinema in the late 1990s led to renewed interest in his work. Although Donisthorpe's experiments had been the subject of derision and disinterest at the end of the 1880s, it was only six years after his film of London had been shot that the first-ever film screening for a public audience took place in London, when the French pioneers of cinema, the Lumière Brothers, brought their programme of short films to the city, to the Marlborough Hall of the Polytechnic Institution (a venue which still exists and now forms part of the Regent Street campus of Westminster University). Film screenings had already taken place in other European cities by that time, with a screening by the German pioneers of cinema, the Sklandanowsky Brothers, at the Wintergarten Hall in Berlin in November 1895, marking the first film show for a paying audience. The Lumière Brothers' screenings in London incited a mixture of excitement and also dismay, since the image quality was initially perceived to be flat and lifeless, especially in contrast with the previous decades' spectacular pre-cinema experiments with visual technologies, which often incorporated intricate live action and cacophonic sound effects as well as image projection. The Lumière Brothers' screenings in London also proved to be a hazardous experience for their urban spectators, since (as with many early film screenings) the projection equipment was liable to ignite and, on one occasion, almost caused the Marlborough Hall to be burned down.

The contemporary digital texture of Donisthorpe's images allows the originating space of filmic London to be intimately read as a dense language of enhanced pixels and pristine urban surfaces: any scratches accumulated on the original celluloid have been digitally erased. The top third of the circular-shaped images holds the sky of London, with the dome of the National Gallery occupying the central part of the images; below that sky, Trafalgar Square carries its momentary human population of traversing figures in movement, and a figure with an umbrella on one of the two horse-drawn omnibuses' open decks suggests that London was recorded as a city of rainfall in its first filmic images. Both of the omnibuses have large, elongated advertisement placards for cocoa products on their side panels. The instant of the originating film image of London coincides exactly with the accidental manifestation within film, for the first time, of the city's determining consumer images, prescient of the computerized urban image-screens that – with their engulfing presence on both the external and interior spaces of contemporary London – may now signal the end of film itself. The wayward and idiosyncratic technology that first created London upon film in 1890 (and then became immediately obsolete and forgotten) exists at acute variance to the corporate digital technologies which, in contemporary London and in all cities worldwide, have worked to annul film and its spaces of projection, in order to instigate new and more homogenized modes of representation for the city.

From the moment of its origin, film formed a preeminent medium for reflection on the ways in which London, as a multiple and intricate venue of human inhabitation and displacement, could be represented to itself. Over the first decades of the twentieth century, film developed its means of cohering the contradictions and paradoxes of urban life within narrative forms, and also gradually meshed itself with literary styles and preoccupations, notably in the adaptation of fictional works and the participation of authors in the screenplays of their books; prominent novelists such as Graham Greene also became involved in the discussion of film's status as a cultural, social and artistic form through such media as newspaper journalism and film criticism, thereby further dissolving the disreputable aura which had been attached to film's origins. As with many other world cities, the history of London itself, from its central areas to its suburban or peripheral zones, now became generated and refigured in large part by film itself. Film's ascendancy as a vital medium for London and as a primary focus for the attention of the city's spectators, over the first four decades of the twentieth century, would also enable it to interrogate the forms of the city in upheaval when, with the bombing of London during the Second World War, those forms were in danger of obliteration.

By the mid-point of the twentieth century, film possessed the capacity to transmit moments of urban transformation or cataclysm in such a way that cinema audiences were able to absorb them instantaneously, as interstitial points of elation or blackout in the duration of urban life. This testing and immediate reformulation by film of the fabric of urban space isolated the medium from literature for the duration of the Second World War, and also largely determined the memory that would take shape of that conflict. Newsreels of the destruction in flames of parts of London carried the intensive and direct transmission of those imageries, delayed only by the imperatives of developing the celluloid before its screening to massive and collective urban audiences; crucially, those compelling images formed part of a narrative charting the endurance by the city into triumph. In his book *The Natural History of Destruction*, W.G. Sebald suggests that the near-absence of a postwar literature of the German cities' own conflagrations (more engulfing by far than those of London) stemmed from the fact that a 'literature of the ruins' was negated even before it began, or else was utilized as 'an instrument already tuned to individual and collective amnesia ... There was a tacit agreement, equally binding on everyone, that the true state of material and moral ruin in which the country found itself was not to be described'.[2] However, it may well have been that the German citizens' own consuming experience, in wartime cinema spaces, of seeing their cities destroyed on newsreel films (with a commentary of fury) effectively preempted the need for a retrospective 'literature of ruins'. By contrast, the destruction of London on film would be perceived, both during and after the conflict, as a kind of salutary cauterizing of the city within a vital process ending in victory. The preeminent documentary films of the destruction of London held their own strategies of elision and absence, with particular literary inflections; Humphrey Jennings's film *Fires Were Started* (1943) never pinpoints the origins of the force instigating the destruction of London, instead focusing on the intricate human rapport between the firemen combating the spectacular dockland fires. London under bombardment is a surreal and engagingly unique space for Jennings, rendered both in his film images and also in the poetry he wrote at that time on the 'thousand strange sights in the streets of London', such as the burning in daylight of a church clock-face, and the traversal of human figures through fire.

The film image formed the supreme medium for the representation of urban ruination, both during the wartime period and also in films of the subsequent years that scanned the human and material debris of Europe, such as Carol Reed's *The Third Man*

(1949). In analysing what he calls the 'intoxicating vision of destruction' of cities, W.G. Sebald cites an evocation by Hitler of his plans to carry through the wartime obliteration of London; Hitler's evocation is itself a cinematic one in conception, imagined topographically and accumulating into a frenzy of vivid detail:

> Speer describes Hitler at a dinner in the Reich Chancellery in 1940 imagining the total destruction of the capital of the British Empire: 'Have you ever seen a map of London? It is so densely built that one fire alone would be enough to destroy the whole city, just as it did over two hundred years ago. Göring will start fires all over London, fires everywhere, with countless incendiary bombs of an entirely new type. Thousands of fires. They will unite in one huge blaze over the whole area. Göring has the right idea: high explosives don't work, but we can do it with incendiaries; we can destroy London completely. What will their firemen be able to do once it's really burning?'[3]

Ironically, it would be precisely the filmic response of London's firemen, depicted or invented by Humphrey Jennings, which infused the city's population with their response to such panoramic ambitions to inflict destruction: that response was one of contemptuous oblivion to the instigators of the firestorms.

Film remained the medium that most closely examined London's layers of absence and points of fracture in the postwar decades, although their excavation often required the disparate perspectives of filmmakers from other origins and cultures than that of London itself. Those urban preoccupations had become far more internalized by the mid-1960s, with the surfaces of the city imprinted by film with imageries generated from subjective crises and lassitudes. In the Italian director Michelangelo Antonioni's 1966 film *Blow-Up*, the defining substance of London has almost entirely vanished; Antonioni's narrative follows the endless movements at speed of a young fashion photographer through a contrary and unseizable city of transitory spaces and profound human unease. The city's cohering signs and indicators have evanesced (they can only be reconstructed retrospectively, as Roland-François Lack has done in his essay for this book), and the photographer seeks to pinpoint the surviving corporeal traces of London by photographing in a night-shelter for the city's excluded drifters. While himself wandering through the space of a deserted park in a run-down area of the city, he photographs two figures embracing; when he develops large-scale prints from his photographic images, taken randomly and accidentally, they gradually reveal to him the fragments of a tangible narrative of murder that was imperceptible and invisible during his actual inhabitation of that space.

The intersection of film and photography in *Blow-Up*'s depiction of London carries all of the unsolvable tension and ambiguity of the relationship between those two media: the vital evidence of the city can be contrarily generated only by the photographic images located within the film images, and those photographs immediately become the seminal elements of the film's narrative. But the alliance of film and photography possesses only a momentary revelation, in allowing the photographer the impetus to return to the park under darkness and locate the body of the figure murdered within his photographs; when he returns to his studio, the photographic prints and all evidence of the images have vanished, and when he returns to the park a second time, the body is gone too. The city deflects and annuls its own discoveries, empties out itself and also empties out all images of itself; all that remain are its capricious styles and corporate spectacles. The film ends at the moment when the active sensation of absence in London has reached its most acute point. That provocative absence itself sustains an inciting force for filmmakers exploring the history and contemporary visual forms of London. By the final decade of the twentieth century, filmmakers attempting to probe the representation of London – after the amassing of a century of film-images of the city – experienced the now image-encrusted city surfaces as uniquely resistant to being brought to light.

The presence of contemporary London on film possesses unique challenges for filmmakers intent on generating original imageries of the city: London's multiplicitous and contrary façades – from the rapidly annulled image-screens of its central spaces to the profoundly layered historical surfaces of its abandoned or labyrinthine zones – present screens to which film images now struggle to adhere. The digital city and the filmic city exist in parallel spaces, meeting only in an urban confrontation which the fragility of the filmic image, integrally attuned to vanishing resources of memory and texture, lacks the power to contest. The physical spaces of cinema projection in London have also undergone sweeping transformation in the decades since the city's picture-palaces and repertory cinemas still formed the revealing conduits for the film spectator to retain an awareness of their own corporeal presence in the city while experiencing its representations. With the vanishing of London's network of repertory cinemas in the 1990s, the representation of the city became determined by the prevalence of digital projection and of multiplex exhibition complexes (often situated within London's far peripheries and suburban retail parks, rather than inside the ostensible heart of the city); the image of the city is then inflected with something which is *other* than the city – an imagery which replicates itself incessantly, in autonomy from the space of the city itself. In that process, London remains a presence that is deeply unknown, but still linked into the amassed cinematic histories of the city precisely through that revealing opacity of the urban image.

The contemporary British filmmaker most intent on tracing those contradictions and resistances of the now-vanishing filmic city, Patrick

Figure 7.1: IKEA, Brent Park, from Patrick Keiller's *London* (1994). Courtesy of Patrick Keiller / BFI Films

Keiller, made his exploratory film-essay, *London*, in 1992. In its narrative of two unseen but acutely observant male characters traversing the city, mostly on foot, from the suburban peripheries to the centre and back again, *London* incises the permanent visual fascination and repulsion of its dimensions and surfaces. All of the film's scattered narrative traces are carried by its wryly disabused voiceover, which gently excoriates the city, occasionally uncovering precious images or sites among the sprawling dereliction and engrained squalor. The very mutation of the city provides a valuable source material for the travellers' obsessions: since the film depicts London as an integrally absent, even disappearing presence (to be seized by a 'journey to the end of the world'), the harsh process of that evanescence itself can serve to grip and instructively grate the eye. The nameless narrator of the film and his companion, Robinson, combat the redundancy of their own eccentric reimagining of London by attempting to gather data and evidence of the city's exiles, especially its late nineteenth-century poets of francophone origin (Arthur Rimbaud above all), the traces of whose transient inhabitations of the city are topographically tracked down to crumbling or already-demolished buildings. Apart from those moments of subdued revelation, the film encompasses a corrosive observation of the city's political and social power formations, deploying a glacial eye and advanced irony upon the Queen's 'annus horribilis', 1992: a prescient year of terrorism and violence inflicted both upon the essential fabric of the city and upon its disintegrating human structures. The film ends with a salutary conflagration of the city, as the two travellers attend a vast outdoor

Figure 7.2: Shaftesbury Avenue, from Patrick Keiller's *London* (1994). Courtesy of Patrick Keiller / BFI Films

bonfire, with the figures of London's inhabitants outlined against the flames. In its exhaustive examination of London's mutations, the film scans its way across a raw urban landscape whose substance characteristically resists being easily caught or incorporated by film. In the extended period of the film's shooting, Keiller and his handful of collaborators found themselves often abused or assaulted, subject to hostilities emanating from the city, as they filmed alongside fume-clogged roads or at the boundaries of London's corporate terrains. The urban landscape Keiller generates from that tension is one that possesses a stark homogeneity, from the Tesco and Ikea surfaces of the suburbs, to the recurring architecture of office complexes hastily erected during the 1980s property boom. The film's evidence for what it views as the violently inflected substance of the city is marked by a sequence showing the royal unveiling of a statue to Arthur 'Bomber' Harris, instigator of the wartime bombing raids on such cities as Hamburg and Dresden, and a principal architect of Europe's destroyed cities of 1945. The further the film tracks its way into London, the more urgent becomes its desire to castigate the city's systems of power, and the more poignant the realization of the futility of that desire. Ultimately, the film's own process of visualizing the city is one imbued with solitude and with intimations of perilous displacement: its re-creation of the unwilling city is always executed against the urban grain. Keiller's images are often almost empty of human forms, and his aim is evidently not to trace the course of individual lives in the city, other than the idiosyncratic, self-reflexive meanderings of his two, invisible characters, travelling from end to end of London. The most striking element of the film is that its static, long-take shots carry a haunting sense of urban beauty and stillness, accentuated by the film's spoken narration and its musical accompaniment, while the actual intentions behind the making of the film are more interrogative and combative; that intentional mismatch between image and strategy serves both to foreground an intricate visual attachment and attraction to London, while also intensively probing the city's layers of memory and its social structures in upheaval.[4]

Three years on from *London*, in 1995, Keiller made its sequel, *Robinson in Space*, which carries a driving narrative element of expulsion from London: the first shot of the film is taken from the carriage of a train departing Paddington Station, and the entire structure of the film's journeys (around England's industrial architecture) is generated by the need to avoid and circumvent the space of London. In the early stages of those journeys, while still drawn to London, Keiller's two travellers traverse spaces beyond even the city's suburbs, before gradually detaching themselves entirely from London. In 1999, Keiller published a book of images and texts from *Robinson in Space*:

> After Robinson published the results of his study of London, I didn't see him again for a long time, but I heard that he had been dismissed from his university position, and after a period in which he sank into a deep depression, had taken a part-time job teaching English at a language school in Reading, where he was now living.[5]

When film exhausts the imageries of London (or has itself been exhausted by the contemporary London of digital image-screens and of graffitied layers of engrimed history), there still survives the book, at whose core is the very absence of London and its imageries.

Notes

1. The Dutch animator Charl Lucassen's website has a digital animation based on the ten surviving frames of Donisthorpe's film of Trafalgar Square (alongside other digitally reanimated examples of early cinema), and can be viewed at: http://web.inter.nl.net/users/anima/pre-cinema/donisthorpe/donisthorpe.htm.

   Other useful sources on the context of Donisthorpe's work are Stephen Herbert's *Industry, Liberty and a Vision* (London, 1998), and John Barnes's *The Beginnings of the Cinema in Britain* (Exeter, 1998).
2. W.G. Sebald, *On the Natural History of Destruction*, London, 2003, 9–10.
3. Ibid., 104–5.
4. This paragraph is drawn from a number of discussions of *London* with Patrick Keiller.
5. Patrick Keiller, *Robinson in Space*, London, 1999, 2.

CHAPTER 8

SHUTTING OUT THE CITY: REFLECTIONS ON THE PORTRAYAL OF LONDON IN 1960S *AUTEUR* CINEMA

Hugo Frey

J.G. Ballard's recent novel *Millennium People* charts the rise and fall of an urban terrorist cell, the secret headquarters of which is located in an exclusive Chelsea Marina housing complex. Ballard's band of middle-class rebels express their alienation by targeting the symbols of their own class. In the course of their revolt they rampage across West London and Surrey or, as the title of one chapter suggests, 'from Guildford to Heathrow's Terminal 2'. In so doing, the group raze to the ground various tennis clubs, Waterstone's bookstores and Pret à Manger coffee shops. Little of West London is spared: beware Barnes, Putney and Fulham! Therefore, it is only a matter of time before Ballard's gang start to target more iconic national institutions, like the BBC or the Proms music concerts. When the activists escalate their campaign, the first prominent raid that they organize is launched against the National Film Theatre (NFT). The new target is the innocuous three screen art house that is secreted under Waterloo Bridge, on the Southbank riverside parade. For Kay Churchill – one of the angry brigade from the novel – the NFT represents everything that is wrong with Britain. For her, the screens of NFT1, NFT2, and NFT3 are a bourgeois memory factory that spoonfeeds culture to the intelligentsia so as to disguise their perilous position in society. Kay's attack on the NFT is a success. The complex is burnt to the ground. A pall of black smoke drifts across the river Thames and the NFT is no more. In fact, Ballard's apocalyptic vision echoes an earlier revolt that took place at the same Southbank location. Intentionally or otherwise, the episode in *Millennium People* nods to Jean-Luc Godard's

Figure 8.1: Catherine Deneuve starring in Roman Polanski's *Repulsion*: a vision of claustrophobia and despair. Courtesy of the British Film Institute and Euro-London Films.

infamous rebellion of November 1968. In an event that has subsequently passed into folklore, Godard was so upset with the studio cut of *One + One*, premiering at the arts centre, that he punched the offending producer. Next, he exhorted his audience to leave the auditorium. Outside, they were treated to the spectacular show of students projecting an alternative version of his film onto the concave underbelly of Waterloo bridge.[1]

Today, Ballard's literary treatment and Godard's minor revolution dramatically illustrate how contemporary cinema and London form an important, incendiary and complex partnership. The focus of this chapter will be to continue to examine the London/cinema axis through a case study of the portrayal of the city in a number of well-known *auteur* films that were made throughout the 1960s. Here, I am thinking of several key works from prominent international directors, including Joseph Losey's *The Servant* (1963) and Michelangelo Antonioni's *Blow-Up* (1966). Similarly, there is the now relatively neglected piece set in South Kensington, Roman Polanski's *Repulsion* (1965). From towards the end of the decade, the Donald Cammell and Nicolas Roeg collaboration, *Performance* (1970) must also feature. Predominantly, but not exclusively, filmed in Powis Square, Notting Hill, it shares many topographical aspects with the earlier works. Furthermore, when discussing *Performance* and the other 1960s films, the important forerunner remains Michael Powell's *Peeping Tom* (1960).[2] As Peter Wollen rightly suggests, that film can be seen as the opening episode of this unofficial quintet of London encounters. For, as is quickly apparent, Powell's vision of the city cast a long shadow over the *auteur* tradition.

The *auteur* pictures offer violent and disturbing portraits of life in 'swinging sixties' London. The earliest film from the sequence, *Peeping Tom*, remains the most extreme narrative. Focusing on the world of an alienated young man working in the film industry, Powell notoriously revealed the inner life of a ruthless killer. Losey's *The Servant* shares the same basic motif of psychological torment. However, it is founded on a growing class conflict between a master, James Fox, and his man-servant, Dirk Bogarde. *Blow-Up* is the least overtly violent piece, but for all Antonioni's restraint and self-denial at its heart there is an unresolvable murder. Following Powell and Losey, this is a London conceived of as collective mental asylum, a clinical cinematic dissection of a photographer's psychological fallibility. *Repulsion* and *Performance* deployed comparable thematic arcs, with Roeg and Cammell next redeploying James Fox to play against aristocratic type as a vicious gangland hit-man. In short, the quintet of films chart a series of disruptive actions, performed by violent and deranged individuals.[3] Like the Rolling Stones, whose star Jagger features in *Performance*, the *auteurs* revelled in the dark underbelly of the social revolution. Their films were the sharp-suited antithesis of the Beatles, running counter to the gentle northern humour first visualized in *A Hard Day's Night*.

London itself draws the films closer together. In each case the directors established relatively bleak snapshots of urban life that reflected and supported the violence of narrative and characterization. Any sense of even faded imperial grandeur or metropolitan might is rejected in favour of a series of drab locations. Distinctively, the films weave together bland images of sidestreets, crossroads and anonymous junctions. None of the major thoroughfares is chosen for any extended attention. Well-known buildings of architectural or historical importance are excluded from view. Instead, the preference is for what might be called a banal London of the ever-expanding suburbs. While, of course, the borough of Chelsea and Kensington features in *The Servant*, its opening shots provide a telling commentary. After the credits have passed across the screen, Losey's camera pans leisurely over the dimly lit Georgian square to focus on a shop frontage. The establishment selected is that of Thomas Crapper, manufacturer of water closets, by appointment to 'Her Majesty'. A similar sense of ironic despair is captured in the glimpses of social life that are provided in each of the other films. Public houses feature in both *Repulsion* and *Performance*, but they are relatively characterless affairs, simply drinking holes in which to shelter from the rain. These hostels offer little immediate comfort other than via the alcohol that they purvey. The only public buildings that figure to any extent in any of the films are in fact railway stations. However, they too are depicted as drab points of departure and arrival. The single open space to be filmed in an extensive fashion is the famous park sequence from *Blow-Up*. However, this is a deliberately anonymous site that lacks all identifying features. Comparable to the deserted golf courses that figured in *I Vinti* and *La Notte*, it is a windswept hillside, an ultra-green lawn reimagined as a virtual prison.[4]

The sites that are selected are immediately indicative of London (a red phone booth there, a black taxi cab here) but they also consciously overlook glamorization. They provide an imaginary space that favours the banal street geography of pelican road crossings and other characteristic English urban street furniture. The *auteurs* measure out London through some of its most idiosyncratic and atypical landmarks so as to reinforce a sense of weariness, if not collective social frustration. One is offered a sinister metropolis in which the camera appears to be trapped at ground level. As viewers we are instructed to forget St Paul's Cathedral, Westminster Palace or the Royal Festival Hall. The sight of a panorama or an aerial perspective are simply distant fantasies. Deploying a more theoretical perspective when writing on *Blow-Up* Anthony Easthope quickly ran into the anonymous nature of it all. He remarks: 'London as the contemporary city is no longer imaged by contrasting a false present with a fuller past, according to a logic of historical temporality which, arguably, presupposes the knowable coherence of classical space. That sense of space within which the city may be held as the object of knowledge is not so readily available.'[5] – a sense of space that was not so readily available precisely because Antonioni's London is constructed via marginal, ordinary and banal locations, idiosyncratic venues that were already being charted out by Powell and Losey and further ground into the popular mythology of the city by Polanski, Cammell and Roeg.

Detailed and elaborate interior and exterior images of town house apartment blocks and shared Victorian dwellings dominate and pull the works even closer together. For instance, in *Peeping Tom* one finds a series of depictions of suburban properties, subdivided into separate small apartments. The same type of construction is the main setting for *The Servant* and it is again repeated in *Repulsion* and *Performance*. These buildings are maze-like structures, including extensive basements, attics, shared landings and hallways. Like the exterior footage from the films, they represent a constrained and restricted space. Indeed, the world outside of the apartment is predominantly shut out from view. There are few, if any, elaborate window shots. Windows are obscured and incidental footage of the outside world is deliberately limited. Here, Polanski's *Repulsion* is surely the definitive example. As Carol's (Catherine Deneuve) psychosis takes hold she literally imagines the walls of her apartment closing in on her. Slowly, she boards up the windows and creates her own prison cell, a site that is a denial of all that lies beyond her inner space.

Deeper feelings of entrapment are asserted through the recurrence of secret rooms and concealed or darkened chambers. Often the flats that are the central dramatic sites are attached to private annexes or are isolated from everyday public life altogether. Intriguingly, special emphasis is given to photographic dark rooms, private cinemas and the seedy film sets of the pornographic film industry.[6] So, to chart this visual micro history: in 1960, Powell introduced *Peeping Tom* and his extensively renovated rooms, filled with threatening cameras and mysterious film-screens. In 1962, Losey concentrated on the narrow stairwell that linked the master's quarters to the servant's domain. Later, Antonioni partially revisited the same narrow spatial territory by providing his photographer with his own extensive studio. And later still, the crumbling mansion block from *Performance* confirmed this persistent indoor mythos, including both basement den and intoxicating private sound recording studio.

Productively, Geoffrey Nowell-Smith has argued that city cinemascapes revolve around two characteristic types: dystopian cities, which tend to be shot 'in studio' and which block out the reality of setting in favour of fantasy (eg: Lang's *Metropolis*; Polanski's *Chinatown*); and those more realistic works that seek to engage with aspects of the reality of the cities in which they are set.[7] Such distinctions do not easily map out on to the *auteurs'* visions of London. On the one hand, their films are clearly located in the capital and speak to that location; on the other hand, the London setting is rigorously manipulated to support narrative and psychological tension, irrespective of the urban reality. A more productive theoretical anchor through which to analyse this particular cinema city is therefore found in Anthony Smith's work on film and national and social identity. Smith formulates that film, like painting before it, offers audiences snapshots of their 'homeland', the very visual fabric of how a society imagines itself to be.[8] Here, filmed cities are important not because they are dystopic or real but because of how they function to colour the social imagination; how cultural discourses are established that instruct us how we imagine our past and future to be. Let us now continue to reflect on how the *auteur* representation of the capital operates to form just such an imaginary London 'homeland'.

Importantly, the films worked through relatively traditional British and European conservative attitudes towards urban life. Intentionally or otherwise, Powell, Polanski and the others toyed with long-standing anxieties about modernity and urban living. In the classic British and European conservative mindset cities are traditionally perceived as sites of alienation, decadence, perversion, physical and mental dangers. In fascist ideology they were frequently associated with internal subversions of the nation. In both the conservative and fascist anti-urban mythologies, the city is juxtaposed with romantic rural spaces. It is here in the countryside and not in the metropolitan

Figure 8.2: *Peeping Tom*: the start of an obsession with cameras and secret cinemas?
Courtesy of the British Film Institute / Canal+Image UK Ltd.

areas that family values, social harmony and order are founded,
preserved and organically recreated. Perhaps unintentionally, a work
like *Repulsion* reemploys comparable stereotypes. By showing London
as a site of danger and entrapment the films contributed to a deep
reservoir of anxieties about being a city dweller. Aside from their
potentially more complex sexual or psychological subtexts, the films
harbour a series of implicitly anti-urban codes that warn off
audiences from the decadent capital. While Colin MacCabe has
suggested that *Performance* is a reflection on sexual awakening and
carnivalesque transgression, on a different (perhaps indeed more
banal) level, it is also a deeply violent and depressing encounter with

municipal life.[9] *Auteur*-London operated as a grim welcome to the corrupting 'Smoke'.

Robert Murphy rightly suggests when discussing *Blow-Up* that these films do not blandly celebrate London in its libertarian 'swinging' heyday.[10] Instead, this 'London homeland' is an obliquely pessimistic commentary on the capital, the nation and its future. The depiction is subtle and should not be confused with an outright attack on the idea of London. Rather, the films intersect with wider intellectual preoccupations with contemporary decay. For example, writing in 1963, Arthur Koestler announced that Britain was experiencing nothing short of the suicide of a nation. While her European rivals, Italy, Germany and France, had moved into a period of social and economic revival, Koestler and other London-based intellectuals despaired of Britain's trajectory. They saw the nation entering a phase of retreat in which the entrenched class system was holding back development. Stagnation was the norm, Koestler excitedly reporting on the crisis: 'What ails Britain is not the loss of empire but the loss of incentive. We hear the news at nine o'clock, but where are the eagles and the trumpets?'[11] *The Servant, Blow-Up* and the other works visualize this type of critical intervention. *Auteur*-London is as marked by images of 'old world' stagnation as it is celebratory of that now much overused phrase 'the swinging 1960s'. Similarly, the gender politics of the films mark their distance from the 'sexual revolution' or the growing feminist movement of the period. Here too the films fall closer to conservative discourses on male and female roles than perhaps might be expected in the light of nostalgic film histories of the 1960s. To an extent the male protagonists are shown to be more at ease in the city, and thereby are identified with it. On the other hand, *grosso modo*, women are frequently constructed as victims, cowering insanely indoors for fear of contamination from the streets.

There is a profoundly bunker-like aspect to the dominant topography. In relying so heavily on a sense of enclosure, I think that the films reflect the profound military importance of the city in the twentieth century. The general preference for enclosed spaces and random violence implicitly recalls the genuine militarization of the preceding wartime period. The combination of sudden brutality and enclosure was very much at the heart of the experience of London during the Blitz. Powell's choice of casting Austrian actor Karlheinz Böhm as the psychopath Mark Lewis is especially disturbing in the light of this mood. While Powell's narrative explains Mark Lewis's symptoms as the consequence of his father's psychological experimentations, the fact that this blonde Germanic figure continues to wreak havoc is suggestive of terrors that date from 1940. Powell's work subconsciously provided an unpleasant reminder of dangerous times past.[12] However, each of the films' geography of concealment and secrecy equally underlined the latent but continued violence of the Cold War: the hidden underground atomic shelters and specially designed tube lines to be used in case of emergency.[13] Moreover, beyond the *auteur* work, it was in the popular espionage film genre that a comparable spatial orientation was most resonant. For instance, *The Ipcress File* (directed by Sidney Furie, 1965), an adaptation from Len Deighton's novel of the same title, and initially planned as a working-class franchise competitor to James Bond, manipulates a comparable symbolic geography to that articulated in the art films. Herein, Harry Palmer's (Michael Caine) world is presented through further series of constricted and tight spaces. In that film Palmer's Intelligence Headquarters are concealed behind a shabby exterior, buried inside a fake shell. Like *Peeping Tom's* loft-apartment they too contain a private cinema. Bureaucratic offices, train stations, a research library and abandoned warehousing are all filmed in *The Ipcress File* through the oppressive and confined style. Indeed, in the light of these parallels one can speculate that had Mark Lewis (Böhm in *Peeping Tom*) not been drawn to working in the British film industry, his skills would have been valued by one of the intelligence services. Here, Powell's casting of Böhm is again rich with intertextual meaning, the actor's Austrian background now recalling Harry Lime and Graham Greene's *The Third Man*, as well as hinting at Peter Lorre's memorable performance as the foreign spy from Hitchcock's *The Man Who Knew Too Much* (1934).

For the most part the films in question were made by outsiders, exiles and visitors to England. Looking in on London from this vantage point, the directors captured aspects of our identity that perhaps only they could so explicitly imagine. The London and the Londoners found in these films frequently display characteristic English hypocrisy. On the outside, in the streets, everything is plain and anonymous, if just a little sad and dull. However, at home, behind closed doors, one is invited to witness all manner of obsessions, transgressions and disturbed passions. Thus, the 'London homeland' used in the films can be read as a metaphor of double standards. This is a bleak and unflattering reading of the English psyche but one that strikes a raw nerve.

The emphasis on apartments, private cinemas and studios underlines another disturbing issue. The London viewed in these films is composed of individuals and their privatized homes and lives. The metropolis of secret chambers, of individuals' rights to privacy in their domestic lairs, evokes a genuinely important political aspect. Each of the films anticipates a world of atomization and alienation that is typical of late capitalism. Here, the spatial context which the characters inhabit is important because it is illustrative of a retreat from public life and a rejection of wider social values. *Auteur*-London predicted the Thatcher era's attacks on the social arena. Furthermore, it asserted just how damaging isolation and extreme privacy can be. These films imply that when individuals find themselves utterly at a loss in a modernizing urban space the resulting alienation is dangerous for all concerned. The anti-heroes from *Peeping Tom* and *The Servant* anticipate, or even predict, the better known acts of random violence that have been committed in recent years. I am not thinking here of the organized, systematic and politicized terrorism of the Irish Republican Army, but rather of those lone, alienated terrorist figures that are more closely foreshadowed by a character like Mark Lewis – such as the murderers of Stephen Lawrence, and the assassin who executed television presenter Jill Dando (who coincidentally is discussed in the aforementioned novel, *Millennium People*). The classic case to note here is nevertheless that of David Copeland, who in April 1999 decided to nail-bomb a well-known gay bar in Soho, following his targeting of migrant communities in Brick Lane just one week earlier.[14] Copeland's disturbed attack brought chaos and fear to a city that temporarily looked uncertain of its own identity. As the United States's uneasy response to the Oklahoma bombing and the Columbine school massacre demonstrated, violent internal threats to the social order are especially difficult to come to terms with. This was a very modern crisis that Powell, Polanski and Roeg and Cammell warned of through the disturbed individuals that populate their films.

To summarize, it is helpful to pose the question whether the works are implicitly anti-London pieces, six interlinked anti-London films. *Peeping Tom*, *The Servant* and *Repulsion* certainly fall closest to this description. They each provide damningly critical insights on the city; broadly speaking they also parade hostility towards modern metropolitan life. The work of Powell et al emphasizes violence and urban decadence in ways that are rarely favourable to the capital. Nevertheless – and it seems to me to be an essential point – the films never completely condemn. Each work has a far more symbiotic relationship with its setting than such a simplistic outlook allows. None of the films includes directly polemical arguments against London. Moreover, one even senses that a director like Powell revelled in the charming normality of the setting of his particular suburban nightmare. Ironically, in the longer term, the decision of these international filmmakers to work in England in the 1960s lent instant prestige to the city, irrespective of the final content of their work. Indeed, in a global market dominated by Hollywood and the USA, any kind of British/London imagery is now in short supply and so even the most negative representation is at least a reminder that London exists as cultural discourse. Perhaps the moral of the story is that it is preferable to be known for the bad weather, the criminal underworld or the psychotic loner than to be culturally forgotten altogether. For such a scenario would mean London falling to the rank of a provincial American city, condemned to being just another 'wrong answer' in a thousand failed geography essays – or to become a new cultural ghost town, already at risk of being outflanked by mid-ranking art-film powers like the Danish *Dogme* movement, who have at least carved out their own niche market.

By way of an extended and impressionistic conclusion, let us briefly speculate on the longer-term impact of these representations that shut the city out. Of course, as any number of recent cultural historians will remind us, the 1960s gave way to the 1970s and thereby ended a distinctive period of political and cultural change. Slowly, the 1960s, its art and attitude, drifted into the distant past to return only as the subject of political and historical polemic. Directors like Antonioni quit town and London's fashionable status diminished. Nevertheless, the imaginary space that had been articulated was not so easily displaced or disrupted. From the 1970s to the present day aspects of the core portrayal found in the original *auteur* films have recurred in important new films. Probably one of the best examples is David Lynch's historical drama *The Elephant Man* (1980). Once again, one finds in that work a combination of hidden rooms, concealed hospital wards and interior spaces that lock up secrets from the outside world of unflappable bourgeois contentment. Later, like Lynch, Louis Malle also picked up on the tensions of the original *auteur* films in the filmic adaptation of Josephine Hart's novel, *Damage*. Like *Repulsion* before it, *Damage* (1993) is set in South Kensington and further emphasizes the city as an ultimately traumatic space. Such recurrent echoes of the 1960s vision are indicative of its haunting power. Even a recent attempt to make a portmanteau film devoted entirely to life in London chose to use the underground railway network as its defining motif. In so doing *Tube Tales* followed a visual topographical attitude established as a cultural norm through Powell to Roeg and Cammell. Now, their claustrophobic apartment blocks were replaced by sweltering tube train carriages.[15] Most famous British television depictions have been similarly reluctant to depart from a variation of the patterning that I have been analysing. It remains a remarkable fact that the soap opera *EastEnders* rarely abandons its Elstree set to film on location. Aside from the maps that open the title sequence to each evening's slice of daily life, I do not recall a single episode that has shown the actual river Thames, its often beautiful bridges, or the major buildings that make up the waterfront. Other highly acclaimed television programmes as different as *The Bill* or *This Life* also broadly occupy the same anonymous zones once used in *Peeping Tom* and *The Servant*. These popular television pieces thrive on a discrete, gray and pessimistic scenery that revels in wastelands, outmoded public houses and cheap cafés. Ironically, the picture-postcard London that is enjoyed by millions of inhabitants and visitors everyday has been abandoned by much of the mass media. Such choices certainly are in part derived from the powerful domestic social realist tradition, but equally they develop out of the psychotic lower-middle-class encounters with suburbia that I am exploring in this essay.

The sheer resilience of the drab vision of the 1960s films carries important implications for contemporary identity politics. Recently, scholars like Kevin Robins have sought to use the idea of London as a model for future postnational identity formation.[16] Optimistically, it has been suggested that the capital is an exemplar of contemporary civic identity, blending sociocultural differences together in a successful modern civic community. This conceit frames London as the venue for 'Cool Britannia' – that pre-Gulf War New Labour paradise, where Tony and Cherie restage G.K. Chesterton's *Napoleon of Notting Hill* to Islington's Upper Street ... In Robins's argument, London is presented as an open and forward-looking place in contrast to the reactionary conservatism of the rural provinces. (So the story goes, beneath the spires of most cathedral county towns lies a sea of pro-hunting mob rule, fuelled by low-key racism and tabloid euroscepticism.) Certainly, Robins's theoretical project is a promising and attractive idea. However, it is in danger of being permanently frustrated by the sheer volume of ambiguous cultural-visual markers that are attached to London. For how is one to celebrate the successes of postwar London if one of its dominant representational modes remains as pessimistic as I have suggested? Certainly, the treatment found in the selected 1960s films will not provide fertile cultural ground from which a new identity is likely to flourish. There are a range of usable London pasts to support this kind of new identity formation project but they are not provided in the terrifying profile of *The Servant*. The more promising origin of cultural markers for a new liberal city identity in fact probably lies in the success of London character actors (Caine, Hoskins and the other younger versions) than in any direct vision of the place itself.

Finally, critics have bemoaned the popularity of the 1990s fairy-tale films, *Notting Hill* and *Four Weddings and a Funeral*.[17] These works replicate basic American comedy plotlines and transfer them to the exotic foreign shores of Britain. In many of these films London is simply reduced to the status of Hugh Grant's hometown. As Pamela Church Gibson rightly emphasizes, the capital is now constructed as if it were a nostalgic rural idyll. It is perceived in Hollywood as a village made up of whimsical eccentrics waiting to be amused by an American visitor. Church Gibson's critique is brilliantly executed but ultimately it is over-anxious and under-confident. Put crudely, London can afford to occasionally offer itself a positive fantasy or two. The sheer cinematic and cultural persistence of the iconic *auteur* films means that no one is in any grave danger of suddenly believing London to be an exclusively glamorous place. The long shadow of the 1960s *auteur* tradition is a timely defence against the fantastical excesses of the recent comedies. Of course, the Hugh Grant films will still draw in cinema audiences, but they will not be able ever to fully displace the London that was originally evoked by Powell, Losey and the others. The scope of the portrayal found in the films I have discussed might well fade over time but it will not be superseded.[18]

Notes

1. See J.G. Ballard, *Millennium People*, London, 2003. For a further account of the Godard episode see Colin MacCabe, *Godard*, London, 2004, 212. The dramatic event is also detailed in the sleeve notes to the British Film Institute video edition of *One + One*.

2. The underlying interrelationship between each of these 1960s films was first noted but not fully analysed in the insightful commentary on *Performance* provided by Peter Wollen. See his article, 'Possession', *Sight and Sound*, vol. 5, no. 9 (1995), 20–23. *Blow-Up* and *Performance* were also linked in Jon Savage, 'Snapshots of the Sixties', *Sight and Sound*, vol. 5, no. 7 (1993), 14–18.

3. In addition to the thematic issues which pull the films together, the history of their making also contains a series of intriguing interactions and overlaps. For example, David Bailey, on whom the main protagonist of *Blow-Up* was based, later married the star of *Repulsion*, Catherine Deneuve. A good, albeit journalistic, backdrop to the period is Shawn Levy, *Ready, Steady, Go!: Swinging London and the Invention of Cool*, London, 2002.

4. For a full catalogue of the actual locations used in the films see Tony Reeves, *The Worldwide Guide to Movie Locations Presents: London*, London, 2003. Incidentally, the famous park used in *Blow-Up* is Maryon Park, off Woolwich Road.

5. Anthony Easthope, 'Cinécities in the Sixties', in David B. Clarke, ed., *The Cinematic City*, London, 1997, 137.

6. It is important to note that one of the most highly regarded London novels of recent years has also engaged with this topography; see Christopher Petit, *Robinson*, London, 1993.

7. Geoffrey Nowell-Smith, 'Cities: Real and Imagined', in Mark Shiel and Tony Fitzmaurice, eds, *Cinema and the City*, Oxford, 2001, 101.

8. Anthony Smith, 'Images of the Nation: Cinema, Art and National Identity', in Mette Hjort and Scott Mackenzie, eds, *Cinema and Nation*, London, 2000, 45–59.

9. Colin MacCabe, *Performance*, London, 1998.

10. Robert Murphy, *Sixties British Cinema*, London, 1992.

11. Arthur Koestler, *Suicide of a Nation?*, London, 1963 [1994], 13. It is a matter of historical accuracy to note that an intellectual argument on British decline had started before the heyday of the 1960s, that very period which in later classic right-wing versions of declinology is held to be the cause of this very process.

12. The wider impact of cultural memory on European city films is underlined by Stephen Barber, *Projected Cities: Cinema and Urban Space*, London, 2002, 63. One would precisely expect such intersections with the wider European tradition in work from directors like Antonioni and Polanski. Indeed, the bunker geography of enclosure which I am analysing is repeated in perhaps the most challenging and claustrophobic of city-memory films, Liliana Cavani's Viennese work, *The Night Porter* (1974), a film that is very much prepared for by Dirk Bogarde's original role in *The Servant*.

13. Details of the Cold War/Intelligence Services' impact on the geography of London are provided in the fascinating work of Ed Glinert, *The London*

Compendium, London, 2003. For a wider national picture see also, Wayne Cocroft, Roger Thomas and P.S. Barnwell, eds, *Cold War: Building for Nuclear Confrontation 1946–89*, London, 2003.

14. Copeland was a commuter to London, travelling in from Aldershot, Hampshire.

15. *Tube Tales* (1999) sequences directed by Gaby Dellal, Stephen Hopkins, Bob Hoskins, Menhaj Huda, Armando Iannucci, Amy Jenkins, Jude Law, Charles McDougall and Ewan McGregor. The film might be profitably compared to the much-discussed work of Patrick Keiller, *London* (1994). Although Keiller's film is hardly an optimistic piece it at least does provide a fascinating visual record of London that breaks with the claustrophobic approach I am discussing. For that alone it is a genuinely unique film.

16. Kevin Robins, 'To London: the City beyond the Nation', in David Morley, and Kevin Robins, eds, *British Cultural Studies*, Oxford, 2001, 473–93.

17. Pamela Church Gibson, 'Imaginary Landscapes, Jumbled Topographies: Cinematic London', in Joe Kerr and Andrew Gibson, eds, *London: From Punk to Blair*, London, 2003, 363–69.

18. Much of the work for this chapter was conducted in the months before the July 2005 suicide bombing attack. Rereading the text, one can see the shadows of many contemporary anxieties influencing my thinking.

≈ CHAPTER 9 ≈

LONDON CIRCA SIXTY-SIX: THE MAP OF THE FILM

Roland-François Lack

Paris, circa 1964: 'We need a plan ... A plan? What for?' The men in Godard's *Bande à part* need a plan of action, but in French the word 'plan' also means a camera shot, and when the woman asks 'What for?', with a look straight to camera, she actualizes the second meaning of the word. A third meaning of the word in French is actualized when a topographical reading of the film discovers its easterly orientation (from Bastille out to the suburbs, with excursions back to the centre): plan means map, and a reader of *Bande à part*, of all Godard's ciné-cities (Paris, Geneva, Rome ... and London), needs a map.

London, circa 1965: 'That's what her legs are walking her into.' The young woman in *The Knack* arrives at Victoria Coach Station, to the sounds of comments from elderly onlookers who anticipate her going astray. She wanders off westward in search of lodgings, and finds herself at a variety of London locales (Mary Quant's Bazaar boutique on the Brompton Road, the old barracks on Knightsbridge, a Golden Egg restaurant in Queensway, the tube station at Warwick Avenue, and Buckingham Palace). An air of *flânerie* pervades her solitary *errance*: encounters with salesmen, prostitutes, street surveyors, short-order chefs and guardsmen might all be Baudelairean or Benjaminian tropes. She might be the famous missing *flâneuse*, though there is little residual glamour in her luggage-laden quest for the YWCA. Like any movie tourist in London, what she really needs is a map.

This essay considers the usefulness of visiting the cinema of 1960s London, and by implication all films with a topographical premise, map in hand. My map of choice is a 1966 edition of the *Geographer's A to Z of London*.[1] My film of choice is Antonioni's *Blow-Up*, though I

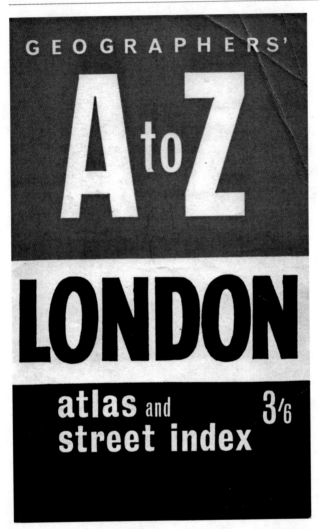

Figure 9.1: *The A to Z of London* (c.1966). Photograph by the author.

have taken a comparative approach to its topography, consulting and discussing several others from the period.[2] 'Swinging London' films have helped me calibrate the swing of *Blow-Up*, a work emblematic of London in the 1960s and central to the ciné-city canon. *Blow-Up* is, in this reading, the London film.

Map and film both offer an image of the city; both show those paths, edges, districts, intersections and landmarks identified in 1960s urbanism as defining elements of the city image.[3] Ciné-theorists have recently explored deeper analogies between urban cartography and film,[4] but my first model here is another consumer of the ciné-city, the location tourist, who remembers watching a film and then takes that memory into the streets, reoccupying, for a moment, the film's place in time. *Blow-Up* is a good object for such ciné-tourism, with at least six different places to visit listed in the London volume of *The*

Worldwide Guide to Movie Locations (including a restaurant to eat in and a park to stroll in), and several of the other films discussed here can be revisited with the aid of such guides. Without these, or the kind of research on which they are based, the serious study of a film's relation to place is impossible.[5]

Serious visitors to this ciné-city circa sixty-six will bring maps, directories, works of reference and picture books, as well as novels, biographies and other sources of detail. But it is the videos, DVDs and memories of films shot in and about London in the 1960s that are their chief research tools. A number are listed at the end of this essay: they are the image of the city seen then, by locals and tourists, by local and visiting filmmakers, and by their audiences. These films are often the only image visible now.

Visitor's London

Almost every sight the visitor to London in the 1960s might wish to see is on view somewhere in the period's cinema. See, for example, Buckingham Palace in *The Magic Christian*, Big Ben and the Houses of Parliament in *The Bliss of Mrs Blossom*, Piccadilly Circus in *Col Cuore in Gola*, Leicester Square in *Georgy Girl*, Trafalgar Square in *Darling*, Tower Bridge in *Alfie*, the Tower of London in *Fumo di Londra*, St Paul's Cathedral in *Kaleidoscope*, the GPO Tower in *Bedazzled*, the Albert Hall in *The Knack*, the Albert Memorial in *Thirty Is a Dangerous Age, Cynthia*, the Royal Opera House, Covent Garden in *The Intelligence Men*, Portobello Market in *Tonite Let's All Make Love in London*, Carnaby Street in *Smashing Time*, the King's Road in *Dorian Gray*, etc. None of these sights is shown in *Blow-Up*. A sequence shot for the film in Carnaby Street was never used, and the only tourist sight we do see is St James's Palace, with its single red-coated guardsman serving – like buses, phone boxes and red-painted shops – as part of a colour scheme. Antonioni came to London as an artist, not a tourist.

London in the 1960s was an important stop on the European director's Grand Tour. Before and after Antonioni came Polanski (*Repulsion*), Truffaut (*Fahrenheit 451*), Brass (*Col Cuore in Gola*), Godard (*One + One*) and Skolimowski (*Deep End*). Each in turn documented an outsider's gaze upon the unhomely city, constituting a corpus of London films on the premise of an initial dislocation. Of these art-house itinerants, Polanski, Brass and Godard stayed to make more films in England, but always from that external viewpoint.

The *'viaggi per Londra'* of Italian filmmakers made a particular contribution to the city's image in the late 1960s, counting, alongside *Blow-Up* and Brass's films, Sordi's *Fumo di Londra*, Monicelli's *Girl with a Pistol*, Grieco's *Fuller Report* and *Argoman*, Comencini's *Italian Secret Service*, Baldanello's *Nest of Spies* and Tessari's *Kiss Kiss Bang Bang*. (Taking, as I do here, a long view of the 1960s, we can add Castellari's

Cold Eyes of Fear, Fulci's *Lizard in a Woman's Skin* and two films by Dallamano, *Dorian Gray* and *What Have They Done to Solange?*). Italian producers also came: Ponti followed *Blow-Up* with *Smashing Time*; Grimaldi followed Zanchin's *Rebus* with Pasolini's *The Canterbury Tales*.[6]

The 'stranger in London' category also accommodates films by displaced Americans like Donen (*Arabesque*, *Bedazzled*, *Staircase*), Lester (*A Hard Day's Night*, *Help!*, *The Knack and How To Get It*), Losey (*The Servant*, *Modesty Blaise*, *Accident*) and Kubrick (*A Clockwork Orange*). The Canadians Narizzano (*Georgy Girl*) and Furie (*The Young Ones*, *The Leather Boys*, *The Ipcress File*, *The Naked Runner*) and the Australian Clavell (*To Sir with Love*) can also be seen as outsiders looking in.

My Fair Lady and *Mary Poppins*, the period's most remunerative visions of London, were both set in the past and made in Hollywood, but several US directors arrived to make one-off genre films with a contemporary London setting, usually using tourist guides as location managers: see Quine (*The Notorious Landlady*), Tashlin (*The Alphabet Murders*), Preminger (*Bunny Lake Is Missing*), Wyler (*The Collector*), Lumet (*The Deadly Affair*), Huston (*The List of Adrian Messenger* and *Casino Royale*), Parrish (also *Casino Royale*, and *Duffy*), Smight (*Kaleidoscope*), Richard Donner (*Salt and Pepper* and *Twinky*), Paris (*Don't Raise the Bridge*), Aldrich (*The Killing of Sister George*), and Wanamaker (*The File of the Golden Goose*).[7]

Remarkably, almost all of these outsider gazes are framed and toned by an insider. The look of London in 1960s cinema is the work of local lighting-cameramen: artists such as David Watkin, Walter Lassally, Otto Heller, Douglas Slocombe, Ken Higgins and Ken Hodge. (The rare foreign contributions are Italian, especially Silvano Ippoliti's work for Tinto Brass and Carlo di Palma on *Blow-Up* and *Girl with a Pistol*.)

Foreign filmmakers brought exotic faces to London, international stars whose appearance against a London backdrop alters for that moment the look of the ciné-city. If we include those who came to feature in films by British filmmakers, at some time or another on the streets of 1960s London could be seen: Monica Vitti, Sophia Loren, Simone Signoret, Catherine Deneuve, Leslie Caron, Anna Karina, Anne Wiazemsky, Ewa Aulin, Ursula Andress, Anita Ekberg, Kim Novak, Ann Margret, Shirley Maclaine and Shelley Winters; Marcello Mastroianni, Franco Nero, Jean-Louis Trintignant, Oskar Werner, Helmut Berger, Warren Beatty, Sidney Poitier, James Coburn, Yul Brynner, Charles Bronson, Frank Sinatra, Sammy Davis Jr, Gregory Peck and Orson Welles.[8]

Antonioni would have played a bigger part in thus beautifying our streets if Monica Vitti had accepted a role in *Blow-Up*. He discovered his London as a visitor, accompanying Vitti when she came to shoot scenes for *Modesty Blaise*, in which Vitti is seen passing the Savoy (Antonioni's base while in London) in a Rolls Royce convertible (though not the Silver Cloud seen in *Blow-Up*). Vitti visited London again two years later, in *Girl with a Gun*, framed and toned by *Blow-Up*'s Carlo di Palma.

The cast of *Blow-Up* is largely local. The one exotic presence in *Blow-Up* is the Prussian aristocrat and model Veruschka, confined to interiors but conduit of the film's showpiece gag about displacement. The scene is a drugged-up party in Cheyne Walk, Chelsea:

Thomas (David Hemmings): 'I thought you were supposed to be in Paris.'

Veruschka (stoned): 'I am in Paris.'

Alien presences (directors or actors) may be thematized as such, and those that are complement a different corpus of London films, where the narrative foregrounds the look of the outsider, in terms of both what they look like and how they look. 'Look at her looking', says the voice in *The Knack*, observing Nancy, newly arrived from the North ('London? Lovely!' says she). This theme's emblematic actress is Rita Tushingham, a strange-looking stranger in London in *The Knack* and *Smashing Time*, and its emblematic scene is the stranger's arrival, whether by foot (Leslie Caron in *The L-Shaped Room*), bus (Sidney Poitier in *To Sir With Love*), coach (Tushingham in *The Knack*), lorry (Carol White in *Cathy Come Home*), car (Jane Asher in *Alfie*), train (Tushingham and Lynn Redgrave in *Smashing Time*) or aeroplane (Alberto Sordi in *Fumo di Londra*). Its emblematic story is either that of the outsider who does not adapt and goes home, or that of the visitor who makes London home, who successfully makes the move from outside to inside. The first is summed up in the last words of *Smashing Time*:

> Well what the hell do we do now, then?
> I've still got them, Yvonne.
> Still got what, Brenda?
> Our return tickets.
> Smashing. Let's go home then.[9]

The second is Nancy's story: at the beginning of *The Knack* she is on the coach into London, reading a magazine article about love, illustrated by a photograph of a couple strolling amorously along the Albert Embankment; by the end of the film she is herself strolling amorously with her beloved in the same location, in her London.

London Belongs To Us

'You obviously don't know your London.' 'I don't know your London. I suppose a lot of London actually is yours.'[10] This exchange between property entrepreneur and girl about town, from *Darling* (Raphael's 1966 novel of Schlesinger's film), is a reminder that 1960s London really belongs to the entrepreneurs and developers, and only figuratively to the dwellers romanticized twenty years before in

London Belongs to Me (Gilliatt's 1948 film of Collins's novel). Thomas, the photographer in *Blow-Up*, makes both a figurative claim on London by capturing its image, and a literal claim by moving into property speculation in an up-and-coming area.

Paris nous appartient (1958–60), the nouvelle vague's first city film, is named in vague memory of the romantic London trope, and names perfectly a relation between subject and situation, person and place. Only a few London films of the 1960s attempt to foreground in their titles a relation to place. Documentaries do so, directly (*London in the Raw*, *Primitive London*, *The London Nobody Knows*, *Tonite Let's All Make Love in London* [a.k.a. *The London Scene*]); fictions either directly (*Fumo di Londra*, *That Swinging City*, *Up the Junction*) or obliquely (*The L-Shaped Room*, *Popdown*, *The Bed-Sitting Room*, *Wonderwall*, *Deep End*). Unlike his films made just before and after *Blow-Up* (*The Red Desert* and *Zabriskie Point*), Antonioni does not give his London film a place-name. As the conclusion to this essay will argue, the '*blow up*' names a quite different kind of place.

More often, the titles of London films express an attitude, sentiment or demeanour that may characterize life in the city (*Nothing But the Best*, *A Hard Day's Night*, *Help!*, *The Knack*, *Repulsion*, *Smashing Time*, *Kaleidoscope*, *Bedazzled*, *Laughter in the Dark*, *Performance*, *Cool It Carol!*). A striking number of London films are named for the central character, fixing attention on the body that will move from place to place, on the personality for whom the city is home. London, at least figuratively, belongs to Darling, Georgy Girl, Joanna, Twinky and Carol, to Alfie, Morgan, Otley and Dorian, even to What's 'Isname, Poor Cow, the Sandwich Man and the Sorcerers.

Of these, the one who seems most at home in the city is the philanderer Alfie: his claim on London is commensurate with his claim on the women he finds there. He is pictured in various characteristic locales (pub, park, hospital, deluxe hotel room, deluxe or dingy flat, high street, back street, embankment, canal side) and in a number of identifiable districts (SW1, W10, W9, EC1, N1). Alfie moves through a London that belongs to him: the variety of locations signifies a power invested in mobility. In her important reading of London circa sixty-six through film and architecture, Katherine Shonfield identifies Alfie as a mix of types – traditional Don Juan and Baudelairian *flâneur*, though unlike the *flâneur*, his quarry cannot be the female passer-by:

> he cannot risk the possibility that she is as mobile as himself. His licence is dependent not only on an absence of communication between the women themselves, but also on the predictability of their immobility within their assigned place, the prerequisite which allows Alfie to drift with impunity around the city sampling Woman.[11]

This overstates the prerequisite immobility of the women he visits. Every one of the women with whom he has contact is herself a transient of some sort, is seen walking, running, on buses, in cars or lorries (the chest doctor even has a mobile clinic). London is also theirs.

Alfie in 1965 is more premodern Don Juan than nineteenth-century *flâneur*. He does not actually 'drift' until the late sequence that brings him, in the same movement, from the Ladbroke Grove area to Brixton then to Battersea, overlooking the Thames. Even then, his *errance* has a heavily symbolic endpoint: by St Mary's in Battersea, his gaze shifts from the river upwards to the church spire, then pans down to see his own child emerging from the church, at which the camera zooms in. The child is pictured behind gravestones, as the stepfather comes to retrieve him. Alfie moves forward and is framed by the panning camera in a loaded composite of architectural past and present: St Mary's Church, from 1777, and the twin towers of the Somerset Estate, dated 1964.[12] In contemplation of these temporal motifs Alfie has abandoned his anachronistic donjuanism. His directionless wandering was reflected in the Brixton shop windows he passes,[13] and in the water of the canal by King's Cross (abandoning another Baudelairean trope, as this mirror-fixated dandy ignores his reflected image in favour of introspection).

Even before the undoing of his worldview, Alfie had been too purposeful to be a true *flâneur*. He always knew exactly where he was going and when (he keeps appointments). Moreover, there is a planned topographical logic to his displacements. At the opening of the film he has been having sex in his car by a canal behind King's Cross, convenient for his flat (near Exmouth Market). Then he drives his lover to the Embankment near Temple tube station, some distance away but apt for a postcoital romantic stroll and, more importantly, convenient for her connection with the overground train that takes her home. (The husband is waiting for her at St Margaret's station, Twickenham, convenient for the film's production base at Twickenham Film Studios, just opposite the station.)

Less feasible topographically (and chronologically) are the displacements of the film's true *flâneur*, the emblematic dog from the opening sequence: he moves from Waterloo Bridge in one shot to the streets behind King's Cross in the next (where he picks up another dog and has sex next to Alfie's car). He is seen again at the close of the film, two or three years later, in a chance encounter with Alfie on Waterloo Bridge. Both head southward, towards the Royal Festival Hall: away from Alfie's home, away from Alfie's London.

Thomas in *Blow-Up* is the anti-Alfie. (If Terence Stamp had, as envisaged, played both roles, he would have had to play them as opposites.) Though both drive Rolls Royces, have meaningless sex and take photographs for a living, Alfie is a 1950s throwback and Thomas is modern. They think differently. Alfie couldn't say what Thomas says of the city and its women: 'I've gone off London this week. It doesn't do anything for me. I'm fed up with those bloody bitches.' They dress differently: Alfie is seen in a variety of smart ensembles, including a blazer with Royal Air Force crest and tie, whereas Thomas is always in exactly the same very casual clothes.[14]

They look different, and look at London differently. Alfie the street-photographer snapshots affluent tourists; Thomas the reportage-artist photographs the homeless in a doss-house. A point-of-view shot when Alfie fixes his camera on Shelley Winters by Tower Bridge shows us his looking, but all we ever see him looking at are his sexual conquests (briefly), his son (more lingeringly), and the camera, us (repeatedly). He never sees the London that we observe around him. *Blow-Up* is about what Thomas sees in his photographs (above all, of course, the murder in Maryon Park), but what he sees or does not see around him when not taking photographs is as exactly identified, either by the camera's examination of his undeviating gaze, or by the camera's movement away from Thomas to look at what he does not see: he pays no attention to a tramp near St James's Palace, to the red buildings on Stockwell Road and the blue building in Woolwich, or to the spectacular towers of the London Wall development. But he does see – that is, we see him seeing – the rag-week revellers in St James's, the protest march on Victoria Street, the 'queers' on Tamar Street near the park, and the 'buildings going up around the place'. In a road off Victoria Street he also sees (though we spectators blink and miss it) the grey Rover in which the woman he photographed in the park is following him, and later he spots her on Regent Street, staring into a shop window (though she inexplicably disappears, almost before our eyes).

The disappearance of the woman anticipates the disappearance of Thomas from Maryon Park, in the last shot of the film, where a cinematic sleight of hand removes from the screen the subject to whom London has belonged hitherto. What remains, of course, is London, specifically an expanse of lawn in an obscure suburban park. The ciné-urban myth according to which the director altered at whim the reality of the London he filmed (erecting fake houses and trees, painting buildings red or blue, painting paths black and trees green)[15] makes of this grass, painted a greener green, a piece of London that belongs now to Antonioni ... or, by extension, to cinema.

Le vieux Londres n'est plus

It is a function, sometimes even a purpose, of cinema to record its object for posterity. 'The old London is no more', as Baudelaire might have said, and the ciné-tourist often discovers that the things on film no longer match the things before him in the real. One brief sequence in *Blow-Up* illustrates well the factors in the mismatch. The camera is on Victoria Street, opposite the junction with Buckingham Gate. On the corner is The Albert, a 'distinguished pub' dating from 1864 'that has survived the Blitz and 1960s redevelopment',[16] and is known to locals and tourists alike. Coming down Buckingham Gate is a protest march, the narrative motivation for the sequence, since Thomas's interaction with the protesters will express his character. But we could also see the marchers as a trace element of the real, documented and preserved for posterity. That could be said, for example, of the Vietnam War protesters in *Col Cuore in Gola*, seen firstly in a Piccadilly cinema on newsreel (alongside other real events like war in the Near East or Vietnam, and the Torre Canyon disaster), then presented in sharp contrast as part of immediate reality, down the road from the cinema in Trafalgar Square. The same could be said of the CND demonstration in *The Day the Earth Caught Fire* (though not of the fake pro-bomb protesters in the same sequence); of the Vietnam War protest in *Tonite Let's All Make Love in London*; of all those who march through 1960s London cinema: all expose the inauthenticity of the demonstration filmed by Antonioni. The *Blow-Up* marchers' slogans read 'Go away', 'Not this', 'No no', 'On on', 'The end', 'Peace not war', 'De-escalate', 'Not our lads', 'Stop the war'; all feasible messages, but all oddly vague. Missing above all are the names of places, usually an essential part of the message. Nothing identifies who is protesting and nothing identifies what war, where, should be stopped.[17]

The marchers are, like Thomas, actors placed at the scene to serve narrative ends. The scene itself is just backdrop, but that backdrop is a detailed document of London, and a dramatic deployment of the 'changing city' topos. Next to The Albert pub is another piece of old London: the livid white façade of the Windsor Hotel, described by Pevsner as 'the crowning monstrosity of Westminster ... A nightmare of megalomaniac decoration'.[18] Built in the 1880s, it had been converted by 1966 into offices (and would eventually be replaced by Seifert's twenty-storey Windsor House, 1979). To the other side of the pub, across Buckingham Gate, is a construction site, a sight emblematic of the 1960s ciné-city. (A sign indicates that the client is Mobil: a year later and for the next twenty years, Burnet's Mobil House would stand on the site.)

Other parts of the old London documented by *Blow-Up* have gone. The extensive premises of motorcycle specialists Pride and Clarke, stretching far down both sides of the Stockwell Road, with each shop-front painted the firm's trademark red, are hard to visualize now the company has closed, though most of the actual buildings still stand. These red shops were already red before *Blow-Up*, a patch of colour appropriated for the film, found there and not manipulated (as, I suspect, is also the case for the blue-painted building shown immediately after, on the corner of Woolwich Road and Tamar Street).

More spectacular than the changes undergone on the Stockwell Road is the disappearance of Tamar Street, where Thomas considers buying a shop and discovers an entrance to Maryon Park. Here the thing on film was already a modified reality: the antiques shop was installed for the shoot on the site of a grocer's shop. (Like the marchers on Victoria Street, then, the shop is a period confection; for further displays of 1960s antiquarianism, see the clothes shops in *Smashing Time* or the Portobello Road sequences in *Fumo di Londra*, *Tonite Let's All Make Love in London* and *The Italian Job*.) The other old houses on Tamar Street (mid-Victorian, mostly) are filmed unmodified, documented before their imminent demolition. An irony is added to the urbanist theme developed at this point in the film, where Thomas comments on the area's potential: 'What about all the building that's going up around the place? Already there are queers and poodles in the area.' He doesn't anticipate that these building projects will require the demolition of precisely those terraces that have charm for those 'queers' and their poodles.

The filming of Thomas's approach to Tamar Street is organized exactly around contrasts between old and new London. Thomas drives along the Woolwich Road, legibly labelled by the street sign on the blue-painted building. He turns into Tamar Street and the point-of-view pan effected as he turns includes in-shot some modern housing under construction (now the Morris Walk Estate). The shot also includes a Victorian factory chimney and, in the distance, a newly built high-rise block of flats, still encased in scaffolding.

These juxtapositions match the framing of the 1770s church and the 1960s tower block in *Alfie*, all recurrences of the old versus new trope in 1960s London cinema. *Blow-Up* in fact begins with that opposition, cutting between an 1870s workhouse in Peckham and the Smithsons' newly completed Economist Buildings and Plaza, St James's Street. Old and new combine in the shot of Thomas turning from Aldersgate Street into London Wall, or in the framing together of Georgian terraces near Hyde Park and the scaffolded Royal Lancaster Hotel, still under construction at the time.

In other films, this thematic preoccupation is more obvious. *Smashing Time*, the Swinging London film about fashion and photography that *Blow-Up* thankfully is not, is also about the changing look of London through development. When Brenda and Yvonne arrive in London, a montage of things seen includes a building site where once stood Euston Station (built 1838, demolished 1963). They settle in the rundown area around Lismore Road, NW5, a district actually being demolished ('smashed') as the film was being shot. The filmmakers dressed and populated abandoned streets to recreate the cafés, shops and street-market of a working-class community already departed. (A year earlier, a similar and still thriving street was recorded in *Morgan*; by the end of the decade, that part of Walmer Road had gone, to be replaced by the Westway.) *Smashing Time* does not show the cheap modern housing that will replace these Victorian slums. Rather, it contrasts them with the preserved Victoriana of Belsize Park, a middle-class district less than a mile away. The film shows old clothes being bought from a secondhand shop in Lismore Road and repackaged as retro-chic in the 'Too Much' boutique on Belsize Lane, implicating fashion in modernity's assault on London's past. (Cuisine is also implicated in this process, with the 'posh pie shop' – named after Sweeney Todd – making middle-class chic out of the common people's memories.)

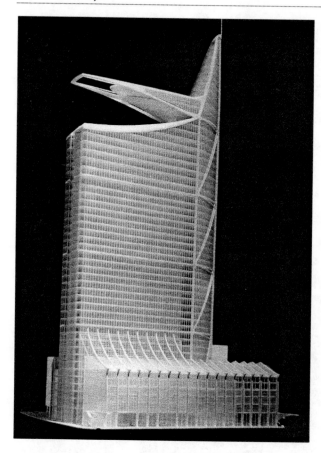

Figure 9.2: Unused scheme (c.1996) for the redevelopment of Britannic House. Photograph courtesy of Santiago Calatrava, Architect and Engineer. Copyright is with Santiago Calatrava LLC.

Yvonne's social progress is expressed in her move from Victorian slum to high-rise 'turned on studio in Chelsea' (actually, from the exterior, Britannic House in the City of London), and the climax of the film is a display of technological modernity, a party in the revolving restaurant of the GPO Tower (built 1964). Here 'swinging' London becomes 'spinning' London, as the restaurant reaches top speed and blows London's fuses, putting out the lights in Piccadilly Circus. The closing sequence, where Yvonne and Brenda decide to go home, frames old and new London: the romantic vista of Charlotte Street with the GPO Tower in the background takes a topographical motif (Northern girls lost in London) and adds a chronological theme.

The newness of London's architecture is on display throughout 1960s cinema. Two primal scenes take place at the beginning of the decade, in films that do not yet swing but are already modern. *Victim* (1961) begins at a building site, the substantial development around Stag Place including Esso House (briefly to be glimpsed in the protest march sequence of *Blow-Up*). The location is an explicit metaphor for the film's idea of a new world to be built (one where homosexuality is no longer illegal). *The Young Ones* also begins at a high-rise building

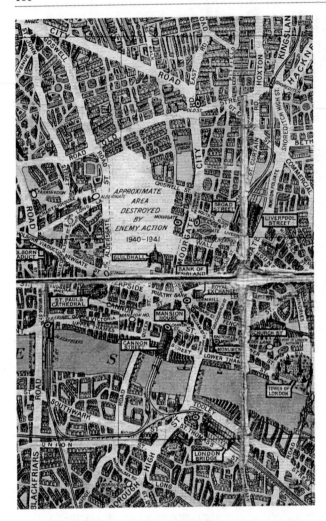

Figure 9.3: The London
Wall area (c.1946).
Photograph by the
author.

site, though here modern architecture expresses not newness but the
rapacity of the old (in the form of the hero's property-developer
father). In the narrative climax, the young ones connect with
London's traditional aspect and architectural heritage by putting on
their show at the splendid Empire Theatre, Finsbury Park (built 1910).
Preserving on film this vestige of the past before its actual demolition
by developers in the next year, *The Young Ones* ends on a note of deep
irony about oncoming modernity.

   London cinema of the 1960s continued to document the old
London that is no more. It also documented a new London now also
gone. Several of the Victoria Street buildings going up in *Victim* came
down again in the mid-2000s (making way for the Cardinal Place
development). Paternoster Square, Lord Holford's 'outstandingly well-
conceived precinct' (Pevsner), was not yet finished when *Darling*
(1965) showed it off as the property entrepreneur's ideal home; after

vilification in the 1970s and 1980s, it was replaced in the 1990s by something ill-conceived and uglier. The brutally elegant Britannic House (1967), Yvonne's pad in *Smashing Time*, survives remodelled as CityPoint, a narrowed, rounded and heightened 1990s fancy.

Panoramic shots over the City in *The Day the Earth Caught Fire* (1961) show the Daily Mirror Building (built 1957–60, demolished in the 1990s), and in the distance, still under construction, two of the five matching tower blocks overlooking London Wall. The thoroughfare can be seen in its finished, pristine state in *The Italian Job* (as Michael Caine hitches a ride on a milk float), and to even better effect in *Blow-Up*, when Thomas's car turns into London Wall and the camera frames the five blocks, all between eighteen and twenty storeys (with the thirty-five-storey Britannic House visible just to the north). The staggered effect as the towers recede is commonly reproduced as a defining image of new London architecture, and there is an exact correspondence between Antonioni's composition and the period's architectural photographers. But London Wall now is unrecognizable. Four out of the five towers have gone or are going. Lee House was replaced in the 1980s by Alban Gate, Moor House by Norman Foster's Moorhouse (2004), Seifert's Royex House is being demolished, to be replaced by an Eric Parry tower, and the demolition of St Alphage House is rumoured to be imminent. Only City Tower, 40 Basinghall Street, will survive (but for how long?).

Buildings come and go, and the map hardly changes. The layout of streets is more likely to change after the kind of bombing that destroyed the London Wall area in the Blitz, obliging postwar mapmakers to represent the area by a blank space, awaiting the developers. If Thomas had moved through this part of the city twenty years before, his movements could not have been mapped. They can be mapped now, forty years on, because though the photographic image of the city has changed, its cartographic image is intact.

The Map of the Film

The movements of film characters through 1960s London can generally be traced on a map. For many, the map need not be one of 'Greater London': something covering the centre and points west would suffice for most of the films examined here. There is a remarkable concentration of ciné-tourist sites postcoded South West 1, 3 and 7, and also West 1, 2, 6, 8, 9, 10, 11 and 14. One explanation is the attraction for filmmakers of tourist landmarks concentrated in these areas; another is the dramatic contrasts afforded by the adjacency of affluent and impoverished residential areas towards the west (the difference between Campden Hill and Ladbroke Grove, more or less). In *Alfie*, Michael Caine goes from his seedy Victorian bedsit (off Chepstow Road, W2) to call on Shelley Winters in her luxurious modern apartment (Campden Hill Towers, W11), quite within walking distance.[19] *Morgan* is centred on the upper-class wife's residence in Campden Hill Square (W8), contrasted with a café in a working-class district less than a mile away in Walmer Road (W11). (The ciné-tourist walking from one *Morgan* district to the other passes a pub seen in *It Happened Here* and another seen in *The Knack*, and then the photographic studio where more than half of *Blow-Up* takes place.)

Maps of *Blow-Up* mark where Thomas is to be seen (except the Economist Plaza, the one place in the film from which he is absent). The narrative structure of the film can then be written as a pattern of postal districts: SE15 (the doss-house), SW1 (the Economist Buildings and St James's Palace), W11 (the photographer's studio), SE7 (the antique shop and the park), SW3 (the restaurant), W11 (the studio again), SE7 (the park again), W11 (the studio once more), W1 (the club), SW3 (the party), and SE7 (the park, finally).

Several topographical factors complicate this narrative pattern, not the least being Thomas's movements across London by car, of which five are shown. The first is from the doss-house in Peckham to his studio in Holland Park: he is seen first near St James's Palace (where he meets the rag-weekers) and then in Tooley Street, SE1 (just south of London Bridge), arriving finally in W11 (his studio). The illogical order of these locations is hardly noticeable, and the second movement shown, from W11 to SE7 (Woolwich), via the Stockwell Road, is logical. The fourth takes him from Sloane Square to Holland Park via Victoria Street (a deviation understandable if he knows he is being followed), but the incoherence of the third movement has no such logical explanation in the narrative: Thomas drives east to west from Woolwich to Sloane Square via Victoria Street, Hyde Park, Kensington Church Street and London Wall (i.e. the sequence: SE7, SW1, W2, W8, EC1, SW3). A fifth movement, from Holland Park to Chelsea, takes Thomas inexplicably into the centre of London, to Regent Street.

Movements one and three, at least, cannot be traced as lines on a map. Their incoherence as trajectories are cinematic effects, dependent on montage: sequences of shots following Thomas in real time would necessarily show feasible movements, allowing displacements to have the topographical coherence of the real world. As it is, these opposed topographical motifs point to a thematic opposition that is central to *Blow-Up*: places too are shown to lack coherence.

At the centre of the film, topographically, is the West End club sequence, with The Yardbirds playing an anthem to *flânerie* ('Stroll On') before an unfeasibly immobile audience. The place is labelled as the Ricky Tick Club, with authentic posters inside and electric sign outside. The original Ricky Tick Club was in Windsor, with branches in other areas outside London (e.g., Hounslow, Staines, Newbury and Guildford). The relocation of this club to central London is one of the film's manipulations of reality, though considerable effort is made to make the displacement feasible, down to producing posters for this staged event at the new location: 'Ricky Tick London W1 | Wednesday 20th December | Yardbirds'.[20] Not so feasible is the new club's location on the map of the film. Though shot in the MGM studios at Elstree, the sequence situates the club somewhere between Regent Street and Oxford Street. Thomas enters from a rear entrance that he reaches by running down New Burlington Place, a turning off Regent Street. He emerges from the club's front entrance onto Oxford Street, which requires that the club cover an unfeasibly large area (including the whole of Hanover Square).

This unreal place between real places is the still centre of a topographical opposition, as the film moves between the west and the east of London (from St James's to Peckham to Holland Park to Woolwich to Chelsea, etc.). These are also movements from north to south of the river and back, but *Blow-Up* never shows the river being crossed, and no meaning is invested in that movement (unlike the ending of *Alfie*, for instance). The only sight of the river in *Blow-Up* is a distant one, through a window in Chelsea.

The pattern of *Blow-Up* was announced in the opening architectural exchange between the Economist Buildings and the Peckham workhouse buildings, and repeated in other visual contrasts throughout the film. Less exactly than the succession of districts, but more usefully for the reader of big differences, the west-east alternation maps the meanings of *Blow-Up*, and is – in short – the map of the film.

The Map in the Film

Tom Conley has suggested that the sight in a film of a geographical map, 'which refers to the real world, complicates the imaginary space of the diegesis as well as the space in which spectatorial subjectivication takes place'. What is a complication for the spectator positioned vis-à-vis the imaginary space of the narrative is, however, for the spectator who has already abandoned imaginary spaces for the real world of street names and postcodes, a spectacular sanction. He can, for example, enjoy the solecism when the detective in *What Have They Done to Solange?* points on a map to the positions for a stake-out of Battersea Park, South London, but actually is pointing to Hampstead Heath, in North London. The space between these two parks is, for the map-reading ciné-tourist, the space of spectatorial subjectivication.

As informational image the map-shot is common in documentaries, but its symbolic mise-en-scène is more familiar from the openings of historical romances and war pictures, where it establishes a shared perspective, a community of interest, and a set of assumptions between teller and audience that allows a story to be told. No 1960s film I have seen shows London in this way. Rather, there are dramatic instances of maps that refer, contra Conley, not to the real world but to an imaginary space from which the real-world spectator is excluded.

Filmic map-reading occurs in the opening sequence of *It Happened Here*. As Katherine Shonfield has pointed out, a familiar map is made radically strange by the arrows that show the advance of German troops across England. The effect is to break any shared topographical perspective and disorient the spectator. In a different mode and to different effect is the mise-en-scène of maps in the James Bond parody *Casino Royale* (1967). The operations room of SMERSH is dominated by a large map laid out horizontally on a large table. (This refers to the communitarian mapping in the operations room of a war film, where viewers identify their threatened country on a map: the scene is reprised for 1960s audiences in *The Battle of Britain*.) Initially, the viewer cannot identify its topographic detail, and it signifies only that someone within the narrative has a cartographic vision of the world. Three other maps are fixed to the back wall. They are equally schematic but an eye open to topography might find correspondences between the map on the table and one of these. The same eye might recognize the line traced across the three wall maps as the River Thames, with the map to the right showing the Thames at London. A Bond film is usually placed in London by showing recognizable tourist sites: in *Thunderball* (1965), the sight of guardsmen marching places us in London; *On Her Majesty's Secret Service* (1969) opens with the Houses of Parliament reflected in a brass plate, with passing red buses for good measure. Inversely, the map in *Casino Royale* places London in the Bond film, as a thematic concern, a theme located in the film's topographical ironies. (Briefly put: Is the Swinging London of cinema a place on the map, or a figment of cinematic fancy?). When the map of London becomes readable in extreme close-up, the viewer's cartological competence is ironized, since London is shown traversed by a north-to-south frontier separating England to the east from Scotland to the west: the borderline crosses the Thames via Vauxhall Bridge. (This is, of course, just a gag in the film, but there are too few map-shots among the films of my corpus under examination for the rare instances not to bear close reading.)

The close-up map-shot offers a correspondence of the spectator's view with the camera's that ultimately is unsustainable or, at least in the two instances cited, is rejected by the film. A more acceptable position offered the spectator is that of a map-reading character within the narrative, a place available for identification (an identification that the film may of course ironize). For all cartographic cinema the *locus classicus* is the map-reading scene in *The Red Desert* (1964), Antonioni's film before *Blow-Up*. Antonioni is not only, as Mitchell Schwarzer and others have pointed out, deeply preoccupied with place; his films are, as Giuliana Bruno notes, consistently cartographical:

[In *The Red Desert*] Giuliana seeks a lover who is at home travelling the world. It is no wonder that she finds herself with him, staring at a map, in a hotel room that changes tones ... Homelessness is a perennial condition for the maker of *The Passenger* (1975). In this restless landscape, maps and *vedute* appear frequently. They generally function as potential sites of opening, places to escape to, views of an elsewhere that is nowhere. For Antonioni, cartography is an existential situation.

But the map-shot is missing from *Blow-Up*; indeed, it is rare in the body of films here on view. Three further situations might be existentially pertinent.

The first revisits one of the common places for map-reading on film, the police detective's office. *The Hunchback of Soho* (1966) is a London film shot almost entirely in Berlin studios and locations, save for a second-unit shot of Piccadilly Circus and another of the Houses of Parliament. What situates the film more effectively is a vast map of London covering a wall at police headquarters. The map is seen being closely scrutinized by detectives, emblematically seeking cartographical elucidation. It is, moreover, dotted with bright lights that flash in sequence, denoting the site of crimes, no doubt, but connoting London as spectacle.

A map of London is *de rigueur* decor for a scene at Scotland Yard, and can be seen distinctly behind the superintendent's desk in *Help!* (1965). This map of 'Greater London' remains a background detail until attention is drawn to it by an arrow, with paint-filled balloon attached, fired into the office: the arrow lands on the map (somewhere near Richmond) and is followed immediately by a second arrow that bursts the balloon, covering most of West London with red paint. As well as parodying the French artist Nikki de Saint-Phalle's ballistic art of the early 1960s, this rendering illegible of the map derides the ciné-tourist's cartographical obsessions, since the most obsessive of all movie-location hunters for our period are Beatles fans,[21] and the area obliterated includes key sites from *A Hard Day's Night*, *Help!* and other Beatles-related projects such as *Wonderwall* and *The Magic Christian*.

My last map-shot from 1960s London cinema is the most relevant to *Blow-Up*, appearing in a film that consciously employs topographical tropes missing from Antonioni's film, and expressly occupies that film's intertextual space. Tinto Brass's 1967 *Col Cuore in Gola* is, like *Blow-Up*, an amateur's investigation of a murder conducted in Swinging London. Hero and heroine escape from gangsters outside the London Pavilion cinema, where *Blow-Up* is playing: the camera zooms in on the publicity still of Thomas and Veruschka, in case audiences miss the allusion when *Col Cuore in Gola* also shows an erotic fashion shoot in a photographer's studio.

The map in the film is of the London Underground, shown as part of the credit sequence that places Jean-Louis Trintignant in and around Piccadilly Circus, reading the signs around him: 'Stop', 'Right Turn', 'Underground'. He reads the map of the tube system, shown in a panning close-up that follows the Central Line west to east (from Notting Hill Gate to Liverpool Street: not quite the line drawn in *Blow-Up*). The exact trajectory of and in this map-shot is belied by the confused and inconsistent topography of the narrative that follows (just as the smooth left-to-right pan is belied by Brass's experimental montage, including rapid cutting, jump cuts, split screens, cartoon inserts and chromatic shifts to rival the best of 1960s Godard).

The map of Brass's film covers much of Greater London, going in all directions from the West End around Piccadilly Circus and St James's, to Clapton Greyhound Stadium in the east, Richmond Park in the west, Kensal Green Cemetery in the northwest and Alexandra Palace in the north. These topographically confused movements over the surface of the city, on a horizontal plane, contrast with precise symbolic movements on a vertical plane, in particular a downward movement, 'underground', precisely. A sequence near the film's denouement rapidly intercuts the faces of hero and heroine (Ewa Aulin) with the red and blue 'Underground' sign, preceding their descent into Holborn tube station. The final narrative twist, however, comes at a point where the meaning of 'Underground' is reinterpreted. The end of *Col Cuore in Gola* takes Trintignant and Aulin to Muswell Hill in North London, to the 'Fourteen Hour Technicolour Dream' event at Alexandra Palace.[22] This 'happening' happened on 29 April 1967, marking a point when London's 'Underground' art and music scene came spectacularly to the surface. *Col Cuore in Gola* documents the event as effectively as Peter Whitehead's better-known *Tonite Let's All Make Love in London*, even while pursuing its own narrative line. The closing murder is filmed on a balcony with, as its backdrop, the spectacular panorama over London that Alexandra Palace offers. The topographical shift from underground to the top of a hill (and from Central up to North London) is answered in the film's last shot, a tilt of the camera movement downward from the panoramic view over London to a view of the victim on the balcony floor. (The shot is also, in itself, the hyperbolic overcoming of the cinematic difference that underscores this essay, a difference between reading the locations and reading the plot, between place and what takes place.)

Col Cuore in Gola is the anti-*Blow-Up*, topographically speaking. The axis of *Blow-Up* is west-east, with no northerly orientation. Nor is *Blow-Up* interested in the verticality of London, never going underground or heading skyward. The high-rise buildings at London Wall or behind Hyde Park are in the far ground of horizontal shots fixed on Thomas's car (points-of-view from the car following him): the camera never adjusts vertically to take in architecture. The opening sequence films the Economist Buildings, for example, but always at ground level, showing the bases of the three blocks, the Plaza and a sculpture by Brian Wall on display there;[23] not one of the five shots points upwards to show the fifteen storeys of the principal tower.

Figure 9.4: Brian Wall, *Four Elements II* (1965). Photograph courtesy of Brian Wall.

Compare this with the opening of *I'll Never Forget What's 'Isname*, a year later: four ground-level shots of the Plaza (including a sculpture by Barbara Hepworth) are followed by an upwards pan to take in the top of the tower against the sky, and the following sequence shows panoramas over London from the top-floor penthouse. This film is, in so many ways, also the antithesis of *Blow-Up*.

A film that stays at ground level is relatively easy to plot onto the map. In *Blow-Up*, the horizontality of the London shown from sequence to sequence is replicated on a smaller scale within sequences. Character movements up or down in *Blow-Up* are only between the two floors of the photographer's studio, up the six steps into the back entrance of the Ricky Tick Club, and up and down the stairs and slopes of Maryon Park. A few angled shots, mostly related to a character's point-of-view, vary the dominant horizontality of the compositions, the emblematic image of which is John Cowan's 'Camel Train in the Desert', a photograph that dominates the decor of Thomas's (actually Cowan's) studio.

The film's human-scale angles of vision are linked to motifs of perception. For example: Thomas lying flat on the studio floor sees from that angle the laid-out corpse in the photograph, though the angled shot shows Thomas looking, not what he sees; when he returns to Maryon Park, the camera looks down with him at the actual corpse, and looks back up at him (with the corpse?); soon after, he looks down on his neighbours making love, but the reverse-angle is the view of the woman, a living and seeing subject.

There are two striking exceptions to the film's general horizontality and human-scale vision. Driving home from the Peckham doss-house, Thomas is briefly filmed from directly overhead, though the shot is remarkable above all for inadvertently showing the camera and operator reflected in the car's windscreen. More significant, in compositional terms, is the film's last shot, showing Thomas against an expanse of grass from a high-angled crane position, diminishing the hitherto dominant human scale.

When Thomas disappears from the shot, we return to the very opening of the film, where the credit sequence had imposed its wording on the same view of the same expanse of grass. But on the lawn of the credit sequence there was no human subject to indicate scale or angle. Nothing indicated that the camera was close to or far from the grass, that the lawn was actually a place that might be located on a map. That location becomes possible only after the narrative has closed, once events have been played out in the park; but when Thomas disappears at the end of the film, we have returned to that primary, abstract place (a place not on the map).

Panoramic Views

Giuliana Bruno's book *Atlas of Emotion* shows and discusses many films and many maps, but very few films of maps.[24] Instead, discussing 'cartographic film practices', she shows that cinema habitually employs an equivalent of the map-shot: 'A clear example of cartographic transference is the cinematic convention of the "establishing shot". Here, a travel practice is quite materially transformed into filmic mapping.' Bruno goes on to compare the spectator's position at the beginning of a film with that of a traveller on arriving in a city, who is thought to confront a geographic emotion. This may range from a simple desire to know the location, to a fear that develops into the need to be reassured of one's whereabouts. The establishing shot is the conventional response to this destabilizing 'space effect'. It is a way of securely mapping the viewer in space.

But for the ciné-tourist – a film spectator who is a traveller arriving in a city – the space in which he is to be secured is not that of the narrative, to which he is indifferent. What establishes his position is not a shot that maps him, but one that can be mapped.

Long panoramic views may serve as establishing shots, and there may be reasons to believe they serve well the purposes of the map-reading ciné-tourist: firstly, because they tend to include landmarks which the tourist can identify, and secondly because, in scale, they may resemble the map in the tourist's hand. But on both counts they actually unsettle his or her position. On the second: the suggestion that a panoramic view is map-like would only be of use if the view were readable like a map, but it is not. There are no words to read, of course, in a panoramic view (unless it takes in the neon signs of Piccadilly Circus),[25] and words are what make a map readable.

Further, it is necessarily an oblique view, offering angled perspectives on the city's topography which require of the viewer a calibration, positioning him- or herself above the thing viewed in order to adjust it to the proportions of the map in his or her hand. Only vertical or near-vertical views (such as the shot over West London near the opening of *Darling*, or over the docks to the east from a helicopter in *The Magic Christian*) are adequately map-like, and these are rare.

On the first count, there is little virtue in identifying London or some part of it by a sighting of Big Ben or a familiar gasometer: for these shots, unlike ground-level views of streets or buildings, the location to be identified is the camera position, and the evidence thereof tends not to be in the view but in the shots that surround it.[26] We know that the end of *Col Cuore in Gola* is filmed at Alexandra Palace not because we have seen what can be seen from there, but because we have seen and identified the location of the viewpoint in other shots. Moreover, by showing London from Alexandra Palace, the film is showing something of Alexandra Palace, not of London. The view from the building is part of the building – something Antonioni demonstrated in the credit sequence of *La Notte*, combining the Pirelli Building and the view from it of Milan in one striking and justly famous shot.

The place from which a view is taken can be fabricated for a film, as in the shot in *Mary Poppins* charting Mary's descent towards London on a cloud, or in more modest helicopter or crane shots, but otherwise, in the London films sampled in this essay, panoramic views tend to come with evidence that situates the viewing position. In 1960s London cinema, the best high-placed view is from a high 1960s building. These are more frequently shot from below, a motif pointing to the 'little man, big city' theme in, for example, *The Young Ones* (Castrol House, now Marathon House), *Darling* (Sudbury House in Paternoster Square), *The Intelligence Men* (the Vickers Tower, now Millbank Tower), *Smashing Time* (Britannic House, now CityPoint) and *The Bliss of Mrs Blossom* (Centre Point). Good high views over London are to be had from Esso House in *Victim*, from 33 Cavendish Square in *The Young Ones*, from the Economist Tower (*I'll Never Forget What's 'Isname*), the GPO Tower (*Bedazzled*), and Alembic House, now Peninsular Heights (*The Italian Job*).

As a dedicated vantage point for visitors to the city, the high hotel room is a good place from which to position the viewer topographically. The Dorchester (built in 1938) serves such a purpose in *Espresso Bongo*, *Alfie* and *Morgan*, but the spectacular views are to be had from the Hilton, further down Park Lane. This viewing point is identified in *One + One* less by what is shown of London than by the disparaging graffiti painted on the hotel-room windows. A more detailed example is the mise-en-scène situating Alberto Sordi in *Fumo di Londra*. On his arrival in London, the voyager from Italy takes a taxi to 'The Queen's Hotel, 49 Park Lane'. When he arrives, the small hotel he had known twenty years before has gone, replaced by speculators with the twenty-nine-storey Hilton. From his high room, he has panoramic views over London, but is told he must not use binoculars or a photographic apparatus. The reason, as an intrusive zoom-in shows, is the proximity to Buckingham Palace, residence of the Queen, whose privacy must be respected. He asks why such a skyscraper was allowed to be built, to which the answer is that the land thus developed belongs to the Queen. She is the all-powerful speculator, with power over the image of London and over who is allowed to look upon that image. 'Marvellous country,' comments Sordi, laughing: '*Che mondo meraviglioso*, my London town.'

Sordi, Tinto Brass and Antonioni are three Italians in London circa sixty-six, discovering there a 'mondo meraviglioso'. But *Fumo di Londra* is the tourist film that *Blow-Up* is not. Antonioni is in St James Street to show the modern architecture (and because his production office for *Blow-Up* was located there); Sordi, however, is there to buy his bowler hat at Lock & Co., as he begins to kit himself out as the perfect English gentleman (he goes to Lobb for his shoes, Swaine Adeney Brigg for his umbrella, Dunhill for his pipe, Fortnum's for his buttonhole, and Piccadilly Circus for his copy of *The Times*). Where Antonioni shows a solitary guardsman outside St James's Palace, Sordi joins in the Queen's Birthday Parade, marching alongside a whole battalion of Irish Guards. Where Antonioni erects a solitary white neon sign to cast a deathly glow over Maryon Park, Sordi is dazzled by the multi-coloured neon lights of Piccadilly, a cliché of 1960s London cinema (see *Gorgo, Smashing Time, Tonite Let's All Make Love in London, Cool It Carol!* and many others). *Fumo di Londra* refreshes the cliché with a gag: Sordi is looking for a typical English restaurant, and all he sees is a succession of neon signs for a dozen or so Italian restaurants (*La Dolce Vita, La Laguna, Hostaria Capri, Il Gattopardo*, etc.: home from home for the Italian tourist). And Sordi's film, unlike Antonioni's, offers panoramic views over London, from his room at the Hilton and from other, yet to be identified vantage points. On identifying them, the real tourist's travel practice will have been turned by the ciné-tourist into filmic mapping.

The *Blow-Up*

Perhaps because he never looks upon it from above, Antonioni cannot say of the city he films: '*Che mondo meraviglioso*, my London town'. Nevertheless, when art-house ciné-tourism becomes the fully fledged industry that is in prospect, guides to 'Antonioni's London' will take us by the coach-load to points west, southwest, west-central, east-central and southeast of this screen city. To the *Blow-Up* sites already identified in this essay will be added *The Passenger*'s London locations (the house in Lansdowne Crescent, W11; the Brunswick Centre, WC1; the shop where Jack Nicholson buys his moustache –

Figure 9.5: Maryon Park, London SE7 (c.1966). Photograph by Carlo di Palma.

once it has been identified), and the settings of the London section of his 1952 film *I Vinti* (Fleet Street, Piccadilly Circus, Sutton High Street, and others still unmapped). The tour will end in Woolwich, where specially drawn-up maps of Maryon Park will trace the paths and locate the landmarks: those still there, such as the gate by which Thomas enters the park, the steps on which the woman accosts him, the tennis court where he watches the mimes, the lawn from which he disappears; and those now gone, like the white buildings that overlook the park, the indecipherable neon sign, the tree under which lay the corpse, the fence behind which the gunman stood.

It will hardly matter that parts of Antonioni's London are hard to recognize now (London Wall, Victoria Street, Gordon Road), that some have entirely gone (most of Tamar Street), and that others were never there (the West End branch of the Ricky Tick Club). Disappearances in the film (the woman on Regent Street, the corpse in the park, the photographs in Thomas's studio, Thomas in the closing shot) prepare the viewer for what's missing in the real. And to compensate, our tracing of paths and identification of places find their analogue in Thomas's investigations of the image. It is tempting to allegorize the film's central sequence, the '*blow up*' moment. An analogy is drawn in the film between the deciphering of Thomas's blown-up photographs and Ian Stephenson's paintings ('They don't mean anything when I do them, just a mess ... then it sorts itself out, it adds up'), and readers of *Blow-Up* have drawn analogies between the arrangement of the photographs and the process of filmmaking (he 'builds a plot by sequencing pictures, turning photography into cinema').[27] But to the reader within this essay, at least, the plotting done by Thomas is not narratorial but cartographic: what the blown-up photographs add up to is a map.[28] Provided with a map reference that he plots directly onto the real, Thomas becomes an effective allegory of the map-reading ciné-tourist. He takes still-images from a moving reality (like grabbing frames from a DVD), enlarges them (zooms in), reads the seemingly illegible detail (for Thomas, the pointed gun; for us, the name on a shop front in Aldersgate Street), traces a path (that of the bullet; of the Rolls Royce turning out of Aldersgate Street onto a dual carriageway), and identifies a place (where the body is: under the tree; where that dual carriageway is, and the five office blocks that frame it: London Wall). Like the ciné-tourist, Thomas can find that the thing found (the corpse, the office blocks) has gone, or else, like the Ricky Tick Club, was never there.

A photograph is not a map. Blow up a photograph and you discover the grain of reality (as well as gunmen and corpses). Blow up a map and you do not get greater legibility, you just get larger words, thicker lines and wider empty spaces between them. And yet these spaces make of the blown-up map a better figure for the kind of film study offered in this book. These wide empty spaces are perfect for filling with the annotations and commentaries that form this map-reading ciné-tourist's contribution to the serious study of the screen city.

Appendix: London in *Blow-Up*

- The Economist Buildings and Plaza, 25 St James's Street, SW1. Built 1962–64 by Alison and Peter Smithson.
- Camberwell Reception Centre, Gordon Road, SE15. Built as a workhouse in 1878 by Berriman & Sons Ltd. Now converted to flats.
- Consort Road, railway bridge, and Copeland Road, SE15. View of number 149, the South Eastern Metal Co.
- St James's Palace, SW1.
- Tooley Street, SE1. View of number 28, Garrad & Sons, marine salvage.
- 77 Pottery Lane, W11. Exterior of Thomas's studio (renumbered 39).
- 39 Princes Place, W11. Interior of Thomas's studio (in reality, John Cowan's studio).
- 'Temple Bar Memorial', Fleet Street, EC4. John Cowan photograph of Jill Kennington, 1962, in Thomas's studio.
- 117–61 and 140–66 Stockwell Road, SW9, Pride & Clarke Ltd, motor car and cycle dealers (the red buildings).
- 754 Woolwich Road, SE7, dining rooms (the blue building). Now demolished.
- 33 Tamar Street, SE7, grocer's shop (dressed as an antiques shop). Now demolished.
- The Morris Walk Estate, Clevely Close, SE7 (under construction).
- Maryon Park, SE7.
- Hyde Park, W2. View of the Royal Lancaster Hotel (under construction), completed 1967.
- Kensington Church Street, W8. View of number 36, Bacchus Wine Co.
- Aldersgate Street, EC1. View of number 184/5, John Foster & Co, furnishing fabrics.
- London Wall, EC1. Views of Lee House (Bernard Gold & Partners, 1961–63), St Alphage House (Maurice Sanders Associates, 1960–62), Moor House (Lewis Solomon & Kaye, 1961), Royex House (Seifert & Partners, 1961–63), 40 Basinghall Street (Sir John Burnet, Tait & Partners, 1962–64).

- Basinghall Avenue, EC1. View of Girdler's Hall (Waterhouse & Ripley, 1960–61).
- Basinghall Street, EC1. View of Gillett House (Ralph Tubbs, 1963–65).
- 8–9 Blacklands Terrace, SW3, the Andreas Restaurant, now El Blason.
- 'Aldgate, E1', a 1965 Don McCullin photograph of a down-and-out man, in Thomas's portfolio.
- Victoria Street, SW1. Views of: number 52, The Albert Pub; numbers 42–50, Windsor House, built as a hotel in 1881–83 by F.T. Pilkington, now demolished; Mobil House (building site), Westminster City Hall and Kingsgate House, all by Sir John Burnet, Tait & Partners (1960–66).
- 151 Regent Street, W1, the Permutit Company Ltd.
- New Burlington Mews, W1.
- 309 Oxford Street, W1. Dressed as exit to the Ricky Tick Club.
- Cheyne Walk, SW3. (A National Trust property let to Christopher Gibbs). View of the Thames (Turner's Reach).

Acknowledgements

My thanks for help with the research and for writing of this essay go to: Karen Alexander, Ruth Austin, Stephen Barber, Tim Hale, Christophe Lack, Jann Matlock, Frederick Raphael, Rita Tushingham, John Tunstill and Brian Wall.

Notes

1. Also visible on the shelves of a pornographic bookshop in Godard's London film *One + One* (1969), and in the hands of the heroine of *Cool It Carol!* (1970), as she crosses Sloane Square.
2. All films referred to are listed at the end of this essay. The general period intertext is vast, so the films I have looked at in more detail tend to have more direct connections with *Blow-Up*, though these connections can be quite diverse, and sometimes trivial: *Morgan* shares an actress with *Blow-Up* (cast and crew interrupted shooting in Woolwich to toast Vanessa Redgrave's Cannes Film Festival award for *Morgan*); *I'll Never Forget What's 'Isname* shares a location (the Economist Buildings in St James's Street); *The Knack* shares a narrative enigma ('did something happen in the park?'); *Alfie* shares the possibility that the male lead could have been the same iconic star, Terence Stamp (he turned down *Alfie* and was eventually turned down for *Blow-Up*); *Col Cuore in Gola* refers explicitly to Antonioni, showing a cinema where *Blow-Up* is playing and mentioning the director by name in the voiceover. Several films share an interest in the fashion photographer as type (*Darling*, *Smashing Time*, *Col Cuore in Gola*, *Wonderwall*) and others offer contrasts with other types of photography (*Alfie*'s job taking snapshots of tourists, or Joy's posing in underwear for local 'enthusiasts' in *Poor Cow*).
3. See Kevin Lynch, *The Image of the City*, Cambridge, MA, 1960.
4. See, for example: Tom Clark Conley, 'Du cinéma à la carte', *Cinémas*, vol. 10, no. 2–3 (2000); Katherine Shonfield, *Walls Have Feelings: Architecture Film and the City*, London, 2000; Mitchell Schwarzer, *Zoomscape: Architecture in Motion and Media*, New York, 2004; Guiliana Bruno, *Atlas of Emotion: Journeys in Art, Architecture and Film*, London, 2002; Peter Wollen, 'Architecture and

Film', in *Paris Hollywood: Writings on Film*, London, 2002. Wollen applies Lynch's terms for mapping perception of the city to the reading of film narrative, and Bruno also takes Lynch's model as a point of departure.

5. A good example of ciné-touristic research contributing to the academic study of film is Ali Catterall and Simon Well's *Your Face Here: British Cult Movies Since the Sixties* (London, 2001), with a chapter on *Blow-Up*, of course. Elaine Shepherd's BBC documentary *The 'Real' Blow Up* (2002) revisits the sites of the film as well as the personae of the period. See also John and Brian Tunstill's 'Reel Streets' site, dedicated to identifying locations in British feature films, (http://www.reelstreets.com/films.htm).

6. In her reminiscences of the period, Janet Street-Porter, an extra in *Blow-Up* and *Col Cuore in Gola*, describes London as invaded by Italian directors (*Baggage: My Childhood*, London, 2004).

7. From beyond Hollywood came quirkier visions of London, all the more strongly adapted to generic demands: see, for example, Fred Marshall (*Popdown*), Joe Massot (*Wonderwall*), Alfred Vohrer (*The Hunchback of Soho*), Alberto Sordi (*Fumo di Londra*), Georges Robin (*Mini Weekend*), Peter Medak (*Negatives*), and Enzo Castellari (*Cold Eyes of Fear*).

8. In 1967, Jean-Pierre Mocky came to London to make *Les carrosses de la mort* with Marlon Brando, but the producer died in a car crash and the project fell through.

9. See also the exchange at the end of *Cool It Carol!*, a downbeat rewrite of *Smashing Time*: 'Are you happy? Is this what you always wanted?' 'No.' 'Let's go home.'

10. From Frederic Raphael's *Darling* (London, 1965, 59), a novelization of his script for John Schlesinger's film.

11. Shonfield, *Walls Have Feelings*, 84.

12. An earlier sequence at the same locale, but without Alfie, had not shown the Estate, preferring to set the church against the Lots Road and Fulham Power Stations, dated 1905 and 1902 respectively.

13. This contrasts with an earlier shop window in Earl's Court Road (analysed in detail by Shonfield), through which he approaches a sexual partner, the dry-cleaning girl who will also press his suits (effectively combining donjuanism and dandyism).

14. Or almost exactly. The film's costume designer Jocelyn Rickards has described the care with which these clothes were chosen (the white jeans modelled on those of the painter John Stephenson, apparently), and the panic that ensued when the jacket was stolen from the set and had to be replaced with an exact copy.

15. The most recent re-teller of these myths is David Hemmings himself, in his posthumously published autobiography *Blow-Up and Other Exaggerations*: 'A massive Alitalia sign in the Elephant and Castle was painted black and whole streets in Brixton were sprayed red. When he told Di Palma, "I want every tree in the park painted green," Carlo understood. But the British set designer, Michael Balfour, gazed at him with puzzled horror. "They are green." "The trunks are brown. I want them green, too," the Maestro ordered lightly ... "to match this fence. And I want all the paths sprayed black"' (London, 2004, 23–24). This is all very well, but there are no shots in the Elephant and Castle used in the film, the street in Brixton was already red, the set designer was actually Assheton Gorton, the tree trunks in the film are all still brown and none of the paths are black. The grass may have been

painted green, but, as Jocelyn Rickards points out in her less exaggerated reminiscences, this was because the sun had scorched it yellow.

16. Says the internet *Pubs.com* guide, adding: 'Far from being intimidated by the skyscrapers that surround it, The Albert stands proud against its bland neighbours.'

17. The 'not our lads' suggests a voice from the general locality, Britain, but if (as the period would suggest) the war being protested is Vietnam, in which 'our lads' weren't fighting, this rather resembles the placard photographed in London circa 1967 reading 'Fuck the draft', reproduced in Shawn Levy's book on London in the 1960s and commented thus: 'If only Britain had a draft ...: A curiously ill-inspired Whitehall protest march' (Shawn Levy, *Ready Steady Go: Swinging London and the Invention of Cool*, London, 2002, 296–97). The demonstration in *Col Cuore in Gola* identifies CND branches from Welwyn, Hampstead and Cambridge.

18. Nikolaus Pevsner, *The Buildings of England: London*, vol. 1, Harmondsworth, 1973, 662.

19. A further explanation for the westerly orientation of these films, at least for those with a studio-shot element, is proximity to major film studios situated in the counties west of London: Shepperton (*Darling, Georgy Girl, The L-Shaped Room, Performance, The Pumpkin Eater, The Servant*), Twickenham (*Alfie, A Hard Day's Night, Help!, Poor Cow, Repulsion, Wonderwall*) and Pinewood (*Victim, The Ipcress File, Billion Dollar Brain*).

20. Oddly, this sign of topographical congruity is also one of chronological incongruity: other posters in the club are contemporary with the shooting and narrative time of *Blow-Up* (e.g., Saturday 2 April, a John Mayall concert), but the December date sets the scene eight months ahead (and on an impossible date: 20 December 1966 was a Tuesday).

21. Their bible is Piet Schreuders, Mark Lewisohn and Adam Smith, *The Beatles' London: the Ultimate Guide to Over 400 Beatle Sites In and Around London*, London, 1994.

22. Curiously, Brass's next London film, *Nerosubianco*, also uses Holborn Station, and shows there the topological map of the Piccadilly Line pointing north, towards Wood Green, Southgate and Cockfosters. Wood Green is the stop for Alexandra Palace.

23. *Four Elements II* (1965). The piece was placed on display by the Economist Buildings, and Antonioni obtained permission from the artist to show it in this opening sequence.

24. Chiefly, maps in different works by Peter Greenaway (Bruno, *Atlas of Emotion*, 298, 305), the *'carte de tendre'* from Louis Malle's *Les Amants* (ibid., 241), and the map-shot from *The Red Desert*, already mentioned.

25. As in, for example, the panorama over London in *Till Death Us Do Part* (1969).

26. A good exception is the opening sequence of *The Young Ones*, offering panoramic views in various directions across London, with identifiable high landmarks such as Big Ben, Senate House and the Upstream Building. Lines drawn on a map converge at a feasible location for the viewpoint in Cavendish Square.

27. Bruno, *Atlas of Emotion*, 302.

28. The Ian Stephenson paintings seen in *Blow-Up* are map-like, as Nicky Charlish, commenting on the 2004 'Art and the Sixties' exhibition at Tate Britain, says of Stephenson's *Parachrome*, from 1964: 'It looks as if an aerial map of a great city has been showered with tiny pinpricks of colour.'

London Films Consulted

Alfie (Lewis Gilbert, 1966)
The Battle of Britain (Guy Hamilton, 1969)
Bedazzled (Stanley Donen, 1967)
The Bliss of Mrs Blossom (Joseph McGrath, 1968)
Blow-Up (Michelangelo Antonioni, 1966)
British Sounds (Jean-Luc Godard, 1970)
Casino Royale (Val Guest/Ken Hughes/John Huston/Joseph McGrath/Robert
    Parrish, 1967)
Col Cuore in Gola [Dead Stop] (Tinto Brass, 1967)
Cool It Carol! (Peter Walker, 1970)
Darling (John Schlesinger, 1965)
The Day the Earth Caught Fire (Val Guest, 1961)
Dorian Gray [Il dio chiamato Dorian] (Massimo Dallamano, 1970)
Fahrenheit 451 (François Truffaut, 1966)
Fumo di Londra [Smoke Over London] (Alberto Sordi, 1966)
A Hard Day's Night (Richard Lester, 1964)
Help! (Richard Lester, 1965)
The Hunchback of Soho [Der Bucklige von Soho] (Alfred Vohrer, 1966)
I'll Never Forget What's 'Isname (Michael Winner, 1967)
The Intelligence Men (Robert Asher, 1965)
It Happened Here (Kevin Brownlow/Andrew Mollo, 1966)
Kaleidoscope (Jack Smight, 1966)
The Knack... And How To Get It (Richard Lester, 1965)
The L-Shaped Room (Bryan Forbes, 1962)
The Magic Christian (Joseph McGrath, 1969)
Mary Poppins (Robert Stevenson, 1964)
Modesty Blaise (Joseph Losey, 1966)
Morgan: A Suitable Case For Treatment (Karel Reisz, 1966)
My Fair Lady (George Cukor, 1964)
Nerosubianco (Tinto Brass, 1969)
On Her Majesty's Secret Service (Peter R. Hunt, 1969)
One + One (Jean-Luc Godard, 1969)
The Passenger [Professione: reporter] (Michelangelo Antonioni, 1975)
Poor Cow (Ken Loach, 1967)
Repulsion (Roman Polanski, 1965)
Smashing Time (Desmond Davis, 1967)
The Sorcerers (Michael Reeves, 1967)
Thirty Is A Dangerous Age, Cynthia (Joseph McGrath, 1967)
Till Death Us Do Part (Norman Cohen, 1969)
Tonite Let's All Make Love in London (Peter Whitehead, 1967)
To Sir With Love (James Clavell, 1967)
Twinky [aka London Affair] (Richard Donner, 1969)
Victim (Basil Dearden, 1961)
I Vinti (Michelangelo Antonioni, 1952)
What Have They Done to Solange? [Cosa avete fatto a Solange?] (Massimo
    Dallamano, 1972)
Wonderwall (Joe Massot, 1968)
The Young Ones (Sidney J. Furie, 1961)

CHAPTER 10

REPRESENTATIONS OF DYSTOPIA AND THE FILM CITY OF LONDON

Sara de Freitas

Introduction: Anxiety and Change

Perhaps the most striking feature of London's cinematic profile, gauged over a century of film, is just how seldom the city has been shown in a positive light. In fact, as this essay will explore, by far the majority of films – which feature the city in any notable way – tend to show London, not merely in a poor light, but as the archetype of the modern civic dystopia. The dystopia, a Victorian concept, inverted the notional and idealized city or state articulated in works such as Plato's *Republic* and Thomas More's *Utopia* so that the ideal constituents of the perfect society are articulated through their diametric opposites. Thus, in the Victorian model, the Classical and Renaissance visions of 'heaven on earth' are replaced with the worst imaginable landscape of inequality, poverty, crime, chaos and absolute social determinism. The dystopia is quite literally a vision of hell on earth, and while this might seem an unfortunate identity for a city to have gained, it is not hard to fathom how London came to be stereotyped in this way, or indeed why the cinematic tendency for dystopic portrayals of the city still persists today.

As one might expect of a city which displays two pagan dragons supporting the Christian cross on its heraldic logo, popular perceptions of the city of London have traditionally involved an element of mythology or fantasy alongside the historical. Within the British Isles, this fantasy element usually involves, at the very least, an exaggeration of the bloodiness of London's history, so that Roman Britain is seen through the lens of the Boudiccan revolt, the Middle Ages are viewed only through tyrannical Norman monarchs and plague, and the calamities of the Restoration, together with the destruction of the Blitz, are all remembered, whereas such events as the founding of the royal societies, or the Abolition movement, are by and large ignored. Almost by convention, native writers and filmmakers have generally, and for very obvious reasons, preferred to focus upon the most dramatic and catastrophic moments in the city's history. That London itself has probably enjoyed as much peace and prosperity as any European city over the last two millennia is neither here nor there. As far as the domestic audience is concerned, London is the 'big smoke', the 'heart of darkness', and the bloody capital of a violent realm.

However, this domestic point of view has also been augmented over the last century or so by a more global perception of the city – conveyed through a host of well-known films – which incorporates a range of supernatural and often apocalyptic elements. The fact that London, at the turn of the twenty-first century, should be perceived by filmmakers and audiences alike as such a natural backdrop for Egyptian mummies, Transylvanian vampires, werewolves, dragons, plagues, and even as the residence of the Antichrist, can be traced to a representational heritage which has increasingly portrayed London as a dystopic nexus, where modern anxieties, historical events and ancient superstitions all converge.

Clues as to why London has become so closely identified with so many supernatural icons can of course be gleaned from the city's own heraldic self-image and the wider British opinion of the city, but perhaps the most important element in the creation of the dystopic cinematic identity of the city should be sought in its unique position as the world's first truly modern industrial capital. At the time of the invention of film, London was enjoying the greatest growth in population and prosperity in its history, and the influx of workers from the countryside, foreign traders, refugees and intellectuals into the city undoubtedly resulted in a highly beneficial exchange of ideas and manners. Inevitably, however, it also resulted from time to time in confrontation, when those from different cultural backgrounds with incompatible ideas found themselves in opposition. These differences grew with the city and were as likely to centre on financial competition, class or religion as they were on the different nationalities that made up the city's population. In this kaleidoscopic environment, any unifying cultural narrative, or indeed any book, play or film which hoped to make money had to appeal to what was common to all of those culturally diverse groups without transgressing into the divisive areas of politics or religion. And, in the end, what was common to all of these people from so many different backgrounds, packed together on a scale previously unknown, was not origin, religion, custom or language; what the people of London had in common, and what the populations of all modern industrial cities still have in common, are their anxieties and fears. In this sense, London's cinematic profile mediates that of any city undergoing the change from a rural hub to a truly modern national capital, where the fear of isolation, crime, poverty, disease, conflagration and pollution necessitates a rapid and often traumatic period of adaptation for the incoming population. Both of these themes – anxiety and change – are central components of London's cinematic profile, and can be detected in all of the films discussed in this essay. However, what is perhaps more interesting is the way in which these themes have been interwoven with English gothic horror, Middle Eastern apocalyptic mysticism, Eastern European superstition, technophobia, medieval folklore and Victorian social commentary, to form the familiar dystopic cityscape that cinema audiences have expected and enjoyed throughout a century or more of film.

Social Commentary and the Criminal Gang

Charles Dickens's vision of London, which is among the most influential in print or on film, has provided historians and filmmakers alike with a wealth of social commentary that was intended to show the dehumanizing consequences of urban chaos. The dystopic themes of poverty, crime and inequality that Dickens explores in much of his work represent careful studies of Victorian society and have perhaps become most associated with London through two narratives in particular, *A Christmas Carol* (1843) and *The Adventures of Oliver Twist* (1837–39). The first of these is an overtly supernatural narrative, which combines the otherworldliness of the old pagan mid-winter festival with a redemptive Christian allegory. The popular appeal of the narrative ensured that it would make the transition to film more frequently than any other of Dickens's works, and it is notable that this was a rare departure from his tendency for realism. Moreover, the inclusion of a populist supernatural element has ensured that this narrative has survived the transition from book to film by and large unchanged.

The Adventures of Oliver Twist, on the other hand, is an altogether less uplifting narrative which underwent a notable transformation between the monochrome misery of David Lean's film *Oliver Twist* of 1948 and the vibrant textures of Carol Reed's 1968 colour musical-film *Oliver!*, scored by Lionel Bart. The 'rags to riches' narrative of young Oliver starts in a workhouse, and follows his journey to London where, through destitution, he joins a gang of pickpockets led by Fagin. The darkness and moral dilemmas of the narrative, however, reside in the psychopathic and criminal character of Bill Sykes and his abuse of his girlfriend Nancy, who acts as the moral guardian of Oliver's welfare; the apotheosis of the narrative comes with the murder of Nancy, Bill Sykes's violent death and Oliver's return to his family home.

Few representations could have underlined the change in London's postwar fortunes so well as the transformation in the telling of this familiar narrative over twenty years, bringing London from rationing, hardship and the brink of annihilation in the Blitz to the prosperity and colour of the 'Swinging Sixties'; in Reed's musical, the Dickensian portrait of London is indeed subverted into something more akin to Disney's *Mary Poppins* (1964) than to the satanic landscape of the original narrative. Nonetheless, Oliver Reed's portrayal of Bill Sykes as the abusive and psychotic lover who kills Nancy remains starkly at the heart of the piece, which in the final analysis is still essentially a story about poverty, inequality, exploitation, prostitution, murder and child abuse.

A number of themes are played out within filmic explorations of the politics and customs of the criminal gang that are central to the Victorian conception of the dystopia, not only in terms of poverty or inequality as motivators, but also through the autocracy of the criminal hierarchy and the resultant chaos which inevitably results from the struggle for power by the ambitious 'lower ranks'.

Building on an urban tradition that can be traced back to Chaucer, filmmakers from the 1930s onwards have portrayed London's criminal fraternity according to conventions that would have been as familiar to Karl Marx as they would have been to Charles Dickens. In films such as *Get Carter* (1971), *The Long Good Friday* (1979), *Mona Lisa* (1986), *The Cook, The Thief, His Wife and Her Lover* (1989), *The Krays* (1990), *Gangster Number 1* (2000) and *Mr In-Between* (2003), a highly dystopic and sociopathic criminal culture is shown for what it is: chaotic, greedy, fascistic, brutal and self-destructive. The chaos and incompetence which are endemic to these kinds of feudal criminal groups have equally been played as dark comedy in *The Ladykillers* (1955), *The Italian Job* (1967), *Lock, Stock and Two Smoking Barrels* (1998) and *Snatch* (2000). Whether the protagonists from these films are from London, or are just passing through, as in *Trainspotting* (1996), the characteristic common to all criminal fraternities that try their luck in London is their flippant and fatalistic acceptance of the bleak social determinism governing their destiny. As with the outlaws of the Middle Ages who elected to poach rather than starve, London's criminals are pre-destined by adversity to commit their crimes, and having committed them, they enter another world, outside of society. In this sense, the term 'underworld' is loaded with metaphorical resonance, and in the genre of criminal fantasy, the moral pay-off for any sense of escapism is always clearly signposted. Moreover, the individual's attempts to prosper and survive in these close-knit and violent alternative societies is often used to highlight the brutish and Faustian nature of gangland relationships; the portrayal of these dysfunctional groups constitutes an effective cinematic shorthand for the exploration of the innate sociopathy that characterizes any rigid hierarchical society or dictatorship.

Liminal States

The logical extension of the criminal gang – the dictatorship or totalitarian state – has no real contemporary native example in Britain during the era of film, but in a century dominated by totalitarianism it was not surprising that writers such as H.G. Wells and George Orwell would try to conceive what a domestic version would have looked like. Wells adapted his own novel *The Shape of Things to Come* (1933) for the film *Things to Come* (1936), in which a prescient and dystopic vision of war and totalitarianism is finally countered with a resolution in which technological and scientific planning are, rather unusually for the sci-fi genre, posited with positive advance. However, the somewhat forced optimism of this film seems at odds with Wells's earlier and more celebrated novels, *The War of the Worlds* (1898) and *The Time Machine* (1895, adapted for film in 1960).

In the film version of *The Time Machine*, the main character's journey from 1890s London to a future thousands of years hence functions as an exploration of the individual's struggle to adapt to a rapidly changing social order. Social commentators have described the process of changing from one state to another in terms of three transitional phases: separation, where the individual is removed from the existing social situation; marginality or liminality, where the individual is regarded in contrast to the social situation; and aggregation, where the individual is replaced back into the social situation, having undergone transformation. Many anthropologists consider liminality the most dangerous of these phases, as the person is neither one thing nor another, and the inherent danger is obviously that the individual may be permanently trapped in this in-between state. This theme, of change or metamorphosis – not just in the landscape or society, but also in the individual – crops up time and again in London's cinematic portfolio, and always serves to emphasize the rapid adjustment and evolution that the city forces upon its citizens.

In *The Time Machine*, the traveller's innate disenchantment with his own society at the outset of the narrative, and his subsequent disowning of it, when he witnesses the persistent ravages of war over the future course of London's history, reaches crisis point as he discovers the near-bovine future of human society in the shape of the cooperative and unquestioning Eloi. The further discovery of the Morlocks, a subterranean society descended from the city dwellers of the past, provides the final shock for the time traveller as he realizes that the descendants of his society are breeding the passive Eloi for food. The transformation of the environment is highly significant in this narrative, and is emphasized in the contrast between the cavernous industrial underworld of the Morlocks and the garden paradise of the Eloi. The fact that one part of humanity has maintained machinery and a sense of cooperative society is beside the point. In Wells's view, the Morlocks' descent into cannibalism and their exploitation of the Eloi symbolize a dreadful but logical outcome of urban sociopathy. Although the narrative culminates in an epiphany of existential purpose and belonging, Wells's outlook was far from sanguine. The monstrousness of the Morlocks and the docility of the Eloi are a consequence of the ebb and flow of civilization, which, over time, has polarized between utopic and dystopic societies; an uncharacteristically pessimistic Wells could only conclude that the psychopathic and the monstrous would prevail over time.

Metamorphosis and the Monster

The portrayal of the urban monster is one of the most familiar themes to have been woven into London's folklore, and the fear of the serial killer in particular has been the subject of numerous films which mingle fact with fiction. However, even the earliest films dealing with this subject connected with the traditions of Georgian and Victorian melodrama, in which the dramatic portrayal of characters such as Spring Heeled Jack, Sweeney Todd, and the London Monster of the 1780s, all came to define popular preconceptions of what an urban psychopath was like.

A revealing example of this occurred between 1888 and 1891, when London's theatre-goers were being entertained and terrorized in equal measure by the Lyceum Theatre's production of R.L. Stevenson's *The Strange Case of Dr Jekyll and Mr Hyde* (1886); the Whitechapel murders of Jack the Ripper were taking place simultaneously with the three-year run of the show. Only four of the eighteen murders which occurred during that time are now firmly attributed to Jack the Ripper, but the almost immediate melding of folklore and sensationalist reportage, which drew consciously or subconsciously from the imagery of the celebrated West End show, profoundly influenced the way in which those crimes and their perpetrator have been remembered, right up to the present day. On 8 September 1888, the *East London Advertiser* noted that the murderer went out at night 'like another Hyde to prey on the defenceless unfortunate class'. While the blending of a fictional monster such as Hyde with a real-life murderer had many precedents in Georgian and Victorian melodrama, particularly when real-life perpetrators proved in any sense elusive, the iconic melding of Jack the Ripper and Mr Hyde has had a powerful effect on the popular perceptions and portrayals of London ever since, particularly among international audiences.

The cinematic merging of fact and folklore that helped to promulgate the amalgamation of the characters of Mr Hyde and Jack the Ripper in the popular consciousness began with *Pandora's Box* (1929), and continued with *The Threepenny Opera* (1931), *Dr Jekyll and Mr Hyde* (two versions: 1932 and 1942), *The Lodger* (1944, remade as

The Man in the Attic, 1954), *Jack the Ripper* (1958) and *Lulu* (1962). In the film *A Study in Terror* (1965), the waters are muddied further when the fictional Sherlock Holmes and his companion Dr Watson are brought in to solve the murders, and an even more fantastical version of the story is presented in the Hammer Films production, *Dr Jekyll and* – the now feminized – *Sister Hyde* (1971). *Murder by Decree* (1979) again brought in Sherlock Holmes (Christopher Plummer) and Dr Watson (James Mason). In another outlandish remake, *Time after Time* (1979), Jack the Ripper (David Warner) steals H.G. Wells's (Malcolm MacDowell) time machine and travels to twentieth-century New York, pursued by Wells himself. The most recent film adaptation of the story, *From Hell* (2002), follows the same populist tradition; Jack the Ripper appears more than ever an agent of the supernatural. The title of the film, taken from a letter that was believed at the time to have been written by Jack the Ripper, encapsulates London's cinematic profile very succinctly, and the metaphor is not limited to this film alone.

Less than ten years after Jack the Ripper's Whitechapel murders, the profile of the violent and overtly sexual psychopath was further illuminated, in 1897, by Bram Stoker's novel *Dracula*; in that novel, which would result in as many cinematic remakes as the narrative of Jack the Ripper, the first of many rural monsters is given a distinctively urban makeover. One hundred years on, seen through recent films, it has become harder than ever to distinguish between these three characters – these monsters – who together not only circumscribe the serial killer genre, but also provide an unholy triumvirate around which Hollywood studios such as Universal and Hammer would centre an entire pantheon of Gothic Horror.

However, in nearly all of these films, as in Georgian and Victorian dramas, as well as in contemporary serial killer genres, the idea of the monster is explored through a set of popular conventions that subvert or at least distract from an obvious and painful truth. Even respected commentators can be seduced by these conventions; Michel Foucault declared in a 1975 lecture that Jack the Ripper was, in fact, Prince Albert Edward, heir to the British throne – demonstrating that he had accepted the unfounded myth that the killer was an urbane, mannered and charming individual, whose aura of power and sophistication hypnotized his victims into powerless submission. While the Jekyll and Hyde scenario of the top-hatted, drug-crazed 'toff' with the mad staring eyes has always been very popular – call him Jack the Ripper, Mr Hyde, Count Dracula, or even Hannibal Lecter – the fact is that the vast majority of murderers and serial killers turn out to be ordinary figures who, without effective forensic detection, would probably never be suspected. As the films discussed in this essay demonstrate, however, this is not a fact that most people really want to think about (let alone pay to think about in the cinema), and writers and filmmakers have been happy to enshrine the far more palatable notion that serial killers are not 'one of us', that they are barely human, and that if someone does evil, they will tend to look evil.

The monster, the antithesis of the human, is synonymous with everything that can be defined as other, and opposed to the interests of society; throughout human history, murders – and particularly murders that involved sexual violation – have been explained away in terms of monstrosity or bestiality. Thus, the rites and rituals of the monster are most often articulated through the ancient mythologies of anthropomorphic beasts and virginal sacrifice. In this sense, the metamorphosis of Dr Jekyll into Mr Hyde is no different from the change that overtakes the werewolf or the vampire of rural folklore. In the same way, the ancient sacrifice of youth and innocence to a monster such as the Minotaur is only slightly updated in the portrayal of the somewhat less innocent young men and women who fall victim to the modern serial killer. These rural myths and ancient superstitions have little directly to do with London, but they provided a treasure trove of popular iconic figures with which to portray the unseen but imagined killer who lurks in the city's shadows and alleys.

Apocalyptic Fantasy, Mythology and Mimesis

Within this same context of superstition and mythology, it is also instructive to consider how folklore and religion are interwoven into London's cinematic profile. The interconnection of native folk history with more exotic imported religions, superstitions and myths has many precedents. Most notably, the dissemination of Christianity throughout Western Europe was facilitated, if not achieved entirely, through a set of adjunctive embellishments which meshed traditional Celtic/pagan imagery and folklore with the more supernatural elements of Christianity. This kind of folk history, with its characteristic overlaying of characters, is undoubtedly Homeric and Bardic, and is typical of the oral tradition and of other forms of dissemination that are regulated by the popular imagination. The Grail cycle in particular, and the Arthurian Romances in general, serve to this day as a wholly contradictory and yet pragmatic, enduring remnant of an almost subliminal attempt to codify a common cultural origin, which could unite the Western, Christian world.

This largely invented Christian folklore served as a unifying force not because it dealt with the minutiae of theology or with the dominant issues of faith, but because these issues were under heated contention throughout the early history of the Christian world. What the Grail cycle succeeded in doing was to unify its audience through the *peripheries* of their beliefs. Playing on both rational and irrational fears, these stories used overtly pagan imagery to fuel the superstition that natural and supernatural disasters are wrought by human misdeed. It was of no consequence that the supernatural element to these narratives was entirely inappropriate and anachronistic, as far as the portrayal of Christianity was concerned. The mythical cycles, concocted from apocryphal sources, Celtic tradition, and Roman and Jewish history, and incorporating some of the most universal elements of human narrative, had a huge impact upon the way in which the British, in particular, came to perceive their own national identity. Retold over centuries, such narratives invented a pervasive perception that became a very real historical force; much of what is central to British culture today can be attributed to the establishment of common perceptions of the past, rather than to genuinely common origins. Just how influential this unifying narrative turned out to be can be seen in London's coat of arms, in which the two dragons and the red cross are 'lifted' directly from the grail legends.

Many filmmakers have also drawn from the same apocryphal sources, and in London's case, a specifically urban mythology has evolved, which conflates the day-to-day anxieties of the city dweller – poverty, disease, isolation, crime, vice, the collapse of social order, and a host of other primal fears – with a rich combination of apocalyptic mythology, pagan superstition and Christian millenarianism. This conflation has worked its way into the popular conscience through, for example, the portrayals of quasi-biblical Egyptian mummies, the apocalyptic themes of films like *The Omen* trilogy (1976, 1978, 1981) and *Reign of Fire* (2002), and more technophobic fantasies such as *28 Days Later* (2002).

Once again, it is the ancient superstition that natural and supernatural disasters are wrought by human misdeed which underpins urban mythology, just as it did in the Grail folklores. This determines the dystopic and millenarian scenario of *28 Days Later*, in which an outbreak of plague is caused by animal rights activists, who unwittingly free a group of apes, infected with a deadly rage-inducing virus, from a government laboratory. The plague hits London and soon infects the population, transforming all of those infected into psychopaths, driven to kill and to infect, until they are killed themselves, or else starve to death. The population is quickly decimated, and when the main character awakens from a coma, he finds that most of the inhabitants of London have already died. The powerful moral centre of the film lies in the sequence in which the main protagonist walks around a deserted London; his journey through the city, over Westminster Bridge to Piccadilly Circus, provides a symbol of the internal and external emptiness and desolation of a postapocalyptic landscape.

However, along with its 'medieval' themes of apocalypse, plague and social collapse, *28 Days Later* incorporates a more contemporary fear of technology and terrorism. The human misdeeds which lead to disaster are threefold. The first misdeed lies in the scientists' interference with nature, in creating the virus; the second is in the government's original commissioning of the work; the third is located in the misguided, irresponsible zealotry of the animal rights activists. The contemporary inspiration behind *28 Days Later* (released soon after the real-life outbreak in Britain of 'mad cow' disease) was not hard to determine, but it is notable that in its use of the wasteland, the female guide and the questing hero, the film's style and conventions are entirely consistent with the imagery of the Arthurian Romances.

Reign of Fire (2002) also holds to those conventions; but its inspiration is overt and literal. Drawing upon the same legend from which London takes its coat of arms, *Reign of Fire* reintroduces the dragon – that most pagan of symbols – to London's skyline. Workmen digging underground disturb a hidden dragons' lair beneath the city; the dragons escape and storm the planet. London is totally destroyed; with nothing left to eat, the largest of the dragons starts to turn on the others. In Robert de Boron's seminal twelfth-century version of this narrative, itself an adaptation of one that can be found in the *Mabinogion*, there were just two dragons – one white and one red, as shown on London's coat of arms – and their destructiveness was confined to themselves. In *Merlin and the Grail* (1190s) the fighting dragons quite literally undermine the stability of the kingdom, and so they are disinterred and forced to fight in the open, until the white dragon kills the red, before itself dying of its wounds. In de Boron's narrative, this struggle is symbolic of the turmoil and upheaval that is about to overtake the kingdom; that upheaval takes the form of the coming war in which the king will be deposed by the two brothers from whom he usurped the throne. Popular imagination, however, as evidenced on London's coat of arms, enshrines the notion that the dragons' fight actually symbolized the struggle between the pagan and Christian worlds, and the eventual victory of Christianity. As a result, the dragons have ended up supporting the cross on London's coat of arms, thereby revealing how representations of London have a way of drawing in and adapting stories to urban folk history.

In *Reign of Fire*, which also incorporates elements from the narratives of *Beowulf* and from the legends of St George and the Dragon, it is the questing hero who kills the only dragon capable of breeding, and thus puts an end to their brief, near-apocalyptic domination of the world. An old narrative is reworked to provide a human solution, to halt the disintegration of the city and of society; however, the apocalyptic themes, of social collapse, reordering and rebuilding contained in films such as *28 Days Later* and *Reign of Fire* still reveal the basic dystopic anxieties which writers and filmmakers have set out to probe and reconfigure. Released just months after the terrorist attacks on New York in 2001, both of these films were, in the tradition of H.G. Wells, very timely explorations of themes which have resurged to the forefront of contemporary urban anxieties, not just in London, but in every city on the planet.

Conclusion

While the dystopic themes of the films and genres discussed in this essay are relevant to any large modern city, it is London which is perhaps most closely associated with this type of dark fantasy. However, this representation was intricately built from amalgamated and interwoven folk histories, brought together as a consequence of industrialization and urbanization. These folk histories have propagated traditions and representations in many cities; in Berlin, New York, Paris or Tokyo, just as in London, there is a symbolic reification of the kinds of human struggle that takes place daily within the city's confines. In each case, a mimesis of ancient narratives, which articulated primal human fears, is adapted in order to form a bridging cultural narrative, between the ancient superstitions of the agrarian past and the urban anxieties of the postindustrial present.

Crucially, both the ancient and modern narratives rely upon an oscillation between different states: the actual and the imagined; sanity and madness; virtue and sin; poverty and wealth; man and beast; life and death; faith and desperation; heaven and hell. In the urban narrative, however, the city becomes the place of otherworldliness and timelessness. Whereas the site of transformation and metamorphosis would once have been articulated through overtly liminal spaces, such as that of the underworld of Hellenic tradition, or of the forests of the Arthurian Romances, the industrial metropolis provides a modern equivalent in which an ancient and constantly changing narrative flow continues to replicate, mutate and adapt, in order to reflect an urban society's evolving fears and anxieties.

Within the dystopic cinematic tradition, what is seen is every bit as important as what is implied or imagined, in order to represent and reflect individuals and societies in flux, and the processes of changing from one state to another. The internal turmoil of change is equated with the social transformation occurring in the spaces of the city, and is often portrayed in narrative terms as leading to situations of dissociation, mass murder and societal collapse.

While these cinematic representations of the city contribute to the fantastical status of London, they concurrently preserve and perpetuate more ancient and established mythological narratives. This process of repetition and reinforcement makes it possible to see how the mythology and folklore of the city, as much as its history, will continue indefinitely to inform dystopic representations; London, in particular, provides a familiar landscape in which fearful and evil imaginings may be conceived, considered and worked through, if not altogether exorcised. Over a century or more of cinema, filmmakers have recognized and contributed to London's unifying but dystopic folklore, and have laid out the modern conventions of crime, horror and apocalyptic fantasy with which today's global audiences have now become familiar.

CHAPTER 11

POODLE QUEENS AND THE GREAT DARK LAD: CLASS, MASCULINITY AND SUBURBAN TRAJECTORIES IN GAY LONDON

Martin Dines

In the anglophone West, the narration of gay sexuality and identity is conventionally structured by a traversal of a set of spatial and temporal coordinates: from suburb or small town to the big city, and from childhood to the edge of adulthood. The most successful genre of gay writing (and film), the coming-out story – which recounts an individual adolescent's discovery, acceptance and declaration of his or her homosexuality – exemplifies this narrative trajectory, by typically concluding with a metropolitan 'homecoming' or otherwise alluding to some kind of urban relocation. As Kath Weston has found, the continual retelling of the same story of gay people getting to the city – or rather, of people getting to the city to be gay – constructs an 'imagined community', to use Benedict Anderson's term, through a metropolitan/nonmetropolitan 'symbolics' that 'locates gay subjects in the city while putting their presence [elsewhere] under erasure'.[1] Frequently writers compound Weston's symbolics by articulating a gay erotics of the city that is distinctly defined in opposition to the suburban environment and culture of their origin. Philip Gambone is typical when he declares his suburban hometown of Wakefield, Massachusetts to be 'unsexy'. He continues: 'Esthetically and culturally, the town felt parental'; 'I could never have the kind of "erotic" relationship with Wakefield that I could have with an urban area like Boston.'[2] For Gambone, as for many other gay writers, gay sexuality implies both a personal and a physical journey. The attainment of gay identity necessitates a spatialized trajectory, an evacuation of a hostile or asphyxiating familial home environment for the centre of a city which holds the promise of a more enlivening existence.

Of course, it is not just lesbians and gay men who are likely to find the suburbs of their childhood unsexily parental. Similarly, all kinds of people have claimed an urban 'homecoming' as a defining element of their personal and social identity. Indeed, Gambone characterizes the journey to the city as approximating a universal experience:

> The city enriches and deepens one's experience of the world and of the self. Towns cannot do this, especially childhood hometowns. Which is why, for instance, the classic shape of the bildungsroman, the novel of self-discovery, often takes the form of a journey from the town to the city. Think of *Great Expectations*. Think of *Tom Jones*. Think of *The Beautiful Room is Empty*.[3]

The latter title is of a well-known gay text, Edmund White's autobiographical novel *The Beautiful Room is Empty*, which narrates a young man's escape from Midwestern suburbia to New York City in time for the Stonewall riots, which are usually understood in the USA – and beyond – to mark the beginning of gay liberation. Hence the 'classic' status of gay narrative in its most conventional form is easily ascribed. Yet, gay and lesbian people are still understood to need the city more than heterosexuals; only a metropolitan existence can sustain the new and diverse forms of life that lesbians and gay men are pioneering. For as long as Wakefield 'remains a town and not a city', Gambone argues, 'it cannot offer us, its gay sons and daughters, what we need. Which is the chance to put together lives and families in new and different ways, ways that are much more diverse, global, unpredictable, erotic, and celebratory'.[4] So, unlike heterosexuals, Gambone suggests, gay and lesbian people tend not to return to suburbs. By remaining in the city they further perpetuate the perceived heterosexuality of suburbia.[5]

Usefully, Robert Aldrich notes not only how a 'persistence of a vernacular linkage' between homosexuality and the city has been repeatedly alluded to in the titles of novels – Gore Vidal's *The City and the Pillar* (1948); John Rechy's *City of Night* (1963); Armistead Maupin's multivolume *Tales of the City* (1978–89) – but also that such texts illustrate the changing face of homosexual subcultures. Whereas Vidal's and Rechy's novels access hidden homosexual underworlds, Maupin's chronicle an altogether more open milieu, featuring 'the coming-out of small-town boys come to enjoy the Bay City in an ebullient period of gay liberation prior to the physical and emotional trauma of AIDS'.[6] Aldrich cites three texts which centre on US metropolises; the inclusion of *Tales of the City*, however, relates the ambivalent adoption of American formations by British gay subcultures. *Tales of the City* has certainly proven extremely popular with British readers – the series came top in a recent poll to find the nation's favourite gay book[7] – which probably reflects how many aspects of gay identity and subculture in Britain are effectively transatlantic imports. Some elements, however, have been understood to be culturally incongruent. Sinfield notes that this 'cultural interchange' is registered by Maupin himself in *Babycakes*, set in 1983. When the character Michael Tolliver visits the Coleherne (a leather pub in Earls Court) he declares: 'there was something almost poignant about pasty-faced Britishers trying to pull off a butch biker routine. They were simply the wrong breed for it ... Phrases like "Suck that big, fat cock" and "Yeah, you want it, don't you?" sounded just plain asinine when muttered with an Oxonian accent'. Sinfield complains that Maupin's 'is a tourist perception of Britain – the characters who don't have Oxonian accents are broad cockneys.' 'Even so', Sinfield acknowledges, 'he has a point.'[8]

One explanation for why it is hard to characterize a particularly British gay urbanity is that metropolitan gay subcultures in Britain are not as substantial – in both real and mythic terms – as those in the States. Quite simply, in Britain, London simply does not have the gravitational pull on the gay imagination as, for instance, San Francisco in the USA, a site which has become virtual metonym for gay homecoming. Beyond the continual retelling of the coming-out story, as discussed above, there are two likely reasons for the greater metropolitan bias in American gay subculture. Firstly, the more rapid expansion of gay urban centres in the USA from a smaller base since the Second World War has rendered them more conspicuous than London's longer-established, but far less obvious homosexual milieus.[9] Secondly, during the cultural and political upheaval of the 1960s and 1970s, the American gay liberation movement readily drew upon other models of identarian activism, in particular, the black civil rights movement, which claimed parts of certain cities as their cultural and political constituency.[10] British gay and lesbian activists have historically been firmly located in London and certain provincial cities, and have certainly sought – and to an extent continue to seek – to foster strategic alliances with feminist, racial and ethnic minority and other progressive movements. Yet, the make-up of British cities has offered not nearly as much scope for fashioning an ethnicity and rights model of gay and lesbian identity.

The perceived unoriginality of the gay milieus of Earls Court and Soho further prompts many recent narratives of gay London to turn their backs on the city in order to tell tales of the suburbs. Three recent texts – Paul Burston's travelogue of his journey around gay Britain *Queens' Country* (1998), Oscar Moore's novel *A Matter of Life and Sex* (1992), and to an extent also David Leavitt's novel *While England Sleeps* (1993) – challenge the conventional spatialization that organizes gay subcultures in Britain. In so doing, these texts not only show disillusionment with gay urban subcultural formations, they demonstrate that suburban environments and motifs can potentially retain a considerable erotic appeal for gay men. In contesting the conventional trajectory of gay narrative, these three texts attempt to search for more genuine expressions of homosexuality, though, as I will show, 'authenticity' typically equates simply with younger men and lower-class masculinities.

Burston admits that the motivation for writing his travelogue, which includes an account of his penetration of suburban Essex, is a feeling of 'metropolitan world-weariness'.[11] His disaffection stems from an increasing frustration with the ways gay men organize themselves in London; Burston is particularly antagonized by the infantilization and commercialization of the 'Scene'. Burston imagines a two-way flow of traffic in and out of the capital: young gay men escaping to the metropolis from the limiting or hostile environments of their provincial or suburban lives, and those older men who, having tired of the youth-oriented scene, seek to distance themselves from London. This model depicts Burston's own life exactly, from his early flight from his small home town in South Wales to the capital, to his search across Britain for fresh inspiration in *Queens' Country*.

Burston undoubtedly concentrates on Essex partly because of the county's nationally infamous reputation for crass heterosexual promiscuity. Certainly, Essex, in the metropolitan gay imaginary, is resoundingly straight. Burston contends that 'for a lot of gay men especially, Essex represents everything that is hopelessly provincial, tediously straight and therefore ... *not at all sexy!*' And yet, he continues: 'Of course, the irony is that those same gay men would probably drop to their knees at a moment's notice if a man with half a pulse and a strong Essex accent paid them the least bit of attention. ... "Provincial straightness" can be a powerful aphrodisiac.'[12] By referring to Essex Man as the 'great dark lad', Burston invokes Quentin Crisp's formulation of the 'great dark man': that 'impossible' object of desire; impossible because, if he were to turn out to be homosexual, he would not be the 'real man' sought after by Crisp's kind. The great dark lad shows how modern metropolitan gays remain sexually fixated on masculine (and working-class) men. After all, Burston asks, how else is it possible to explain the ubiquity of the personal ads that specify 'SA' (straight-acting)?[13]

But, more than Burston appears to be aware, the Crisp reference is appropriate. Venturing into the dark heart of Essex he encounters, as elsewhere, a considerable amount of 'traffic' heading in the opposite direction. Most young gay men are desperate to leave for London. (In fact they are not the only ones who are eager to depart: ironically, the suburb of Seven Kings is said by one inhabitant not to be 'a bad place to grow up gay ... largely because everyone living there seemed to be on their way somewhere else and was far too preoccupied with their own upward mobility to even notice when the next-door neighbour's son started acting a bit funny.'[14]) When Burston eventually finds his 'great dark lad', in Southend, he is disappointed that he too is heading off to the bright lights of the capital:

Naturally I could understand why someone in his situation would want to get out of Southend as fast as they could. But the thought of him moving back to London worried me deeply. At this moment in time, Jamie possessed something that most gay men spend half their years trying to recapture. And I don't mean his youth. There was something very special about him, something unstudied, something rare and precious. He was real in a way that the men who place ads describing themselves as 'Essex Lads' are never quite real, and all the more sexy for it. Moving back to London would be his undoing, I was certain of it. Six months from now he would be dancing on a podium in a little leather G-string, working hard at being sexy and wondering where all the hordes of admirers had gone. And it just didn't seem right somehow.[15]

In the same way that Crisp's 'Great Dark Man' is only desirable so long as he shows no interest in gay men, Essex Lads only maintain their allure if they express no interest in gay culture. They are defined by their suburbanity, and if tainted with any of the false sophistication or hedonism of London gay life, they lose all authenticity for good. This is what has happened to the ad-Lads, they are no longer 'real' and 'unstudied' like Jamie; in London, they can only perform their Essex-ness. Whilst few would seek to escape there themselves, Essex is constructed as the 'natural' and sustaining habitat of the most sexually desirable kind of man. Yet as Burston has discovered, the space must remain confined to the realms of the imagination, as it is no longer realistic to show such a man still remaining there.

Despite its period setting, Leavitt's *While England Sleeps* enacts an eastward trajectory of a middle-class homosexually identified man in search of working-class men that is quite similar to Burston's chapter on gay Essex. In *While England Sleeps* there is no urban homosexual subculture to speak of; instead, the text constructs sexual identities entirely around suburban locations and the journeys made between them. The novel is narrated by Brian Botsford, a middle-class Englishman (though Americanized since the end of the Second World War) living in central London in the 1930s.[16] Botsford meets a younger man, the East Ender and London Underground worker Edward Phelan, at an 'Aid to Spain' meeting. Their ensuing relationship is troubled by Botsford's fear of exposure and pressure from his family to marry. After Botsford becomes involved with a woman hand-picked by his aunt, the jilted Phelan leaves for Spain, joining the International Brigade. Botsford embarks on a rescue mission after Phelan is arrested for desertion, and though he manages to locate his ex-lover, Botsford is ultimately unable to prevent Phelan dying from typhoid.

Botsford rents a room in Earls Court, which is also where Phelan works, at the local Underground station. Earls Court Station, one of the busiest interchanges of the London Underground network then as now, is also a metaphorical junction, representing Botsford and Phelan's cross-class relationship which has been facilitated by the technological developments of modernity. The two men are from opposite ends of the District Line, Botsford from Richmond and Phelan from Upney (which is not quite the line's eastern terminus, but certainly off the edge of Harry Beck's original 1930s diagrammatical map of the Underground). Botsford even defines his relationship with Phelan as being between Richmond and Upney, two very different suburbs indeed.[17]

Botsford is as preoccupied with a third Underground route and a terminus situated in yet another kind of suburb: Cockfosters at the northern end of the Piccadilly Line.[18] Beyond simply signifying class origins, the Underground network's outer reaches represent for Botsford a metaphorical journey. The termini stand for the disappointment of maturity, of adult reality failing to meet youthful expectations (this developmental metaphor only makes sense, of course, if one shares Leavitt's tourist's impression of the city; most Londoners after all live or have origins that are closer to the ends of the lines than to the centre). Botsford is haunted by the incantation 'imagine Cockfosters', a self-penned refrain from his novel 'The Train to Cockfosters'. So great is his investment in the ideal of the end of the line that he is ill-disposed to do anything that might debase it: 'I was afraid that if I actually *went* to Cockfosters, I would discover it was just a place, just like any other place. Shops and houses. Women carting groceries. And that reality, for some reason, my youthful imagination could not dare to contemplate.'[19] *While England Sleeps*, then, can be seen to be rejecting the ordinariness that is so often attributed to the suburbs. Indeed, in his novel Botsford projects Cockfosters as the domain of an artistic – and homosexual – brotherhood, as the antithesis of the feminine domesticity of 'Shops and houses. Women carting groceries.' In this latter respect, its protagonists evince a hostility to the suburbs that is typical of 1930s British intellectuals. Interestingly, however, the anti-suburbanism of Botsford's characters prompts not the familiar tropes of aerial surveillance or bombardment,[20] but occupation: being 'aggressively antibourgeois ... the dreaded suburbs come to embody for [them] exactly the opposite of what they embody for most people; genius lives in semidetached houses'.[21]

Rather like Burston's disappointment upon reaching Essex, after visiting the distant suburbs there remains a persistent disjunction between Botsford's ideas and experience of such places. When voyaging up the District Line to his lover's family home in Upney, Botsford travels with a weight of expectation. For instance, he imagines Edward Phelan's mother to be old and ugly; she is neither. Disappointed, he vows to keep his own creation for his journal. It would seem that, then as now, imagined aspects of the suburbs are not always extinguished after being contradicted through experience. But even more significantly, Botsford's journey to (nearly) the end of the line against the flow of commuters seemingly cannot invoke another terminus, the Richmond of his childhood:

> We were men and women who, like the train we rode, went against
> traffic, who worked nights, or had bedridden parents to tend to, or
> were on our way home after waking up in the flats of strangers – the
> westbound trains, in their normalness, seeming to go backward, to our
> view, though of course it was they, and not us, who were going forward
> into the urban day. I closed my eyes. I was imagining I could join
> them, head home from this nightmare, toward Richmond, childhood,
> the light playing on the river. My mother, alive, with Nanny and
> Charlotte: three women drinking coffee in the garden.[22]

Botsford's conveyance along the clean lines of the Underground map
are eminently reversible: these journeys are just as likely to anticipate
the future, the dreams and disappointments of adulthood, as they are
to conjure the comfort and security of infancy, an environment,
moreover, that is couched in terms of feminized domesticity, as
opposed to a masculine, intellectual domain. Suburban London for
Leavitt, then, is always ambivalent, neither a singular point of origin,
nor a stable site of maturity.

Superficially, the protagonist of *A Matter of Life and Sex*, Hugo
Harvey, is following a familiar, well-trodden path as he flees the stifling
confines of the suburb of Hadley (only a few miles from Cockfosters), for
the liberated and libidinous heart of London. However, all of Hugo's
adventures in central London reveal it to be essentially suburban, or
otherwise dependent on the suburbs, emotionally and economically.
Casting the centre in this way renders it unreachable: it forever
constitutes a replica of, or transports one to, the place that one has left.
The traditional escape route of youth to London town has effectively
been redirected into a cul-de-sac. Watching male prostitutes on
Piccadilly, for example, Hugo is dismayed that his romanticized image
of the rent-boy is hopelessly dated:

> These weren't the boys in the blonde bouffant and the crushed velvet
> jackets, turning tricks and looking for Mr Right. These were runaways
> with spider's web tattoos on their cheeks. Run by black pimps with fat
> bellies and fat gold, they were dumped half-asleep in mini-cabs and
> sent to distant suburbs to be brutalised by shy deviants.[23]

Hugo's depiction of modern-day renters is certainly as caricatured as
his old-fashioned idea of them. But the differences between the two
kinds – gay, effeminate and seemingly bourgeois-aspirant vis-à-vis
straight, hardened and working class – prove less significant than the
spatial reversal enacted here. Instead of tricks having to visit
Piccadilly to hire rent-boys, now the youths must themselves
commute out to the suburbs. So it appears that running away to
London and going on the game is no longer a means of escaping
from suburbia: the job will simply send you straight back.

Hugo's own working experience of prostitution confirms the
suburbanization of the profession. His first client – living at Swiss

Cottage – is fairly typical: 'womanish'; 'he had a black poodle'; 'They talked. They drank tea.'[24] As Hugo is about to be fellated, he looks down on a familiar feminine, suburban scene: 'Saturday afternoon shopping on the Finchley Road. John Barnes. Toys Toys Toys. Lindy's Patisserie. Respectable Jewish mothers parked their two-door Mercedes and ran into Waitrose.'[25] Admittedly, Hugo's work requires him to visit just as many hotel rooms, which are far preferable, he insists, to homes:

> In hotels, loneliness was horny. It was a no-man's land of no holds barred. Anything could happen, anything could be ordered, anybody could pretend to be anyone. At home there was no escape from the man you were, or weren't. It was written in the curtain fabric, the washing-up, the lilac loo paper, the Panadol in the bathroom cabinet.[26]

Recalling Gambone, it is the familial, and arguably feminized, aspects of the domestic interior which are deemed stifling, explicitly asphyxiating masculinity and sexuality. Yet most of the description of Hugo's experiences with his clients is given over to the depressing, home-based variety. Only the instances in hotels where he is paid *not* to have sex are recounted in any detail, as well as the final, abortive encounter which ends his career. Despite his protestations to the contrary, Hugo is more interested in these all-too-familiar home and homely environments.

Earls Court, then London's gay hub, is equally disappointing. Hugo has a preconception that the district represents the quintessence of a sexualized, nocturnal kind of urbanity: 'land of the late-night take away and home of the clone'.[27] But again, Hugo wildly overestimates the sexual glamour waiting to be uncovered in the heart of the city: 'He had always imagined these porn emporia to be seething with young men of every measurement, scantily clad, tongues wagging in each other's throats, a perpetual tableau of sexual spree, snapped by artfully concealed photographers. Instead he was barefoot in suburbia in a draughty studio with a mealy-mouthed clone.'[28] As with Piccadilly, the myth of the alluring sexual metropolis is dispelled and replaced with a dispiriting suburban 'reality'; once again, the search for the city terminates in a vision of gay suburbia. During a soft-porn photo shoot, Hugo realizes that he is being processed to suit the tastes of 'the poodle queens of upmarket bedsit land; the men who went to bed in hairnets and wore chainstore silk dressing gowns; the men who smoked Sobranies and voted Conservative'.[29]

To an extent, the suburbanization of central London in Moore's novel is simply representative of Hugo's failure to achieve gay identity. Hugo insists that he has kept himself 'so firmly outside the scene, standing on the touchline with his back turned'; consequently, he considers the fact that he has caught what he refers to as a 'gay disease' to be a bitter irony. But then, Hugo has little chance to explore questions of identity, dying tragically early from AIDS-related illnesses. As Esther Saxey observes, *A Matter of Life and Sex* is a hybrid text straddling two principal genres of gay writing: the coming-out story and the AIDS narrative.[30] The novel's composition, interweaving the guilt-laden first half of the coming-out story with the later part of the AIDS narrative – the descent through illness and towards death – suggests bleak reading indeed. *A Matter* offers no respite in the form of a sustaining gay subculture, which might have rendered all the anguish of the process of coming out worthwhile, or provided support for those suffering with AIDS.

But, as Saxey argues, *A Matter of Life and Sex* celebrates the pursuit of sensation over the quest for identity and community. That Hugo accepts a premature and painful death as a consequence of his actions indicates not his error in choosing the former path but his commitment to that choice. However, the one place Hugo finds a community of sorts is during his adolescence, in the suburban cottages – that is, public toilets used for sex by men – in Hadley, his childhood home. Hugo's experiences of the cottages are sometimes dismal, but at other times joyous, even carnivalesque: he and his fellow cottagers are said be part of a 'parade', dancing the 'toilet tango'.[31] The cottages constitute a territory, which Moore seems as loyal to as any writer before or since who has defended identifiably gay streets, from Soho to Sunset Boulevard. The walls of the cottages, after all, are inscribed with decades of desiring scrawl – a genre sometimes referred to as 'loiterature'. One of the functions of graffiti is, after all, the demarcation of territory. And indeed, non-cottaging toilets are referred to as 'Dead territory. The writing was on the wall' – both figuratively and literally – one merely featuring 'a few football slogans, some furious racism, a half-rubbed off story [about a] man whose wife wanted three men in a bed and was horny as hell but that was two years ago according to the date at the bottom.'[32]

But despite this apparent territorialization, Moore's cottages are not a decentred equivalent to an Earls Court or any other gay urban community, in that their discovery does little or nothing to foster identity formation. Rather, the cottages suggest a homosexuality that is firmly imbricated with the family home. Despite Hugo's castigation of gay subcultures as suburban and feminized, his preoccupation with suburban imagery, and in particular with the supposedly feminine space of the domestic interior, demonstrates his erotic investment with such environments. In his celebration of the cottage, Hugo continually evokes the suburban-domestic household. For instance, he extols his favourite cottage's virtues with an estate agent's patter (punning on the word 'cottage');[33] elsewhere he refers to the venue as the cottagers' 'parlour',[34] an ironic reference to the epicentre of the bourgeois suburban home. Casting the homosexual space of the cottage as domestic reconnects the likes of Hugo with the thrill of the risk of parental detection, but also gives the equally exciting sense that one is engaging in a sacrilegious act, that one is subverting familial authority. Indeed, when Hugo's lovemaking progresses to the interiors of suburban semis, he expresses precisely this eroticization of transgression: 'the chintz and quilts and ornamental mantelpieces of their suburban sitting rooms only made him more randy. It was desecration and blasphemy in the sitting room'.[35] In this example, the very fabric of suburbia stands metonymically for the hegemony of the heterosexual family. In contrast to Gambone's insistence that he could never have an 'erotic relationship' with his suburban hometown, Hugo finds Hadley sexy precisely because it is parental.[36]

Yet, the eroticization of domestic space is hardly helpful to one attempting to flee the suburbs. If anything, Hugo's sexual tastes are a little too close to those of the poodle queens encountered earlier for comfort. Whilst Hugo's constant search for dynamic, authentic forms of homosexuality ultimately draw him away from the suburbs and towards the city, which he believes to be the habitat of an urban sexual underclass, all he appears to achieve is bringing the suburbs in train with him. Hugo's attempts to enter into a déclassé brotherhood are thwarted – not least because such communities are shown to be the fanciful elaboration of an adolescent mind – but also because his own membership would be inauthentic. Such is the inevitable conclusion of 'the daydream of the schoolboy ... who wanted to enter the fraternity of hustlers ... who wanted to be exotic but knew he was suburban'.[37] In the suburbanized London of Moore's novel, a domesticated middle class is the only social landscape that is realistically representable: urban lower-class homosexualities are pushed into the realms of the imaginary.

If Hugo is seen to spread his wings and travel to foreign cities, all of his adventures abroad are equally precipitately suburban. Paris shares precisely the same promise as London: 'sex ran in deep seams through its centre, titillating, inviting, provoking, preoccupying'.[38] The nightclubs, however, prove to be as tired and unalluring as the ones back home; the only pleasure Hugo finds lies in the soft furnishings of the apartment of the one man who picks him up (a rather unappealing short, balding, bespectacled professor): 'Hugo felt that rush of comfort, that first ache for the softness of a deep carpet and the sinking of the sofa.'[39] Ironically enough, the one domain which does escape the reductive appellation is America. When watching some 'specialized' pornographic films manufactured in the United States, for instance, Hugo makes the explicit distinction: 'they weren't suburban. They were American'.[40] And it is in New York, 'the charnel house of the Western World',[41] where Hugo would appear to have finally given suburbia the slip. The novel's transatlantic trajectory rather serves to foreground the American heritage of gay narrative. It rather seems that London and other European metropolises are incapable of offering an authentically urban homosexual world that is distinct from a familial suburban habitat; quite simply, a sexualized urbanity is still too closely associated with a vision of the American city.

Ultimately, however, even in New York Hugo still cannot shake off his origins. His inability to do so renders his existence on these streets of Sodom as transparently inauthentic: one of Hugo's friends, for example, knew him 'for what he was. A sometime hooker, a sometime low-grade porn star, sometime teenage cottage queen with a smart head and a nice suburban home waiting for him anytime if things got too strange.'[42] More significantly, the text strongly suggests that it is in some dank New York sex club that Hugo contracts the HIV virus, and from this point the narrative rapidly concertinas into Hugo's funeral, which takes place just down the road from Hadley. It is hard not to interpret the denouement crudely, as somehow punitive of Hugo's last attempted escape from suburbia. His mother dominates the wake and Hugo is seemingly kept company in the afterlife not by fellow Hadley cottagers or AIDS victims, but by the ghosts of elderly suburban women. The most overbearing of these even eerily reminds him of antimacassars:[43] the soft furnishings of a bygone age are to be Hugo's psychic death shroud. The final insult to Hugo's metropolitan aspirations is his burial in Hendon cemetery. So, far from disordering with his homosexuality the feminine suburban interiors that he so despises, the suburbs seemingly thwart Hugo's ideal of an independent homosexual urban underworld. The constantly repeated trope of the suburban city, then, reflects both the impossibility of realizing in the British capital what is, in effect, a foreign cultural import, and the inexorable centrifugal draw on Hugo's sexual imagination of his mother and of the suburban surfaces of Hadley.

Many gay narratives, whether they are coming-out stories, historical novels or accounts of middle-aged urban ennui, enact a search for a better place to be gay. But Moore and Burston's texts question the faith typically placed in urban subcultures in the last few pages of the standard coming-out story, though seemingly at the cost of using some rather anti-effeminate or even misogynist imagery. And even if they seem to be chasing after an idealized lower-class masculinity that won't stay in the place their protagonists want it to be, *A Matter of Life and Sex*, *While England Sleeps* and *Queens' Country* each demonstrate that London suburbia does not necessarily construct gay identity only in terms of the place that one must flee before becoming a fully fledged gay man. These texts show that suburban habitats and inhabitants can and do form a significant constituent element of gay sexuality: from Enfield to Essex, the suburbs can be sexy.

Notes

1. Kath Weston, 'Get Thee to a Big City: Sexual Imaginary and the Great Gay Migration', *GLQ: A Journal of Gay and Lesbian Studies*, vol. 2, no. 3 (1995), 253–77.
2. Philip Gambone, 'Wakefield, Massachusetts', in John Preston, ed., *Hometowns: Gay Men Write about where They Belong*, New York, 1991, 94.
3. Ibid.
4. Ibid.
5. Recent American sociological studies, however, demonstrate that lesbians and gay men are increasingly choosing to live in suburban environments. See: Rosalyn Baxendall and Elizabeth Ewen, *Picture Windows: How the Suburbs Happened*, New York, 2001, 223; Ken Kirkey and Ann Forsyth, 'Men in the Valley: Gay Male Life on the Suburban-Rural Fringe', *Journal of Rural Studies*, vol. 17, no. 4 (2001), 421–41; Wayne K. Brekhus, *Peacocks, Chameleons, Centaurs: Gay Suburbia and the Grammar of Social Identity*, Chicago, 2003.
6. Robert Aldrich, 'Homosexuality and the City: An Historical Overview', *Urban Studies*, vol. 41, no. 9 (2004), 1720.
7. Maupin's win was announced during The Big Gay Read Literary Festival, Manchester, 7–28 May 2006.
8. Alan Sinfield, *Gay and After*, London, 1998, 103.
9. On the development of American gay urban subcultures in the postwar years, see John D'Emilio, *Sexual Politics, Sexual Communities: The Making of a Homosexual Minority in the United States, 1940–1970*, Chicago, 1983.
10. See Dennis Altman, *Homosexual: Oppression and Liberation*, New York, 1971.
11. Paul Burston, *Queens' Country: A Tour around the Gay Ghettos, Queer Spots and Camp Sights of Britain*, London, 1998, 215.
12. Ibid., 98.
13. Ibid., 99.
14. Ibid., 111–12.
15. Ibid., 121.
16. Leavitt was successfully sued by the poet Stephen Spender, who accused the novelist of plagiarizing his diaries. My analysis refers to the second version of *While England Sleeps* (Boston, MA, 1995), published after Leavitt was obliged to rewrite sections which Spender deemed objectionably too close to his own life experiences.
17. Leavitt, *While England Sleeps*, 47.
18. In the final chapter Leavitt invokes yet another terminus, with Botsford recalling having relations with 'an accountant from Stanmore' (ibid., 265), which in the 1930s was at the end of a branch of the Metropolitan Line.
19. Ibid., 62.
20. Such imagery features frequently in 1930s poetry, from C. Day Lewis's rendition of W.H. Auden as a panoptic visionary in the form of a kestrel or a birdman (C. Day Lewis, 'The Magnetic Mountain 16', in *The Complete Poems of C. Day Lewis*, Palo Alto, CA: 1992, 151), to Betjeman's notorious line, 'Come friendly bombs and fall on Slough' (John Betjeman, 'Slough', in Roger Skelton, ed., *Poetry of the Thirties*, Harmondsworth, 1964, 74).
21. Leavitt, *While England Sleeps*, 60.

22. Ibid., 172–73.
23. Oscar Moore, *A Matter of Life and Sex*, Harmondsworth, 1992 [first published under the pseudonym Alec F. Moran (London, 1991)], 178.
24. Ibid., 206.
25. Ibid., 207.
26. Ibid., 212–13.
27. Ibid., 193.
28. Ibid.
29. Ibid.
30. Esther Saxey, 'Homoplot: The Coming out Story as Identity Narrative', unpublished doctoral thesis, University of Sussex, 2004, 104–12.
31. Moore, A Matter of Life and Sex, 98 and passim.
32. Ibid., 26–27.
33. Ibid., 33.
34. Ibid., 98.
35. Ibid., 116.
36. For more on strategies of subverting domestic space in gay narrative, see Martin Dines, 'Sacrilege in the Sitting Room: Contesting Suburban Domesticity in Contemporary Gay Literature', *Home Cultures*, vol. 2, no. 2 (2005), 175–94.
37. Moore, *A Matter of Life and Sex*, 161.
38. Ibid., 164.
39. Ibid., 165.
40. Ibid., 187.
41. Ibid., 283.
42. Ibid., 297.
43. Ibid., 320.

CHAPTER 12

CODA: WHAT COLOUR IS TIME?
DEREK JARMAN'S SOHO

Jeremy Reed

What colour is time when you try to remember it? In 1984, the year when Derek Jarman took a lease on a studio flat in Phoenix House, above the Phoenix Theatre off Charing Cross Road, a compactly minuscule, but functional base, the uncurtained window set like a grid framing the Soho skyline, I associate time then with aqueous white rain skies over Leicester Square, and as candy-coloured stripes: pink and white, maroon and grey, pistachio and russet bands according to my abstract notation of big city seasons.

Jarman's studio, reached by an anonymous door, with a clunky semi-industrial lift ascending to his fourth floor flat choked with his paintings, books, a fold-up bed, a metal office desk and looking out at the sky-reflecting windows of St Martin's School of Art, was to become the epicentre for a decade of electrifying creativity, AIDS agitprop as Jarman went public about his HIV status, and intense kamikaze forays into the West End club scene. Jarman regularly visited Bang directly opposite his building, Blitz, Pink Panther, Flamingo, Heaven and the Sanctuary, as well as his favourite backroom at the Subway in Leicester Square. Jarman's club topology also extended north of Soho to the Catacombs and The Bell beside King's Cross, to which he travelled by cab, always asking the driver to drop him wide of his destination and walking the remaining distance there. There was also the teeming pub circuit he pursued that took in The Salisbury, Global Village, Brief Encounter, and of course the pyramidically stacked leather crush of expectant bodies in Compton's on Old Compton Street.

Jarman's last full feature film had been the critically acclaimed *The Tempest* in 1979, a homoerotic reworking of myths that continued

Figure 12.1: Phoenix House, Charing Cross Road. Photograph by Catherine Lupton, courtesy of Catherine Lupton

to resonate with his filmic obsessions. In 1984 he found himself in something of a creative hiatus – lacking the finance to commit to the *Caravaggio* project he was researching, and taking advantage of the interlude to review his past through a comprehensive retrospective of his paintings at the ICA and the publication of *Dancing Ledge*, the first of his experimental and intransigently outspoken autobiographies. And, in need of space in which to paint and put up a wall of his books, he rented a small room from Christopher Hobbs at 20 Hanway Works, one of the gun-barrel narrow alleyways just off the Phoenix House complex.

At the same time as Jarman was considering shooting pop videos to provide some necessary income, the singer Marc Almond, living less than a quarter of a mile away on Brewer Street at the heart of Soho's lugubrious red light district, was planning to release his first solo album, appropriately called *Vermin in Ermine*. The exotic, epic-voiced Almond, who had risen to fame with the Northern Soul dance hit *Tainted Love* and who had quickly grown disaffected with Soft Cell's winning electro-pop formula and angry at the commercial failure of Marc and the Mambas as a serious sideline, had for his first solo project embraced his true identity as a torch singer. He was living in a one-bedroom flat on the third floor of a red-brick mansion-block facing out over Madame JoJo's cabaret bar in Brewer Street and the

Raymond Revuebar Theatre with its jumpy chilli-red neon illuminating his windows. Almond's infatuation with sleaze had brought him to live in it as a reality. From the safety of his unlit living room, his voyeuristic eye monitored nocturnal Soho, finding in its fugitive characters the inspiration for many of the finely crafted songs included on *Vermine in Ermine*.

That the two artists were linked by a shared neighbourhood, as well as elective affinities extending to the use of dramatic camp as an expression incorporated into their art, led to Almond suggesting that Jarman shoot the low-budget video for the third single lifted from his album *Tenderness is a Weakness*. Jarman, who referred to pop videos as 'a cinema of small gestures', was attracted to the form largely as a means of helping finance his more serious artistic projects. That he brought imagination to the work and could earn £1,000 for a few days' filming encouraged him to apply his characteristic theatre skills to the medium. In 1983–84, in rapid succession, he made videos of *Touch the Radio, Dance!* by Steve Hale, *Dance with Me* by Lords of the New Church, *Willow Weep for Me* by Carmel, *Dance Hall Days* by Wang Chung, *Wide Boy Awake* by Billy Hyena, *Catalan* by Jordi Vall, *What Presence* by Orange Juice, as well as Almond's *Tenderness Is a Weakness*.

Jarman's dramatic stage-set for the video of *Tenderness Is a Weakness* poses Almond in a full-length black sequinned gown, alternated with shots of him with glittering devil's horns woven into his hair against an urban landscape featuring dustbins and a blank-faced city backdrop, under a blue night sky painted with splashy gold stars and an imposing yellow crescent moon. Almond's sequinned costumes were indigenous to Soho too, and John Carter – who was living at Almond's Brewer Street flat at the time – remembers the singer returning from one of the fabric shops on Berwick Street with bolts of pink and black sequins to be made up for stage clothes worn on Almond's extensive tour of the UK in the autumn of 1984. The bolts were in fact purchased from Aladdin's Cave, one of the shops that gives on to the heckling bustle of Berwick Street market and which continues to this day to have sequinned material on display in ripples of scintillating emerald, cerise, scarlet and ultramarine.

Almond's song – divisively split in gender between she and he, two characters who form a composite in Jarman's portrayal of the girl as indeterminately androgynous, a Weimar cabaret figure with raked back hair complemented by a sandy-haired rent-boy reading at a café table – is a dichotomy continued by Jarman's depiction of Almond as alternately a devil with horns and bright red lipstick, and a naturally posed torch singer in a black sequinned gown. The song's theme, which is essentially one of vulnerability and of the access that provides to a manipulative lover, is taken up by Jarman's ascending and descending screens, in which Almond – in his endeavour to keep a torch burning for disappointed love – is cast as the rejected outlaw, standing under a streetlamp in the night beside a flaming dustbin.

Working with quickly assembled props and employing archetypes recognizably his own – like a scorching red heart, two teenaged girls dressed all in white who appear to be torch-bearing angels, red theatre curtains, a sky full of stars, characters who are sexually ambiguous, and a city on the edge of apocalypse – Jarman added his own torchy signature and theatrical ensemble to Almond's histrionically flavoured pop.

The Soho of Marc Almond's imagination, one in which rent-boys crowded on the black railings at Piccadilly Circus and mini-skirted hookers trafficked in the alleys, had almost disappeared by 1984, airbrushed by omniscient CCTV cameras and the ubiquitous politics of totalitarianism. Soho's disaffected bohemians still convened in cafés along Old Compton Street, at Maison Bertaux in Greek Street almost opposite Oscar Wilde's old nightspot Kettners, and of course in its landmark bars and drinking-clubs such as The Colony, made famous by Francis Bacon.

I asked what colour time was in 1984. It was pearl grey; the skies were consistently opalescent as they so often are over the West End. I associate time with the colours memory constellates. Pearl banded with charcoal and dark blue. When *Vermine in Ermine* was released I bought my copy from the HMV store in Oxford Street and cut into Soho on a simmering autumn day, nitrogen dioxide air quality 40 ppb, and caught sight of Marc Almond's alertly paranoid, wiry, harassed figure cutting it along Berwick Street as though he was being pursued. He was hurrying back home, and I to meet a friend, in a precinct that always seems to me a starting point for London's imagination.

NOTES ON CONTRIBUTORS

Stephen Barber's recent books include *The Vanishing Map* (2006) and *Hijikata* (2006). He is a professor at Kingston University.

Gail Cunningham is Dean of Arts and Social Sciences and Professor of English at Kingston University. She has published widely on the New Woman and on literary representations of Victorian and Edwardian suburbia.

Martin Dines recently completed a Ph.D. on suburban gay literatures and is a tutor at Kingston University.

Roland-François Lack is the co-editor of *The Tel Quel Reader* (1998) and the author of *Poetics of the Pretext: Reading Lautréamont*. He is a senior lecturer at University College London.

Sara de Freitas is a senior research fellow at the Knowledge Lab at Birkbeck College University of London, and researches library and archival forms, and new technologies for the dissemination of knowledge.

Hugo Frey's books include a study of the French film director, *Louis Malle* (2004). He is Principal Lecturer and Head of History at the University of Chichester.

Deborah Parsons is Senior Lecturer at the University of Birmingham. Her books include *Streetwalking the Metropolis* (2000) and *Theorists of the Modern Novel* (2006).

Jeremy Reed is a Leverhulme Trust Fellow, an acclaimed poet, and the author of many books, including *Orange Sunshine* (2006) and a study of the novelist Anna Kavan (2006).

Andrew Smith is Professor of English Studies at the University of Glamorgan. His books include *Victorian Demons* (2004) and *Gothic Radicalism* (2000). With Benjamin Fisher, he edits the series 'Gothic Literary Studies' for the University of Wales Press.

Lindsay Smith is Professor of English at the University of Sussex. Her books include *Victorian Photography, Painting and Poetry* (1995) and *The Politics of Focus: Women, Children and Nineteenth Century Photography* (1998); she is currently completing a book on Lewis Carroll.

Ana Parejo Vadillo is lecturer in English at the University of Exeter. She is the author of *Women Poets and Urban Aestheticism* (2005), and has recently co-edited a special issue of the *Journal of Victorian Literature and Culture* on 'Fin-de-Siècle Literary Culture and Women Poets'.

Roger Webster is Professor of Literary Studies and Dean of the Faculty of Media, Arts and Social Science at Liverpool John Moores University. He has published mainly on Thomas Hardy's fiction and a range of nineteenth and twentieth century literature, including *Expanding Suburbia* (2001).

BIBLIOGRAPHY

Ackroyd, Peter. 2002. *London: The Biography*. London.

Agrest, Diana, Patricia Conway and Leslie Kanes Wesiman, eds. 1996. *The Sex of Architecture*. New York.

Aldrich, Robert. 2004. 'Homosexuality and the City: An Historical Overview', *Urban Studies*, vol. 41, no. 9, 1719–37.

Allbutt, T.C. 1895. 'Nervous Diseases and Modern Life', *Contemporary Review*, no. 67, 210–31.

Altman, Dennis. 1971. *Homosexual: Oppression and Liberation*. New York.

Armstrong, Nancy. 1999. *Fiction in the Age of Photography: the Legacy of British Realism*. Cambridge, MA.

Bachelard, Gaston. 1979. *The Poetics of Space*. Boston, MA.

Ballard, J.G. 2003. *Millennium People*. London.

Barber, Stephen. 2002. *Projected Cities: Cinema and Urban Space*. London.

Barnes, John. 1998. *The Beginnings of the Cinema in Britain*. Exeter.

Barsham, Dana. 2000. *Arthur Conan Doyle and the Meaning of Masculinity*. Aldershot.

Barthes, Roland. 1981. *Camera Lucida: Reflections on Photography*. New York.

Baudelaire, Charles. 1986. *The Painter of Modern Life and Other Essays*, ed. and trans. Jonathan Mayne. London.

Baxendall, Rosalyn and Elizabeth Ewen. 2001. *Picture Windows: How the Suburbs Happened*. New York.

Benjamin, Walter. 1983. *Charles Baudelaire: A Lyric Poet in the Era of High Capitalism*, trans. Harry Zohn. London.

———. 1985. 'A Small History of Photography', in *One Way Street and Other Writings*, trans. Edmund Jephcott and Kingsley Shorter. London.

Besant, Walter. 1899. *South London*. London.

Betjeman, John. 1964. 'Slough', in Roger Skelton, ed., *Poetry of the Thirties*. Harmondsworth.

Blundell Maple, J. 1891. *Cheap Trains for London Workers*. London.

Booth, Charles. 1901. *Improved Means of Locomotion as a First Step towards the Cure of the Housing Difficulties of London, being an Abstract of the Proceedings of two Conferences Convened by the Warden of Robert Browning Hall, Walworth, with a Paper on the Subject by Charles Booth*. London.

Bowker, R.R. 1888. 'London as a Literary Centre', *Harper's New Monthly Magazine*, vol. 76, no. 456, 815–44.

Bowlby, Rachel. 1985. *Just Looking: Consumer Culture in Dreiser, Gissing and Zola*. New York.

Brekhus, Wayne K. 2003. *Peacocks, Chameleons, Centaurs: Gay Suburbia and the Grammar of Social Identity*. Chicago.

Bruno, Guiliana. 2002. *Atlas of Emotion: Journeys in Art, Architecture and Film*. London.

Bullock, Shan F. 1907. *Robert Thorne: The Story of a London Clerk*. London.

Burke, Thomas. 1922. *The London Spy: A Book of Town Travels*. London.

Burston, Paul. 1998. *Queens' Country*. London.

Carter, Paul. 2001. *Repressed Spaces: The Poetics of Agoraphobia*. London.

Catterall, Ali and Simon Wells. 2001. *Your Face Here: British Cult Movies since the Sixties*. London.

de Certeau, Michel. 1988. *The Practice of Everyday Life*. Berkeley, CA.

Church-Gibson, Pamela. 2003. 'Imaginary Landscapes, Jumbled Topographies: Cinematic London', in Joe Kerr and Andrew Gibson, eds, *London: From Punk to Blair*. London.

Clark Conley, Tom. 2000. 'Du cinéma à la carte', *Cinémas*, vol. 10, no. 2–3.

Clifford, Lucy. 1996. 'The End of Her Journey,' in Kate Flint, ed., *Victorian Love Stories*. Oxford.

Cocroft, Wayne, Roger Thomas and P.S. Barnwell, eds. 2003. *Cold War: Building for Nuclear Confrontation 1946–89*. Swindon.

Conan Doyle, Arthur. 1893. *The Great Shadow and Beyond the City*. Bristol.

———. 1981. *The Penguin Complete Sherlock Holmes*. Harmondsworth.

Conrad, Joseph. 1973. *Heart of Darkness*. Harmondsworth.

———. 1965. *The Secret Agent*. Harmondsworth.

Da Costa Meyer, Esther. 1996. 'La Donna è Mobile: Agoraphobia, Women, and Urban Space', Diana Agrest, Patricia Conway and Leslie Kanes Weisman, eds, *The Sex of Architecture*. New York.

Crosland, Thomas W.H. 1905. *The Suburbans*. London.

Davis, Philip. 2002. *The Oxford English Literary History*, Volume 8. *1830–1880: The Victorians*. Oxford.

Day Lewis, C. 1992. 'The Magnetic Mountain 16', in *The Complete Poems of C. Day Lewis*. Palo Alto, CA.

D'Emilio, John. 1983. *Sexual Politics, Sexual Communities: The Making of a Homosexual Minority in the United States, 1940–1970*. Chicago.

Demoor, Marysa. 2000. *Their Fair Share: Women, Power and Criticism in the Athenaeum, from Millicent Garett Fawcett to Katherine Mansfield, 1870–1920*. Aldershot.

Dickens, Charles. 1965. *Great Expectations*. Harmondsworth.

———. 1996. *Great Expectations*. London.

———. 2002. *Dombey and Son*. London.

Dines, Martin. 2005. 'Sacrilege in the Sitting Room: Contesting Suburban Domesticity in Contemporary Gay Literature', *Home Cultures*, vol. 2, no. 2, 175–94.

Drabble, Margaret. 1980. *The Middle Ground*. London.

Duclaux, Mary. 1933. 'Souvenirs sur George Moore', *La Revue de Paris* XV, no. 2, 1 March, 121.

Easthope, Antony. 1997. 'Cinécities in the Sixties', in D.B. Clarke, ed., *The Cinematic City*. London.

Eliot, T.S. 1922. *The Waste Land*. London.

Freud, Sigmund. 1984. *On Metapsychology*, Penguin Freud Library, vol. 11. Harmondsworth.

Frisby, David. 1985. *Fragments of Modernity: Social Theories of Modernity in the Works of Georg Simmel, Siegfried Kracauer and Walter Benjamin*. Cambridge.

———. *Cityscapes of Modernity: Critical Explorations*. Oxford.

Fromm, Gloria G, ed. 1995. *Windows on Modernism: Selected Letters of Dorothy Richardson*. Athens, GA.

Gagnier, Regenia. 1986. *Idylls of the Marketplace: Oscar Wilde and the Victorian Public*. Stanford, CA.

Gambone, Philip. 1991. 'Wakefield, Massachusetts', in John Preston, ed., *Hometowns: Gay Men Write about Where They Belong*. New York.

Gardiner, Bruce. 1988. *The Rhymers' Club: A Social and Intellectual History*. New York and London.

Gerdhaus, Maly and Dietfried. 1979. *Cubism and Futurism: The Evolution of the Self-sufficient Picture*. Oxford.

Glinert, Ed. 2003. *The London Compendium*. London.

Grossmith, George and Weedon. 1965. *The Diary of a Nobody*. London.

Groth, Helen. 2003. *Victorian Photography and Literary Nostalgia*. Oxford.

Guthrie, Thomas. 1860. 'First Plea for Ragged Schools', in Thomas Guthrie, *Seed Time & Harvest of Ragged Schools or a Third Plea with New Editions of the First and Second Pleas*. Edinburgh.

Hartley, W.H. 1885. *In a London Suburb*. London.

Hawthorn, Jeremy. 1979. *Joseph Conrad: Language and Fictional Self-Consciousness*. London.

Hemmings, David. 2004. *Blow-Up and Other Exaggerations*. London.

Herbert, Stephen. 1998. *Industry, Liberty and a Vision*. London.

Hughes, Kathryn. 2006. *The Short Life and Long Times of Mrs Beeton*. London.

Hughes, Robert. 1980. *The Shock of the New: Art and the Century of Change*. London.

Jones, Ernest. 1929. 'Fear, Guilt, and Hate', *International Journal of Psychoanalysis*, 10, 387.

Keiller, Patrick. 1999. *Robinson in Space*. London.

Kellett, John. 1969. *The Impact of Railways on Victorian Cities*. London.

Kestner, Joesph A. 1997. *Sherlock's Men: Masculinity, Conan Doyle, and Cultural History*. Aldershot.

Kirkey, Ken and Ann Forsyth. 2001. 'Men in the Valley: Gay Male Life on the Suburban-Rural Fringe', *Journal of Rural Studies*, vol. 17, no. 4, 421–41.

Koestler, Arthur. 1963. *Suicide of a Nation?*. London.

Leavitt, David. 1995. *While England Sleeps*. Boston, MA.

Lee, Vernon. 1937. *Vernon Lee's Letters. With a Preface by Her Executor*. Privately printed.

Levy, Amy. 1882. 'Women and Club Life', *Woman's World* (ed. Oscar Wilde), no. 1, 366.

Levy, Shawn. 2002. *Ready, Steady, Go!: Swinging London and the Invention of Cool*. London.

Low, Sidney. 1891. 'The Rise of the Suburbs: A Lesson of the Census', *Contemporary Review*, vol. 60, 545–58.

Livesey, Ruth. 2006. 'Dollie Radford and the Ethical Aesthetics of *Fin-de-Siècle* Poetry', *Journal of Victorian Literature and Culture* (special issue: *Fin-de-Siècle Women Poets and Literary Culture* ed. Marion Thain and Ana Parejo Vadillo), vol. 34, no. 2, 508.

Lynch, Kevin. 1960. *The Image of the City*. Cambridge, MA.

MacCabe, Colin. 1998. *Performance*. London.

———. 2004. *Godard*. London.

Marandon, Sylvaine. 1967. *L'Oeuvre Poétique de Mary Robinson 1857–1944*. Bordeaux.

Masson, Jeffrey, trans. and ed. 1985. *The Complete Letters of Sigmund Freud to Wilhelm Fleiss*. Cambridge, MA.

Masterman, Charles F.G. 1909. *The Condition of England*. London

Mayhew, Henry. 1967 (1865). *London Labour and the London Poor*, 4 vols. London.

Moore, Glen M., ed. 1997. *Conrad on Film*. Cambridge.

Moore, Oscar. 1992. *A Matter of Life and Sex*. Harmondsworth.

Moore, Rayburn, ed. 1993. *The Correspondence of Henry James and the House of Macmillan, 1877–1914*. London.

Moretti, Franco. 1998. *Atlas of the European Novel 1800–1900*. London.

Mulvey, Laura. 2005. *Death Twenty-four Times a Second*. London.

Murphy, Robert. 1992. *Sixties British Cinema*. London.

Nead, Lynda. 2000. *Victorian Babylon: People, Streets and Images in Nineteenth-Century London*. New Haven, CA.

Nordau, Max. 1913 (1895). *Degeneration*, London.

Nowell-Smith, Geoffrey. 2001. 'Cities: Real and Imagined', in Mark Shiel and Tony Fitzmaurice, eds, *Cinema and the City*. Oxford.

Olsen, Donald J. 1976. *The Growth of Victorian London*. London.

Ovenden, Richard. 1997. *John Thomson (1837–1921) Photographer*. Edinburgh.

Parejo Vadillo, Ana. 1999. 'New Woman Poets and the Culture of the *Salon* at the *fin de siècle*', *Women: A Cultural Review*, vol. 10, no. 1, 22–34.

———. 2005. 'Immaterial Poetics: A. Mary F. Robinson and the Fin-de-Siècle Poem', in Joseph Bristow, ed., *The Fin-de-Siècle Poem: English Literary Culture and the 1890s*. Athens, OH, 236–39.

———. 2005. *Women Poets and Urban Aestheticism: Passengers of Modernity*. Basingstoke.

Perkins, David. 1976. *A History of Modern Poetry from the 1890s to the High Modernist Mode*. Cambridge, MA.

Petit, Chris. 1993. *Robinson*. London.

Pevsner, Nikolaus. 1973. *The Buildings of England: London*, vol. 1. Harmondsworth.

Porter, Roy. 2000. *London: A Social History*. Harmondsworth.

Prins, Yopie. 2006. '"Lady's Greek" (with the Accents): A Metrical Translation of Euripides by A. Mary F. Robinson', *Victorian Literature and Culture*, vol. 34, no. 2, 571–81.

Pritchett, V.S. 1968. *A Cab at the Door*. London.

Pugh, Edwin. 1895. *A Street in Suburbia*. London.

Radford, Dollie. 1895. 'From the Suburbs', in *Songs and Other Verses*. London.

Raphael, Frederic. 1965. *Darling*. London.

Rappaport, Erika D. 2002. *Shopping for Pleasure: Women in the Making of London's West End*. Princeton, NJ.

Ravenel, Loïc. 1994. *Les Aventures géographiques de Sherlock Holmes*. Paris.

Reeves, Tony. 2003. *The Worldwide Guide to Movie Locations Presents: London*. London.

Reik, Theodor. 1956. *The Search Within*. New York.

Reuter, Shelley Z. 2002. 'Doing agoraphobia(s): A Material-Discursive Understanding of Diseased Bodies', *Sociology of Health and Illness*, vol. 24, no. 6, 750–70.

Richardson, Dorothy. 1979. *Pilgrimage*, 4 vols. London.

Riddell, Charlotte. *City and Suburb*. London, vol. 1.

———. 1866. *The Race for Wealth*, London, vol. 1.

Ridge, William Pett. 1899. *Outside the Radius: Stories of a London Suburb*. London.

Robins, Kevin. 2001. 'To London: The City beyond the Nation', in David Morley and Kevin Robins, eds, *British Cultural Studies*. Oxford, 473–93.

Robins Pennell, Elizabeth. 1916. *Nights: Rome, Venice, London, Paris*. Philadelphia & London.

———. 1929. *The Life and Letters of Joseph Pennell*, 2 vols. Boston, MA.

Robinson, A. Mary F. 1881. *The Crowned Hippolytus: Translated from Euripides with New Poems*. London.

———. 1882. 'The Art of Seeing', *The Magazine of Art*, vol. 4: 462–63.

———. 1884. *Apollo and Marsyas, and Other Poems*. London.

Rossetti, William Michael. 1970. *Some Reminiscences*, vol. 2. New York.

Sala, George. 1859. *Twice Round the Clock; or, the Hours of the Day and Night in London*. London.

Savage, Jon. 1993. 'Snapshots of the Sixties', *Sight and Sound*, vol. 5, no. 7, 14–18.

Saxey, Esther. 2004. 'Homoplot: The Coming out Story as Identity Narrative'. Unpublished doctoral thesis, University of Sussex.

Schaaf, Larry J. 1992. *Out of the Shadows: Herschel, Talbot and the Invention of Photography*. New Haven, CT and London.

Schreuders, Piet, Mark Lewisohn and Adam Smith. 1994. *The Beatles' London: the Ultimate Guide to Over 400 Beatle Sites In and Around London*. London.

Schwarzer, Mitchell. 2004. *Zoomscape: Architecture in Motion and Media*. New York.

Sebald, W.G.. 2003. *On the Natural History of Destruction*. London.

Sharp, Elizabeth Amelia, ed. 1890. *Women Poets of the Victorian Era*. London.

Sharp, William. 1886. *Sonnets of this Century*. London.

———. 1894. 'Some Personal Reminiscences of Walter Pater', *The Atlantic Monthly*, vol. 74, no. 446.

Shonfield, Katherine. 2000. *Walls Have Feelings: Architecture Film and the City*. London.

Simmel, Georg. 1971. 'Freedom and the Individual', in Donald N. Levine, ed., *On Individuality and Social Forms*. Chicago.

———. 1971. 'The Metropolis and Mental Life', in Donald N. Levine, ed., *On Individuality and Social Forms*. Chicago.

Sinfield, Alan. 1998. *Gay and After*. London.

Sitte, Camillo. 1985. *City Planning According to Artistic Principles*, trans. George and Christiane Collins. New York.

Smith, Anthony D. 2000. 'Images of the Nation: Cinema, Art and National Identity', in Mette Hjort and Scott Mackenzie, eds, *Cinema and Nation*. London, 45–59.

Smith, Lindsay. 1998. *The Politics of Focus: Women and Children in Nineteenth Century Photography*. Manchester.

Sontag, Susan. 1978. *On Photography*. London.

Spittles, Brian. 1992. *Joseph Conrad*. Basingstoke.

Stedman, Edmund Clarence. 1882. 'Some London Poets', *Harper's New Monthly Magazine*, vol. 64, no. 384.

Stilgoe, John. 1988. *Borderland: Origins of the American Suburb, 1820–1914*. New Haven, CT.

Street Porter, Janet. 2004. *Baggage: My Childhood*. London.

Symons, Arthur. 1882. 'Mr. Henley's Poetry', *Fortnightly Review*, 52.

Thesing, William B. 1982. *The London Muse: Victorian Poetic Responses to the City*, Athens, GA.

Thiriez, Régine. 1998. *Barbarian Lens: Western Photographers of the Qianlong Emperor's European Palaces*. Amsterdam.

Thomas, Alan. 1977. *The Expanding Eye: Photography and the Nineteenth Century Mind*. London.

Thomson, John and Adolphe Smith. 1994. *Street Life in London* (1877), reproduced in John Thomson and Adolphe Smith, *Victorian London Street Life in Historic Photographs*. New York.

Van Ghent, Dorothy. 1961. 'The Dickens World: a View from the Todgers's', in George H. Ford and Lauriat Lane Jr., eds, *The Dickens Critics*. Ithaca, NY.

Van Zuyle Holmes, Ruth. 1967. 'Mary Duclaux (1856–1944): Primary and Secondary Checklists', *English Literature in Transition (1880–1920)*, 10, 27.

Walkowitz, Judith R. 1992. *City of Dreadful Delight: Narratives of Sexual Danger in Late-Victorian London*. London.

Waltman, John Lawrence. 1975. 'The Early London Journals of Elizabeth Robbins Pennell'. Unpublished doctoral thesis, The University of Texas at Austin.

Ward, T.H., ed. 1880. *The English Poets: Selections* (with critical introductions by various writers, and a general introduction by Matthew Arnold), 4 vols. London.

Wells, H.G. 1980. *Ann Veronica*. London.

Weston, Kath. 1995. 'Get Thee to a Big City: Sexual Imaginary and the Great Gay Migration', *GLQ*, vol. 2, no. 3, 253–77.

Westphal, Carl Otto. 1871. 'Die Agoraphobie', *Archiv für Psychiatrie und Nervenkrankheiten*.

Williams, Raymond. 1973. *The Country and the City*. London.

Willis, Frederick. 1948. *101 Jubilee Road: A Book of London Yesterdays*. London.

Wilson, Elizabeth. 1991. *The Sphinx in the City: Urban Life, the Control of Disorder, and Women*. London.

Wollen, Peter. 1995. 'Possession', *Sight and Sound*, vol. 5, no. 9, 20–23.

———. 2002. 'Architecture and Film', in *Paris Hollywood: Writings on Film*. London.

Wolmar, Christian. 2005. *The Subterranean Railway*. London.

Filmography

28 Days Later (Danny Boyle, 2002)
Alfie (Lewis Gilbert, 1966)
Bande à part (Jean-Luc Godard, 1964)
The Battle of Britain (Guy Hamilton, 1969)
Bedazzled (Stanley Donen, 1967)
The Bliss of Mrs Blossom (Joseph McGrath, 1968)
Blow-Up (Michelangelo Antonioni, 1966)
Bram Stoker's Dracula (Francis Ford Coppola, 1992)
British Sounds (Jean-Luc Godard, 1970)
Casino Royale (Val Guest/Ken Hughes/John Huston/Joseph McGrath/Robert
    Parrish, 1967)
A Christmas Carol (Edwin L. Marin, 1938)
Col Cuore in Gola [*Dead Stop*] (Tinto Brass, 1967)
The Cook, the Thief, His Wife and Her Lover (Peter Greenaway, 1989)
Cool It Carol! (Peter Walker, 1970)
Damage (Louis Malle, 1993)
Damian: Omen II (Don Taylor, 1978)
Darling (John Schlesinger, 1965)
The Day the Earth Caught Fire (Val Guest, 1961)
Dorian Gray [*Il dio chiamato Dorian*] (Massimo Dallamano, 1970)
Dr Jekyll and Mr Hyde (Victor Fleming, 1942)
Dr Jekyll and Mr Hyde (Adolf Zukor, 1932)
Dr Jekyll and Sister Hyde (Roy Ward Baker, 1971)
The Elephant Man (David Lynch, 1980)
Fahrenheit 451 (François Truffaut, 1966)
Fires Were Started (Humphrey Jennings, 1943)
Four Weddings and a Funeral (Mike Newell, 1994)
From Hell (Albert and Allen Hughes, 2002)
Fumo di Londra [*Smoke Over London*] (Alberto Sordi, 1966)
Gangster No. 1 (Paul McGuigan, 2000)
Georgy Girl (Silvio Narizzano, 1966)
A Hard Day's Night (Richard Lester, 1964)
Help! (Richard Lester, 1965)
The Hunchback of Soho [*Der Bucklige von Soho*] (Alfred Vohrer, 1966)
I'll Never Forget What's 'Isname (Michael Winner, 1967)
The Intelligence Men (Robert Asher, 1965)
The Ipcress File (Sidney J. Furie, 1965)
It Happened Here (Kevin Brownlow/Andrew Mollo, 1966)
The Italian Job (Peter Collinson, 1967)
Jack the Ripper (David MacDonald, 1958)
Kaleidoscope (Jack Smight, 1966)
The Knack ... And How To Get It (Richard Lester, 1965)
The Krays (Peter Medak, 1990)
The Ladykillers (Alexander McKendrick, 1955)
The Lodger (Alfred Hitchcock, 1944)
London (Patrick Keiller, 1994)
The Long Good Friday (John McKenzie, 1979)
The L-Shaped Room (Bryan Forbes, 1962)

Lulu (Rolf Thiele, 1962)
The Magic Christian (Joseph McGrath, 1969)
Man in the Attic (Hugo Fregonese, 1954)
The Man Who Knew too Much (Alfred Hitchcock, 1934)
Mary Poppins (Robert Stevenson, 1964)
Modesty Blaise (Joseph Losey, 1966)
Mona Lisa (Neil Jordan, 1986)
Morgan: A Suitable Case For Treatment (Karel Reisz, 1966)
Mr In-Between (Paul Sarossy, 2001)
The Mummy Returns (Stephen Sommers, 2001)
Murder by Decree (Bob Clark, 1979)
My Fair Lady (George Cukor, 1964)
Nerosubianco (Tinto Brass, 1969)
The Night Porter (Liliana Cavani, 1974)
Notting Hill (Roger Mitchell, 1999)
Oliver! (Carol Reed, 1968)
Oliver Twist (David Lean, 1948)
The Omen (Richard Donner, 1976)
The Omen III (Graham Baker, 1981)
On Her Majesty's Secret Service (Peter R. Hunt, 1969)
One + One (Jean-Luc Godard, 1969)
Pandora's Box (G.W. Pabst, 1929)
The Passenger [Professione: reporter] (Michelangelo Antonioni, 1975)
Peeping Tom (Michael Powell, 1959)
Performance (Donald Cammell and Nicolas Roeg, 1971)
Poor Cow (Ken Loach, 1967)
The Red Desert (Michelangelo Antonioni, 1964)
Reign of Fire (Rob Bowman, 2002)
Repulsion (Roman Polanski, 1968)
Robinson in Space (Patrick Keiller, 1995)
Sabotage (Alfred Hitchcock, 1936)
The Secret Agent (David Drury, 1992)
The Secret Agent (Christopher Hampton, 1996)
The Servant (Joseph Losey, 1961)
Smashing Time (Desmond Davis, 1967)
Snatch (Guy Ritchie, 2000)
The Sorcerers (Michael Reeves, 1967)
Study in Terror (James Hill, 1965)
Things to Come (William C. Menzies, 1936)
The Third Man (Carol Reed, 1949)
Thirty Is A Dangerous Age, Cynthia (Joseph McGrath, 1967)
The Threepenny Opera (G.W. Pabst, 1931)
Thunderball (Terence Young, 1965)
Till Death Us Do Part (Norman Cohen, 1969)
Time after Time (Nicholas Meyer, 1979)
The Time Machine (George Pal, 1960)
The Time Machine (Simon Wells, 2002)
Tonite Let's All Make Love in London (Peter Whitehead, 1967)
To Sir With Love (James Clavell, 1967)
Trainspotting (Danny Boyle, 1996)
Tube Tales (Gaby Dellal et al., 1999)

Twinky [aka *London Affair*] (Richard Donner, 1969)
Victim (Basil Dearden, 1961)
I Vinti (Michelangelo Antonioni, 1952)
The Werewolf of London (Stuart Walker, 1935)
What Have They Done to Solange? [*Cosa avete fatto a Solange?*] (Massimo Dallamano, 1972)
The Wolfman (Stuart Walker, 1935)
Wonderwall (Joe Massot, 1968)
The Young Ones (Sidney J. Furie, 1961)

INDEX